German-American Life
Recipes and Traditions

Edited by John D. Zug and Karin Gottier

Gingerbread Cookies

Recipe for Gingerbread Cookies
and Houses: Page 207

Photography: Joan Liffring-Zug and Karin Gottier
Designers: Esther Feske and Patricia Young
Associate editors: Marlene Domeier,
Dorothy Crum, and Miriam Canter

Penfield
Press

*Dedicated to all the omas and opas in America
with a Germanic love of beautiful
flower and vegetable gardens*

Front Cover
German-American children are Greta, daughter of Neal and Melissa Schuerer,
and Will, son of Susy and Randy Reihmann, all of the Amana Colonies, Iowa.
—Joan Liffring-Zug photograph
Cover design of *bauernmalerei* is adapted from the book
Bauernmalerei No. 1, by Scottie Foster.

Back Cover
The charming photograph of folk dancers was taken by a bystander with Karin
Gottier's camera. In photograph of meats, the carving depicts George Schuerer,
long-time manager of the Amana Meat Shop. Favorite sausages and meats are
made from recipes brought to America by immigrants in the 19th century.
—Joan Liffring-Zug photograph

Acknowledgments
In addition to those named with their recipes, articles, or photographs, we thank
dozens of others for their assistance, including Ruth Julin, Maybelle Mays,
Michelle Nagle, Barbara Shepherd, Georgia Heald, and Lisa Schoonover.

Books by Mail:
(Postpaid to one address; prices subject to change)
This book: $15.95; 2 for $28; 3 for $40.
German Proverbs: All in calligraphy with woodcuts by Albrecht Dürer: $8.95
Please send for a complete list of titles
Penfield Press
215 Brown Street
Iowa City, Iowa 52245-5842

ISBN 0-941016-83-8
Library of Congress Catalog Number 91-60706
Copyright 1991 Penfield Press. All rights reserved.
Printed U.S.A. Julin Printing Company, Monticello, Iowa 52310

*Penfield
Press*

2

Contents

*Lithograph by Joseph Prestele (1796-1867), botanical artist from Bavaria and elder
in the religious Community of True Inspiration in the Amana Colonies, Iowa*

From Fatherland to Frontier

Not like the brazen giant of Greek fame,
With conquering limbs astride from land to land;
Here at our sea-washed, sunset gates shall stand
A mighty woman with a torch, whose flame
Is the imprisoned lightning, and her name
Mother of Exiles. From her beacon-hand
Glows world-wide welcome; her mild eyes command
The air-bridged harbor that twin cities frame.
"Keep ancient lands, your storied pomp!" cries she
With silent lips. "Give me your tired, your poor,
Your huddled masses yearning to breathe free,
The wretched refuse of your teeming shore.
Send these, the homeless, tempest-tost to me,
I lift my lamp beside the golden door!"

—"The New Colossus," a poem by Emma Lazarus (1849-1887) inscribed
on the pedestal of the Statue of Liberty, which was a gift from the people
of France to mark the 100th anniversary of American independence.

By Dianne Stevens

According to Norse sagas, the first German to set foot in the New World was Tyrker, Leif Ericson's foster father and a member of Ericson's 35-man expedition to Newfoundland in 1001. Tyrker discovered wild grapes near the settlement the explorers were building, giving Ericson his name for the land—Vinland.

Several Germans helped found Jamestown in 1607. Captain John Smith recruited the hard-working Germans to counterbalance the not-so-hard-working Englishmen in his group. Although he called the Germans "damned Dutch" because they wouldn't kowtow to the "gentlemen," Smith asked authorities to send him 30 Germans or Poles rather than a thousand Englishmen like the ones he already had.

German settlement in the United States began in earnest on October 6, 1683, when the *Concord*, sometimes called "the German Mayflower," sailed into Philadelphia harbor. Aboard were 13 Mennonite families from Krefeld, the first Germans to emigrate to the United States in a group. Under the leadership of Franz Pastorius, a lawyer from Franconia, the families built Germantown, the first distinctly German settlement in America. Pastorius called his group the "forerunners of all German colonists."

Germantown, then six miles from Philadelphia, was part of William Penn's "Holy Experiment" to offer a refuge to Europeans fleeing from religious persecution. Penn, an aristocratic Quaker, lured settlers with an effective marketing strategy—cheap land and religious tolerance.

By the start of the American Revolution, 225,000 Germans were in America. The early arriving Germans included the Hessians, soldiers hired by the king of England to fight against the American Revolutionaries. In 1776, the Continental Congress ordered a message printed on the back of all tobacco wrappers. The message was an offer to give each Hessian soldier 50 acres and the rights of an American. The offer worked. After the war, 5,000 to 12,000 Hessians stayed in the country they came to fight.

In the 18th and 19th centuries, Germans settled in Pennsylvania, New York, Texas, Ohio, Minnesota, North Carolina, Wisconsin, Nebraska, Iowa, California, Michigan, Virginia, Massachusetts, Georgia, and other states. The immigrants built homes, barns, churches, schools, and colleges.

A fresh start in a new country was appealing. In Europe, the never-ending series of wars devastated Germany. Efforts of both Protestants and Catholics to create "100% pure" areas were disruptive. There was the problem of giving up sons to the military. And, all eager for opportunity, as noted by Emma Lazarus, were "the huddled masses, the wretched refuse, and the homeless."

Reports were exciting. In America one could rise "from a servant to the rank of master," claimed J. Hector St. John de Crèvecoeur in his book, *Letters from an American Farmer*. Immigrants wrote home urging friends and family to join them. Iowa and Wisconsin sent pamphlets for distribution in Germany.

One wave of immigrants (possibly as many as 10,000) became political exiles when the 1848 revolutions in Germany failed. Called Forty-Eighters, they included highly educated intellectuals and professionals such as Carl Schurz, of whom it was said that he might well have become president of the United States had he been born in America, a constitutional requirement.

Getting out of Germany was not easy. The bureaucracy required documents including baptismal and marriage certificates; a baptismal certificate for each child; official evidence concerning business, profession or trade; place of residence; name and place of birth of parents; a certified copy of an emigration certificate from a government source; a certificate of good conduct from the congregation; and official information of the financial status of the emigrant.

There were risks at sea. Tightly packed onto ships, some passengers died of hunger, thirst, and disease during trips that sometimes took several months, depending on the weather. Some ships sank, and sinkings were hushed up lest they discourage others from making the journey. Some immigrants paid their passage by promising to work for three to seven years as indentured servants to cover their fare to "paradise." Paradise turned out to be a slave market with families separated and sold, some to cruel buyers. Conditions improved after 1819, when Congress passed laws limiting the number of passengers on a ship and allowing abused passengers to sue the captain.

Despite the hardships, Germans arrived in great numbers. Between 1820 and 1900, at least five million Germans arrived. In 1882 alone, a quarter-million Germans came. Following World Wars I and II, more Germans emigrated. Today, Americans of German descent—about 52 million—outnumber those of any other ethnic background.

Among The More Recent Immigrants

By Karin Gottier

The last major group of German immigrants to the United States came during the years 1946-1956. They were the German-speaking displaced peoples from Pomerania, Silesia, East and West Prussia, Poland, the Danube-Swabians from Hungary and Yugoslavia, the Carpathian-Germans from Slovakia, the Sudeten-Germans and Egerlanders from Czechoslovakia, the Transylvanian-Saxons from Romania, and, from Russia, the Volga and Black Sea Germans and others.

Their settlement history varied from group to group. The Transylvanian-Saxons and Carpathian-Germans were recruited from the Rhineland, Bavaria, and Frankonia during the 13th century by Kings Geza I and II of Hungary. They were assigned land to found villages, and they were given special privileges. Their fortunes waxed and waned during 800 years of turbulent history.

Those Germans who lived in the Danube countries are collectively called Danube-Swabians. After the defeat of the Turks by Prince Eugene of Savoy, they were settled there by the Hapsburg monarchy, notably during the reigns of Empress Maria Theresa and her son Joseph II. The Volga and Black-Sea Germans were called to Russia by Czar Peter the Great and by Catherine the Great—27,000 during her reign alone. During the Stalin era their settlements were erased and the populations were scattered into Siberia and Asian Russia.

Although the original settlers of all these areas came at different times, from different areas in Germany, under different circumstances, and settled in diverse regions among diverse peoples, they all preserved their language, customs, and traditions, adopting some elements of the indigenous culture and in turn influencing it. They developed thriving cultural institutions—academic, literary, religious, and artistic.

At the end of World War II, 12 million ethnic Germans were driven out of their respective homelands, ending as much as 800 years of German culture. Many of these came to America. Among them were scientists, former German prisoners of war, war brides, and others.

Today, groups of these German Americans can be found in large urban centers including Detroit, Milwaukee, Chicago, New York, Cleveland, Akron, Rochester, Cincinnati, Philadelphia, St. Louis, and Los Angeles.

A Brief History of The Germans

By John Zug

*John Zug is co-founder of Penfield Press and a former newspaper editor.
His German-speaking Anabaptist ancestors came to Pennsylvania in 1727.*

If you are an American of European descent, you may have one or more ancestors who came from Germany. No other group is as numerous as the German Americans. Despite the fact that in this century the armed might of the New World has been rallied successfully against Germany in two wars, the interest of Americans in the German heritage is strong and healthy.

The Germanic peoples (or tribes) were known to the ancient Greeks and Romans, but as an entity, the German nation did not exist until 1871—six years after the American Civil War ended. The wise and scheming Otto von Bismarck (1815-1898), who brought opposing factions together in nationhood, wasn't even born at the time of the American and French revolutions, and was only six years old when Napoleon died. The emigration of Germans to America was under way long before and after Bismarck's era.

Germany's background was in the feudal system, which spread through Europe beginning in the eighth century. Under this system, the nobleman held power over his land and its people, up to and including full sovereignty. A sovereign could raise armies, make alliances, and conduct wars. Among other powers, he could collect taxes and tolls. Some people who were emigrating to America paid 20 or more tolls along German rivers.

Out of the feudal system grew the balance-of-power concept. If a candidate for Holy Roman Emperor, together with his relatives and allied friends, was potentially powerful enough to tip the balance, many of the nobility would back a weaker candidate. Secret agreements were common. Breaking of agreements in order to switch sides was not uncommon. Appeals to the cause of freedom, equality, fraternity, and the rights of man were unheard of.

Weaknesses in the feudal system became obvious. Before it became the practice to bequeath all land to the eldest son, a nobleman's death meant that his domain was divided among all of his sons, leading to a steady increase in the total number of independent land entities. By the middle of the 17th century the land that was to become Germany consisted of more than 300 separate entities. No wonder there were so many castles. Revolutions in America (1776) and France (1789) shook the world but not the feudal system or the German peasant. When Napoleon marched through Germany in 1806 many peasants considered it just another change in the managerial class. Continued presence of the French, however, helped stir German nationalistic feelings.

Nationhood would involve centralization of power. Such an increase in power had begun in the 17th century in Brandenburg, a northern area that included Berlin. Brandenburg became Brandenburg-Prussia, later known simply as Prussia.

A few facts about the rulers who built this power:

1640-1688: Frederick William the Great Elector, born in 1620, was one of the seven electors whose votes chose the Holy Roman Emperor. These electors were the Duke of Saxony, the Count Palatine of the Rhine, the Margrave of Brandenburg, the King of Bohemia, and the Archbishops of Mainz, Cologne, and Trier. Frederick William built a strong and disciplined army, dependent in part on revenues from non-adjacent Cleves and Prussia, and after the 1648 peace of Westphalia, of East Pomerania and the former dioceses of Minden and Halberstadt. As duke of Prussia, he owed loyalty to the king of Poland, but chose armed neutrality when Sweden's King Charles X Gustav overran Poland. Fighting both for and against the Swedes in the 1650s, he won full sovereignty over Prussia. He stripped the estates of their power over taxing and spending, and began the establishment of a central government.

1688-1713: Frederick I (born 1657), son of Frederick William the Great Elector, loaned Emperor Leopold 8,000 Prussian troops and in return was proclaimed in 1701 "King *in* Prussia," an attempted limitation which failed as he became king *of* Prussia by general acceptance. In peace treaties Frederick I won the Swiss canton of Neuchâtel and several enclaves on the lower Rhine. He ran up debts, welcomed French and Dutch Protestants, and founded the Academy of Sciences at Berlin.

1713-1740: Frederick William I (born 1688), son of Frederick I, married Sophie Dorothea of Hanover, daughter of George I of England and sister of George II of England. Frederick William I freed the serfs and made primary education compulsory. He is remembered for what he called his only extravagance—bodyguards over six feet tall. His agents kidnapped one of them in Hesse from a religious group that later founded the Amana Colonies in Iowa. This man served several years before escaping, at risk of execution, by swimming upstream as the search for his body (he was believed drowned) went downstream. He walked, mostly at night, back to Hesse. Frederick William I is also remembered for his harsh treatment of his son and heir, the future Frederick II the Great. At 18, the son and his friend and lover, Lt. Hans Hermann von Katte, sought to escape to England but were arrested and tried as army deserters. The future king was forced to witness the beheading of his best friend.

1740-1786: Frederick II the Great (born 1712), grandson of George I of England, decreed an end to religious discrimination, torture in judicial inquiries, press censorship, and the over-six-foot grenadier guards. He ordered the laws codified, and wrote almost daily—in French. With 40,000 men he overran Empress Maria Theresa's Silesia. With 80,000 men he took Prague in 1744. Opposed by Austria, England, Holland, and Sardinia, he fell back, but retained Silesia and at age 33 was called "Frederick the Great." He fought other wars, winning some and losing some, with an army of some 150,000 troops. He participated in the 1772 partition of Poland by Prussia, Russia, and Austria, which gave him the lands that had separated East Prussia and Brandenburg. He successfully defied the Holy Roman Empire, beginning its downfall, and enjoyed a brief friendship with Voltaire, the great French author. Another victory came when Frederick the Great forced the peasants to plant potatoes. From the time of Columbus, they had shunned potatoes, convinced that this bounty from the New World was poisonous. They learned otherwise.

1786-1797: Frederick William II (born 1744), was the son of Frederick the Great's brother (Frederick the Great died childless). In the second (1793) and third (1795) partitions of Poland, which wiped Poland off the map, Frederick William II acquired Ansbach, Bayreuth, Danzig (Gdansk), Thorn (Torun) and a large part of central Poland, including Warsaw. Both Mozart and Beethoven dedicated chamber music to Frederick William II.

1797-1840: Frederick William III (born 1770), defeated by Napoleon in 1806, lost all provinces west of the Elbe, but after the 1813 War of Liberation against Napoleon, Prussia acquired Westphalia and traded certain Polish lands for the greater part of Saxony. This gave Prussia responsibilities in both the west and east of Germany, areas that later would be heavily industrialized.

1840-1861: Frederick William IV (born 1795) was an indecisive and relatively ineffective monarch, first opposing and later somewhat favoring the growing demands for a German state.

1861-1888: William I (born 1797), second son of Frederick William III, became regent in 1858 after his brother suffered a stroke. In 1861 he became king of Prussia. In 1862, William named Otto von Bismarck as prime minister and Bismarck began guiding Prussia on the path that led to German nationhood. Liberal elements indicated they would accept William I as king of all Germany if he were subject to a powerful legislative body. Bismarck and William I insisted on full power for the monarch. Prussian arms resolved the matter in Bismarck's favor. In the Seven Weeks' War against Austria in 1866, Prussia won control of Hanover, Nassau, Hessen-Kassel, Schleswig-Holstein, and Frankfurt am Main, and excluded Hapsburg-controlled Austria from Germany. In the war of 1870, Germany defeated France. In January, 1871, William I, king of Prussia, became German emperor, or kaiser (from Caesar, the family name of the first Roman emperors) at the invitation, not of the people, but of the princes of Germany.

1888: Frederick III (born 1831), son of William I, was the first Prussian king to get a college education. He served in three wars—the war against Denmark in 1864, the Seven Weeks' War in 1866, and the 1870 war with France. He was king of Prussia and German kaiser only 99 days in 1888, during which time he was voiceless and dying of throat cancer.

1888-1919: William II (born 1859) was the son of Frederick III and Victoria, daughter of Queen Victoria of Britain. As kaiser, he led Germany into World War I. After the defeat of Germany and the formation of Germany's Weimar Republic, he lived in the Netherlands until his death in 1941.

Germany's Weimar Republic faced severe problems, including inflation and war reparations. Its work was hampered by the rise of Adolf Hitler (1889-1945), an uneducated agitator whose political, managerial, and military inexperience, combined with his vicious hatreds, led to costly miscalculations as he seized power and started World War II.

A few of Hitler's many mistaken judgments:

• Starting with troops that carried broomsticks, he vowed to build an unbeatable war machine, failing to realize that others could and would build even greater war machines.

• Instead of massing his forces, he scattered them—from Norway to Africa, from the Atlantic to the interior of the Soviet Union—wars on two fronts at once.

• He failed to comprehend the worldwide revulsion that would result from the gassing of millions of innocent civilians.

• He bombed British cities, ignoring the obvious fact that he was thus inviting retaliatory destruction of the cities and war plants of Germany.

• Where oppressed peoples welcomed his troops with flowers and flags, he took ruthless measures, quickly convincing them that he was not a friend.

In a tragic irony, the defeated Germany became a world showcase of the failures of communism, on the one hand, and the prosperity and freedom of a democracy, on the other. One was imposed by the victor in the East, the other was nurtured by the victors in the West. Had the world known, in 1918, as much about management of the affairs of nations as was known in 1945, perhaps there would never have been a Hitler and a World War II. In any event, the future is bright for Germany and for the European Community. Of the 1990 uniting of West Germany and East Germany, H. J. Hungerland of Troy, Michigan, president of Volkswagen of America Inc., said:

"The United States played an essential role in this development. Were it not for the generosity of the Marshall Plan, which invested billions of dollars in rebuilding the Federal Republic of Germany after World War II, there would have been no union. West Germany might still be shackled by the stagnation plaguing the East.

"The union of East and West Germany would not have taken place if the United States had not orchestrated the airlift to Berlin, or if your presidents had not consistently expressed their friendship and commitment to our people, or if your most powerful corporations had not invested in our economy.

"From the United States we have learned lessons of compassion and generosity. I am proud to be a member of a company that is investing $3 billion in a joint venture that promises to provide jobs to as many as 30,000 East German workers by the mid-1990s."

European Civic Coats of Arms

FRANKFURT AM MAIN

DRESDEN

HAMBURG

MUNICH

The German Homeland

By Hannelore Bozeman

In the Ice Age, glaciers covered the north German plain, leaving behind a number of lakes in Mecklenburg. Much of the rest of Germany is criss-crossed by mountain ranges, modest in height. The Harz Mountains are rich in folklore and legends. To the south are the Thuringian Forest and the Erzgebirge, known for wood-carving, especially of Christmas figures and pyramids.

In the south, the dominant mountains are the Black Forest and the Swabian, both in the southwest, and the Bavarian Forest near the border with Czechoslovakia, the site of Germany's first national park. Along its southern border, Germany shares in the Alps.

Coming from Switzerland, the Rhine River flows through Lake Constance and turns northward at Basel. Lake Constance and the southern Rhine Valley are the warmest regions of the country. Spring often arrives in early March. Vineyards dot the mild and sunny valley, and produce some of the world's best white wines.

The famed Danube River begins in the Black Forest, at the confluence of two little rivers. One runs mostly underground, surfaces at Donaueschingen, and flows 1,800 miles to the Black Sea.

Another great river is the Elbe, best known to Americans because Eisenhower and his World War II armies halted there to await the arrival of Russian troops advancing from the east. Flowing from Czechoslovakia, the Elbe passes near Dresden and through Hamburg, Germany's largest port, to the North Sea.

Germany, with 137,768 square miles, is not as large as Texas (267,338), California (158,693), or Montana (147,138). The German population of more than 77,000,000 is triple that of the most populous American state, California, with about 24,000,000.

In population density, the comparison is mixed. Germany has an average of 564 persons for each square mile. The comparable figure for New Jersey is 940, Rhode Island 783, Massachusetts 695, Connecticut 600, New York State 343, and California 151. Roomy Wyoming and Montana have about five persons per square mile.

Nearly everyone in Germany is ethnically German. The leading minority group, Turkish, created its largest settlement in Berlin. The Turks cherish their own culture, customs, language, and religion, but many have become German citizens. The highest European immigration has been from Poland.

German-speaking regions outside Germany include Austria, two-thirds of Switzerland, and Liechtenstein. France has a German minority of about a million in Alsace-Lorraine, across the Rhine from the Black Forest. About 200,000 German-speaking people live in the Alps in northern Italy, adjacent to Austria. Some 3 million are in Poland, Romania, Russia, and the Baltic states.

Visiting an Ancient Land

By Hannelore Bozeman

Castles, museums, historic churches, and cathedrals abound in Germany, many only a short distance from each other. Most overseas visitors fly into Frankfurt am Main, the nation's largest airport. Frankfurt is a logical starting point for many tours. As a first impression of Germany, however, it is deficient. Severely damaged by Allied bombing in 1944, it was rebuilt in a modern, though rather uninspiring way. The cathedral where emperors once were crowned has been reconstructed. Its 14th-century tower escaped bomb damage. The 13th-century Nikolai Church and the old City Hall have been reconstructed. A few blocks away is the reconstructed childhood home of Johann Wolfgang von Goethe (1749-1832), the creator of *Faust* and genius of the written word.

The town of Höchst, now a western suburb of Frankfurt, has medieval charm. Timbered houses huddle behind the town walls, lining the narrow streets leading to a 1,200-year-old church.

West of Frankfurt is Mainz, an ancient city with a ninth-century Romanesque cathedral. Like other cities in the Rhine valley, such as Bonn and Köln (Cologne), Mainz is more than 2,000 years old, having been founded by the Romans. Johannes Gutenberg (1400-1468), the inventor whose Gutenberg Bible was the first book printed from movable type, was born in Mainz. The Gutenberg Museum contains some of the first printed Bibles. Across the Rhine, charming Wiesbaden has the magnificent palace of the Dukes of Nassau along the river bank, complete with baroque facade.

Mainz is the perfect place to join one of the cruise ships for a trip down the Rhine. Although it is possible to cruise on the Rhine from Basel to Rotterdam, a five-day trip, the stretch between Mainz and Koblenz is the most romantic one, with the continuation to Bonn a close second. Here the river is flanked on both sides by steep hills covered with vineyards, with excellent hospitality and samples of local wines. Castles perch above many of the towns. The most famous rock is the Lorelei, 430 feet high. Its echo may have created its legend, which tells of a beautiful woman whose singing lured sailors to their deaths in the treacherous waters below.

Between Mainz and Bonn are no fewer than 40 castles, many of them in ruins. Possession of such castles often meant that the medieval overlord could exact a toll from every ship passing below. Some of these castles can be visited; others are privately owned or occupied. The best example of a medieval fortress is the Marksburg castle at Braubach. A most strategic castle, the Pfalz, was built on a rock outcropping right in the river, near Kaub, reachable by ferry.

The northern Rhine valley and the adjoining Ruhr Valley are industrialized and heavily populated. For history and art lovers, there is Cologne with its magnificent cathedral and an excellent Roman-Germanic museum, with the largest Roman mosaics north of the Alps. About an hour's drive west is Aachen, once the residence of Charlemagne. His marble throne and his 800 A.D. Bible can be seen in the cathedral.

About 50 miles south of Frankfurt is romantic Heidelberg, a stopping point for many Americans in the military because it houses the U.S. European Army headquarters. Historic "Old Bridge" spans the Neckar River. Heidelberg is known for its 600-year-old University and its 15th-century Student Prison, undergraduate dueling clubs, and the world's largest wine barrel (58,000 gallons). Heidelberg Castle on the slopes of the Odenwald is in ruins, but still a center of activities such as concerts in the courtyard, fireworks, and flood-lighting at night.

The Black Forest starts near Karlsruhe, not far from Heidelberg. The forest is named for its dark evergreens. Baden-Baden, a few miles south of Karlsruhe, was the fashionable spa for the social set of the 19th century. It retains its charm and its hot springs, now offered for relief of stress and other ailments. From Baden-Baden the Black Forest High Road leads past resorts to scenic Freuden-stadt. Other scenic drives enter valleys with large, thatch-roofed farm houses, some occupied by both the family and farm animals, all of them remote from the hustle and bustle of modern times.

Southeast of the Black Forest is Lake Constance, shared by Germany, Switzerland, and Austria. The area is known for scenic beauty, mild climate, excellent wines, and rich historic and art treasures. Meersburg on the north shore has a medieval Old Town and two time-separated castles—one about 1,000 years old, the other 200 years old. Nearby Unteruhldingen has a recon-structed stone-age village erected entirely on stilts in the lake. A short drive or hike leads to the baroque cloister church Birnau. The island Mainau near the southern shore of the lake is a huge flower garden.

Old buildings in Konstanz include the impressive cathedral begun in the 11th century, and the Hotel Insel, birthplace of Count Ferdinand von Zeppelin, inventor of the rigid dirigibles that became known as zeppelins.

South of Munich is Oberammergau, a popular resort town famed for its passion plays, performed once per decade; the next one will be in the year 2,000. After more than 80 villagers had died in the pestilence of 1634, the people of Oberammergau vowed that if they were spared any more deaths they would perform in perpetuity a play honoring the passion of Christ. The villagers survived and kept the vow. The play is an all-day, eight-hour production with 1,000 performers—about one-fifth of the villagers.

A rewarding side trip from Oberammergau leads to Linderhof, one of the fanciful, fairy-tale castles built by King Ludwig II, who was known as "Mad Ludwig." Another, just a few miles down the road is Neuschwanstein, the model for the castle in the Walt Disney movie *Snow White and the Seven Dwarfs*.

South of Oberammergau, near the Austrian border, is the foot of Germany's highest mountain, the 9,717-foot Zugspitze.

A visit to that part of Germany wouldn't be complete without a stop in Munich. An easy-going city with 10 times more restaurants than there are days

14

in the year, it is the world's beer capital. The large breweries operate traditional beer halls where waitresses serve huge mugs of beer and plates piled high with food, while brass bands make for a lively atmosphere.

Munich is best known for its annual *Oktoberfest*, held around the end of September. This beer-drinking fest began in 1810 when Crown Prince Ludwig and Princess Theresa became engaged. The festival is held at a site named for her, Theresienwiese.

The Frauenkirche, with its onion-shaped domes, is Munich's most famous church. At Marienplatz are the gothic New Town Hall and the famed Glockenspiel. Folk dancers and knights on horseback move to a melody at the stroke of 11 a.m. and 5 p.m. The Old and the New Pinakothek contain works by master artists including Rembrandt, Rubens, and Van Gogh.

Two scenic routes, the Romantic Road and the Castle Road, cut through southern Germany. From Würzburg the Romantic Road heads south through medieval villages and walled cities to the Austrian border at Füssen. The Castle Road connects Mannheim and Heidelberg with points east. The two roads cross south of Rothenburg, also known as the "Jewel of the Middle Ages." The city walls surround a 13th-century town, completely preserved. The Castle Road leads to Nürnberg, which still has its old city wall and about 60 of its towers. One of the picturesque, half-timbered houses belonged to the great artist Albrecht Dürer, who lived and worked there for nearly 20 years. Nürnberg is famous for its delightful Christmas market, its gingerbread, and its toy museum.

In the north, Hamburg rivals Munich in size but has a different character. It is a stately, sober city built upon trade, and Germany's largest port. It offers a shopper's paradise and an attractive downtown area with lakes, parks, and an impressive City Hall with a Renaissance-style facade. The second largest port is at Bremen which, like Hamburg and Berlin, is both a city and a state. Bremen has many historical buildings from eight centuries, among them City Hall with its ornate Renaissance facade, elegant ballrooms and the Great Hall. Böttcherstrasse, formerly lined with craftsmen's shops, now offers museums and art galleries. Schnoorviertel is an old residential and artists' quarter with popular taverns.

Resort towns line both the Baltic Sea and North Sea. On the Baltic coast is Kiel, an industrial port famous for its shipyards. Twenty minutes from the Baltic Sea lies Lübeck on the Trave River. Once the most important city in the Hanseatic League, Lübeck is an idyllic town with high-gabled houses, ancient towers, a Gothic church with gilded spires, and other historic structures, including the 15th-century Holstein Gate and City Hall, both in black glazed brick. About 90 minutes south of Hamburg is Hannover, another city heavily bombed during the war. From 1714 to 1837 the rulers of Hannover (spelled with two n's in German, one in English) were also the ruling family of Great Britain and Ireland. Hannover is known for its commercial importance and trade fairs; in the year 2,000 it will host the World's Fair. A short side trip leads to Hameln on the Weser river, the town of the Pied Piper. Every Sunday during summer, an outdoor play reenacts his story.

The gem of the east is Berlin. Many attractions cluster around the Tiergarten, a public park and famous zoo; the Kaiser Wilhelm Memorial Church, a burnt-out hull left as a reminder of the horrors of war; the Kurfürstendamm, a shopping and entertainment boulevard; and the reconstructed Reichstag.

The Berlin Wall is down except for a memorial portion near the Brandenburg Gate, which you can simply step through to reach East Berlin's showcase boulevard, Unter den Linden. The Pergamon Museum in East Berlin shows one of the Seven Wonders of the Ancient World, the Altar of Zeus and Athena. Charlottenburg Palace, in the west, shows Prussian architecture.

Potsdam, near Berlin, is a charming city filled with palaces and gardens from the time of Frederick the Great. Most famous are his Sanssouci Palace and Park, and Cecilienhof Palace. The Spreewald nearby is a tranquil, scenic area where the Wends, or "Sorbs," Germany's only indiginous slavic minority, travel on the many canals, and seem to live in an earlier century.

In Saxony, the queen of cities is Dresden, heavily bombed during the war but lovingly restored. Attractions include the Semper Gallery and the Albertinum, with their collections of Old and New Masters. The famous "Green Vault" holds a collection of medieval and baroque goldwork. Picturesque Meissen, nestled in terraced vineyards, is world-famous for pottery and porcelain.

Martin Luther was born in Eisleben, published his "95 Theses" in Wittenberg, and translated the Bible into German in Wartburg Castle near Eisenach. Leipzig, a beautiful ancient city, is famous for its trade fairs. Johann Sebastian Bach once worked at historic St.Thomas Church. Nearby Weimar is central to German literature and was home to Bach, Goethe, Schiller, and Liszt.

It is impossible to explore this country in a single visit. So when you board your plane to fly home, say *Auf Wiedersehen*—"till we see each other again!"

A few of the many sister cities:

Augsburg—Dayton, Ohio
Baumholder—Irving, Texas
Berlin-Spandau—Boca Raton, Flori
Coburg—Garden City, New York
Cologne—Indianapolis, Indiana
Esslingen—Sheboygan, Wisconsin
Eutin—Lawrence, Kansas
Friedrichshafen—Peoria, Illinois
Füssen—Helen, Georgia
Giessen—Waterloo, Iowa
Heidenheim—Cleveland, Ohio
Kleve—Fitchburg, Massachusetts
Krefeld—Charlotte, North Carolina
Mainz—Louisville, Kentucky
Mannheim—Manheim, Pennsylvania
Mühlacker—Tolleson, Arizona

Munich—Cincinnati, Ohio
Morzheim—Frederick, Maryland
Passau—Hackensack, New Jersey
Pinneberg—Rockville, Maryland
Rastatt—New Britain, Connecticut
Ratingen—Vermillion, South Dakota
Regen—Brownsville, Tennessee
Regensburg—Tempe, Arizona
Saarbrücken—Pittsburgh, Penn.
Stuttgart—St. Louis, Missouri
Sülzfeld—El Cajon, California
Trier—Fort Worth, Texas
Tübingen—Ann Arbor, Michigan
Ulm—New Ulm, Minnesota
Walldorf—Astoria, Oregon
Wesel—Hagerstown, Maryland

American Towns With German Names

This is not a complete list. For example, there are many Berlins. Some accent the first syllable (Ohio), and one (Iowa) changed its name to Lincoln in World War I.

Connecticut
Berlin

Iowa
Amana
Allendorf
Germantown
Germanville
Graettinger
Hamburg
Hanover
Holstein
Klemme
Luther
Minden
Reinbeck

Michigan
Bergland
Hamburg
Hanover
Frankenmuth
Frankfort
Westphalia

Minnesota
Danube
Essig
Flensburg
Fulda
Hamburg
Hanover
Heidelberg
Herman
Hoffman
Karlstad
New Germany
New Munich
New Ulm
Schroeder
Zimmerman

Missouri
Baden
Frankford
Freistatt
Hermann
New Hamburg
New Offenburg
Rhineland
Weingarten

Nebraska
Gothenburg
Herman
Holstein
Minden
Pilger
Steinauer

New York
Angelica
Berlin
Dresden
East Otto
Fleischmanns
Frankfort
German
Germantown
Hamburg
Helmuth
Hoffmeister
Keeseville
Mannsville
Mecklenburg
New Bremen
New Berlin
Obernburg
Otto

North Dakota
Berlin
Bismarck

Bremen
Dresden
Hamberg
Hannover
Heil
Heimdal
Karlsruhe
Kramer
Munich
New Leipzig
Osnabrock
Raub
Strasburg

Ohio
Berlin
Bremen
Dresden
Germantown
Gnadenhutten
Hamburg
Hanoverton
Leipsic
New Bavaria
New Bremen
New Riegel
Steuben

Pennsylvania
Ackermansville
Angelica
Baden
Berlin
East Berlin
East Germantown
Fritztown
Germantown
Hamburg
Hanover
Heidelberg

Hummelstown
King of Prussia
Kleinfeltersville
Manheim
Millbach
Muhlenberg
New Berlin
Germansville
Osterburg
Reinholds
Schaefferstown
Wernersville

South Dakota
Frankfort
Kranzburg
Wagner

Texas
Cologne
Fredericksburg
Hochheim
Klein
Lindenau
Luckenbach
Muenster
New Baden
New Braunfels
New Ulm
Rosenberg
Schulenburg

Wisconsin
Amberg
Berlin
Germanis
Hamburg
Hanover
New Franken
New Holstein
New Munster

Growing Up German American

By Bill Eckhardt

*The Rev. Bill Eckhardt is a Lutheran campus minister at the University of Iowa,
Iowa City, Iowa, where he is known as "Pastor Bill."*

The memories which I most closely identify with my German heritage come from characteristics I observed in my grandfathers. Each worked very hard, was frugal, liked to laugh, respected authority, and highly valued education, his profession, and his family. Neither they nor my grandmothers wasted anything and criticized anyone who did. No one ever denied that each grandfather was stubborn. I know of no situation where either of them changed his mind about anything. Period. That was both an asset and a liability in hard times, of which they had plenty. Also, each felt a formidable family responsibility, even toward his grown children. For example, three of my dad's four sisters got a college education in quite another era. My dad and his brothers got a good start in a business in part because of the generosity of their father.

Some details of the daily life of my grandfather, Frederick Eckhardt, reflect values from his German background. He referred to himself as a sausage maker or a butcher. He was that, but he was primarily the owner of a general store. It occurred to me at a tender age that it was ironic that he, a grocer, had the largest garden in the village of Boyd, Minnesota. Although I never saw him work in his garden, neither did I ever see a weed. I probably got up too late in the morning to catch his activity outside. I often saw him admiring his garden, especially at noontime when he came home for dinner, our largest meal of the day. He loved to walk down the straight garden rows, occasionally stopping to pick a ripe tomato, pull some carrots, or just smile at the beautiful flowers.

He also had a small apple orchard between the community fire station and his huge house (I visited there years later, and the house was not nearly as large as I had remembered it). He liked to walk around the orchard, admiring the apple trees, and occasionally giving a critical stare at whatever. My grandmother would call to him that the meal was getting cold, and his large feet would stomp up the back steps into the huge kitchen filled with the savory smell of roast beef, chicken, or cooked sausage, potatoes and gravy, and cooked beans or corn. He would sit, say grace, and eat, and then perhaps take a brief nap.

It is likely that his love for the land came from a combination of his inheritance and the agricultural practices of Germany. Much of the land there was owned by absentee nobility. The little that was owned by families was passed from generation to generation by dividing the property into segments given to each son. Since the land was scarce and that which was owned by each individual became so small, it was gardened intensively. Much of the parents' pride came from the beauty of their gardens, and how well they could feed their children from this source.

Both World Wars I and II were hard on my family's German identity. I was told that my relatives were occasionally accused, during the first World War, of sympathizing with Germany. "Kaiser lover" was the title some of my family had to defend themselves against on occasion. During World War II, I received some teasing, but very little. My father was drafted into the infantry at age 36. I was always proud to be near him, especially when he was in uniform.

It was difficult for me to identify the adversary as something or someone German. I always quietly translated the awful things done by the Axis to the word "Nazis," and I rarely used the word "German" to identify the enemy. This is still true. Years after the war, it is difficult for me to conceptualize how the nation of Germany could have been the culture out of which came so many atrocities and the initiating of war against America. Beginning in my teenage years I learned how Germany is the source of so much excellence in music, engineering, science, theology, and many other fields. This made the source of the war all the more difficult for me to understand.

Our ties to relatives in Germany continued after World War II. I am still impressed with the generosity of my grandfather in the late 1940s in sending relief packages to his cousins in East Germany. Their thank-you letters were always censored with bold black horizontal marks, but we were able to find out that they received and appreciated our help.

My grandparents were ignorant by today's standards, but they had an epic personal vision. This vision formed an attitude of confidence and humility that made it possible for them to face hardship with such a fearful determination that they could desperately pursue the fulfillment of their dreams, feel a personal significance in doing so, and enjoy life in the process.

For them life was an uncertain, hazardous, but exciting journey. They had a God who had expectations of them, but He also had a plan for them that fit them into this world. They knew the tyranny of a society where possibilities for advancement were limited. America allowed them to use their personal energy to take care of themselves and to expand their horizons. This incentive was passed on to the following generations, but can best be appreciated by observing today's generation of immigrants and their drive to succeed.

My grandparents' success and happiness had to do with their view of life. They valued freedom, but even more they valued opportunity. They appreciated America for that gift. Their hope was based on an ethic of hard work, resiliency, fair and generous treatment of others, and trust in a merciful God. They had shortcomings, but they managed better than most people today to further understand the importance of the big picture, which included a rich and ennobling past, and a confident hope for the future even in the middle of adversity. They responded to tragedy with added resolve. Immediate details were important—as building blocks for the future. They believed the decisions they made were significant, but they did not take themselves so seriously that they couldn't enjoy living. They placed the responsibility for the destiny of the person, the society, and the universe on themselves and a personal God Whose rules of conduct governed human lives as surely as they governed nature.

The Germans in Pennsylvania

By Stephen Scott

Stephen Scott of Lancaster County, Pennsylvania, has written about "plain buggies" and Amish weddings. His other books include Living Without Electricity *and* Why Do They Dress That Way?

In 1682 William Penn established a colony in America that offered a refuge to the persecuted, oppressed people of Europe. Some of the first to accept Penn's offer were 13 families of Germans from the city of Krefeld. These people were of Mennonite background but had converted to the Quaker faith. On the ship *Concord*, they arrived in Philadelphia October 6, 1683. Their new settlement was Germantown, then just north of Philadelphia, now a part of Philadelphia.

In later immigration, the largest numbers came from the war-torn Palatinate region. Others came from Würtemberg, Baden, Franconia, Zweibruecken, Hesse, Hanau, Nassau, and Alsace. A considerable number came from Switzerland. By 1750, German settlements were firmly established in southeastern Pennsylvania. In the 1790 census for Pennsylvania, at least one-third (141,000) of the 424,000 inhabitants were of German origin.

The influx of Germans alarmed some English-speaking colonists. In 1717 Governor William Keith spoke of "great numbers of foreigners from Germany, strangers to our language and constitution." A 1727 law asked all ship captains for lists of German-speaking passengers. Male immigrants age 16 and older had to sign an oath of allegiance to the king of England. In 1755 Benjamin Franklin expressed fear that Pennsylvania would be dominated by "Palatine boors."

A longer, ongoing debate concerns whether these people are "Pennsylvania Dutch" or "Pennsylvania German." Those favoring "German" point out that the people came from within the borders of what is now Germany. Others say that the term "Dutch" was an English form of the German "Deutsch." They point out that restriction of the word "Dutch" to the language and people of Holland dates only from the 19th century. Today, many scholars agree that the terms "Dutch" and "German" may be used interchangeably. Many simply refer to "Dutch" with no thought of windmills or wooden shoes.

The popular image of Pennsylvania Dutch people includes black wide-brimmed hats and beards for men, and for the women, distinctive bonnets and long dresses. People who dress this way are in the minority and always have been. The great majority of German-speaking people in 18th century Pennsylvania belonged to the Lutheran and German Reformed churches.

In 1890 Philadelphia's German population reached 75,000, which exceeded even that of Milwaukee. Pittsburgh also was an important center for Germans in America, with 37,000 German-born residents in 1900. Erie, Reading, Wilkes-Barre, and Lancaster also attracted German immigrants.

The descendants of the 17th and 18th century German immigrants largely assimilated into Anglo-American culture. The later arrivals, however, vigorously encouraged "German-ness." In 1835 the *Männerchor*, the first German singing society in the United States, was founded in Philadelphia. There were German theaters, and in 1915 there were more than 200 German clubs in the city.

The German Society of Pennsylvania was established in Philadelphia in 1764. Its library at 611 Spring Garden Street contains a large collection of German-Americana. The Germantown Historical Society at 5214 Germantown Avenue preserves the heritage of America's first German settlement.

On the last Saturday in September, citizens of Germantown reenact the Battle of Germantown (October 4, 1777). Historic homes and buildings include Cliveden, center of the battle; St. Michael's Lutheran Church, where services were conducted in German until the 1920s; the Germantown Mennonite Meetinghouse, 6121 Germantown Avenue, and the Germantown Church of the Brethren, 6613 Germantown Avenue.

Among the 18 nationality classrooms at the University of Pittsburgh, the German room contains details inspired by the academic auditorium at the University of Heidelberg, including intarsia (decorative art of wood inlay), a craft of the Renaissance period, and unique stained glass windows inspired by the fairy tales of the Brothers Grimm.

Many state, county, and local institutions help preserve the Pennsylvania German culture. The following is a partial list:

Berks County (Most German of all Pennsylvania counties)

Pennsylvania Dutch Farm Museum, Kempton. Implements and artifacts. Open weekends May through October.

Folklife Museum, Lenhartsville. Typical Pennsylvania German buildings contain historical items. Research library. Maintained by the Pennsylvania Dutch Folk Culture Society.

Berks County Historical Society, 940 Centre Avenue, Reading. Relics and archival materials.

Berks County Heritage Center, Red Bridge Road, Reading. The C. Howard Hiester Canal Center and the Gruber Wagon Works.

Conrad Weiser Park, Womelsdorf. The 1729 home of a famous Pennsylvania German Indian agent.

Hex Sign Area. Colorful folk designs on barns in northern Berks county, especially around Shartlesville, Hamburg, Shoemakersville, Virginville, Lenhartsville, Krumsville, and Kempton. Milt Hill, near Virginville, is a hex sign designer and artist. A map locating hex sign barns is available from Dutch Hex Tour Association, Inc., Lenhartsville, PA 19534.

Lancaster County

Pennsylvania Dutch Convention and Visitors Bureau, 501 Greenfield Road, Lancaster. Tourist information, slide presentation.

Heritage Center of Lancaster County, Penn Square, Lancaster. Artifacts, antiques in historic building.

Central Market, Penn Square, Lancaster. Established when town was founded 1730. Present building dates from 1889. Open Tuesday, Friday, and Saturday. Pennsylvania Dutch food items.

Trinity Lutheran Church, 31 South Duke Street, Lancaster. The building, topped by impressive white spires, dates from 1766.

Lancaster County Historical Society, 230 N. President Avenue, Lancaster. Library and archives of local history. Exhibits.

Landis Valley Museum, 2451 Kissel Hill Road, Lancaster. 22 buildings devoted to rural and village life of the Pennsylvania Germans. Crafts. An operating 18th-century-style farm.

Folk Craft Museum, 441 Mount Sidney Road, Witmer. Arts and crafts of the Pennsylvania Germans.

Lebanon County

Lebanon County Historical Society-Stoy Museum, 924 Cumberland Street, Lebanon. Period rooms, re-created shops.

Bologna Companies. Lebanon bologna is a Pennsylvania Dutch favorite. Guided tours offered by Weaver's Bologna, 15th Avenue and Weavertown Road, Lebanon; Kutztown Bologna, 689 Kutztown Road, Myerstown, and Palmyra Bologna, 230 North College Street, Palmyra.

Alexander Shaeffer Farm Museum, Shaefferstown. Historic Volkssports Swiss-type farm house. By appointment only or during festivals.

Dauphin County

State Museum of Pennsylvania, Harrisburg. Large, well-organized. Pennsylvania German arts and crafts.

Museum of American Life, Hershey. Culture of Pennsylvania Germans. Chocolate World: Manufacture of chocolate candy is demonstrated. Milton Snavely Hershey, company founder, was of German ancestry.

Lehigh and Northampton Counties

Lehigh County Historical Society, 5th and Hamilton Streets, Allentown. History in a building that once was a courthouse.

Troxel-Stockel House and Farm Museum, 4229 Reliance Street, Egypt. A 1756 house, traditional German architecture.

Montgomery County

Peter Wentz Farmstead, Shultz Road, Center Point. An 18th century farmstead preserved.

Goschenhoppen Folklife Library and Museum, Green Lane. Open on Sunday afternoons except in winter, or by appointment.

Montgomery County Historical Society, 1654 Dekalb Street, Norristown. Library and small museum. The area was originally Pennsylvania German in the north and Quaker in the south.

York County

George Neas House, 113 West Chestnut Street, Hanover. Local culture and crafts in a 1783 house.

Historical Society of York County, 250 East Market Street, York. Items relating to German heritage; works of folk artist Lewis Miller.

Pennsylvania German Folk Festivals

Pennsylvania German Day, Grings Mill Recreation Area, Sinking Spring, PA. (Berks County). Mid-June.

Kutztown Folk Festival, Kutztown, Berks County. A 10-day event that includes the first week of July. Mammoth affair.

Folklore Festival, Shaefferstown, Lebanon County. Mid-July.

Hanover Dutch Festival, Hanover, York County. Late July.

Das Awksht Fest, Macungie, Lehigh County. Early August.

Goschenhoppen Folk Festival, East Greenville, Montgomery County. Mid-August. Strives for complete authenticity.

Harvest Home Jubilee, Pennsylvania Dutch Folklife Museum, Lenhartsville, Berks County. Early September.

Hecklerfest, Heckler Plains Farmstead, Harleysville, Montgomery County. Late September.

Heritage Festival, Gruber Wagon Works, Reading, Berks County. Early October.

German-speaking immigrants spoke a variety of dialects. The dialect of the Rhenish Palatinate (Pfalz) dominated because settlers from that area were the most numerous. The dialect thrives only among the most conservative "Plain Dutch," but others try to preserve the language. High school and college courses are offered. Newspapers have dialect columns. There are radio and television programs, and a number of churches hold annual dialect services.

Eisenhower National Historic Site

The farm home of President and Mrs. Dwight D. Eisenhower at Gettysburg, Pennsylvania, is open daily from April through October. Otherwise it is open Wednesday through Sunday, except that it is closed for 31 days beginning the Sunday after New Years Day. Tours begin at the National Park Service Visitor Center near the Gettysburg National Cemetery.

Ephrata Cloister

On the outskirts of Ephrata in Lancaster County, Pennsylvania, the steeply peaked roofs, small windows, and unpainted siding look medieval. These structures are the remains of a religious order started in the 1740s by Conrad Beissel, who came from Germany in 1720.

Beissel sought the life of a religious hermit, but was drawn to the Dunkers or Brethren, and became a Brethren preacher. Soon Beissel left and became the leader of a new sect.

Beissel advocated keeping Saturday as the Sabbath, communal ownership of property and goods, and celibacy. His white-robed disciples grew in number, but the sect declined after Beissel's death in 1768 and the death in 1796 of the second leader, Peter Miller.

Photo shows site of America's first 18th century religious communal society, administered by the Pennsylvania Historical and Museum Commission.

The Moravians

—Photo by Reginald Banks

*Johann Antes made this violin in Bethlehem in 1759. Probably
the oldest violin made in America, it is in the collection of the
Moravian Historical Society in Nazareth, Pennsylvania.*

After World War II Old Salem in North Carolina was threatened with demolition, but it was preserved. Old Salem is a dozen or so blocks of 18th-century homes, shops, and gardens surrounded by Winston-Salem. Of 111 properties acquired by Old Salem, Inc., 60 have been restored and nine, including a bakery, are open to the public. Old Salem was built by members of the Moravian Church, or Moravian Brethren, founded in 1457 as *Unitas Fratrum* (Unity of Brethren) by followers of Jan Hus. Driven out of their homeland, now a part of Czechoslovakia, they found acceptance in Germany.

Zeal for evangelism was brought to England by Moravians en route to America to do missionary work among the Native Americans. They strongly influenced John and Charles Wesley, who founded the Methodist Church.

The first Moravians to cross the Atlantic came in 1735. In Pennsylvania, they founded Nazareth in 1740 and Bethlehem in 1741. All property was held in common until 1762. The symphony orchestra organized at Bethlehem in 1744 was the first in America. Today there are museums in both communities. In 1766 the Moravians founded Salem (from Shalom, the Hebrew word for peace). They also founded Moravian College in Bethlehem and Salem College in Winston-Salem. The Schoenbrunn Village State Memorial in New Philadelphia, Ohio, is a restoration of a settlement founded in 1772 by a Moravian mission.

Moravians have rich traditions in music and worship. They emphasize mission work among primitive peoples, and consider evangelism a duty. German was the language of the Moravian Church in America until the 1860s. The northern province of the church is centered in Bethlehem and the southern province in Winston-Salem. The church's world-wide mission efforts have resulted in 19 church provinces, including one in Alaska and one in Labrador.

The first Moravians to arrive in America were deeply religious. Unlike the more austere immigrants seeking religious freedom, however, the Moravians, after about 1800, wore brightly colored costumes. They enjoyed good food, good music, and good fabrics!

24

The Harmonists

By Stephen Scott

Father Rapp's home in Harmony, Pennsylvania

Engraving from 1875 book of the Communal Societies of the United States.

Three National Historic Landmarks preserve the story of the Harmonists, or Rappites, a group of German Pietists. In Harmony, Pennsylvania, site of their first community, is the Harmony Museum. New Harmony, along the Wabash River in extreme southwest Indiana, combines restored buildings with a lively post-Rapp intellectualism. The Old Economy Village at Ambridge, about 10 miles northwest of Pittsburgh, is operated by the state of Pennsylvania. Its restored shops, homes, and gardens are open to the public.

The Harmonists, or Rappites, began in 1787 when George Rapp (1757-1847) started a new religious movement in Würtemberg, Germany. Not tolerated, they emigrated in 1803 and founded the community of Harmony, where Rapp had purchased 5,000 acres. Here they adopted communal ownership of goods and property, and organized as the Harmony Society. In 1807, during a religious revival, they adopted the practice of celibacy.

In 1814 the community was sold to Abraham Ziegler and became a Mennonite settlement, while the Harmonists purchased 20,000 acres in Indiana and founded "Harmonie." They built their church, in the form of a Maltese Cross, along with a school, homes, barns, a factory that doubled as a fort, and other buildings. Rapp laid out his vineyards with bends and twists to symbolize the tests that await those who choose the straight and narrow path in life. In 1817 they were joined by a sizable group of friends and relatives from Würtemberg.

In 1824 the Harmonists sold this, their second community, to Welsh-born utopian Robert Owen, who renamed the town New Harmony. The Harmonists, about 800 strong, moved back to Pennsylvania. Their third settlement was ideal and the community prospered. Several textile mills operated, and orchards and vineyards yielded abundantly. In 1831 about 200 members departed; they sued for a share of the properties, causing bitterness. After the death of Rapp the community carried on until 1905. The end was gradual but certain. No new members were joining and celibacy precluded any natural increase.

All three of the Harmonist-founded communities draw visitors. The noted German theologian Paul Tillich so admired New Harmony's Roofless Church that he had his ashes buried in a restful, tree-shaded spot across the street.

The Plain People

Some very visible groups of German Americans are called "plain people" because of their simple life style and distinctive dress. Most trace the origin of their beliefs to the Anabaptist movement that began in Zurich, Switzerland in 1522. The Anabaptists believed in adult baptism and voluntary church membership. They were called Anabaptists (rebaptizers) because they baptized adults who had been christened as babies. At that time, this practice was a crime punishable by death, and many were executed.

The Anabaptists believed in total separation of church and state. They were opposed to participation in war and violence of any kind, and did not swear oaths. Anabaptists generally interpreted the Bible quite literally. They believed it was the final authority on all matters of faith and life, and that church members should live holy lives. Europe was not ready for such beliefs in the 16th century. Both Catholics and Protestants severely persecuted the Anabaptists, who were among the Germans coming to America in search of religious freedom.

The four major groups of "plain people" are the Mennonites, Amish, Brethren (Dunkers), and River Brethren.

The Mennonites were named for a prominent Dutch preacher, Menno Simons. The Amish were followers of Jacob Amman, a Swiss Mennonite who decided his church was "too worldly." Two branches of the Mennonites developed separately: the Swiss and the Dutch. Many Swiss Mennonites found homes in the Palatinate area of Germany. From there many came to Pennsylvania in the 18th century. Many Dutch Mennonites moved to Prussia beginning in the 16th century. In the late 18th century Catherine the Great invited Prussian Mennonites to settle in the Ukraine.

Of the nearly 640,000 members of Anabaptist churches in America, about 500,000 have become outwardly assimilated into the larger society and are not "plain people." About 75,000 have retained a distinctive style of dress and worship, but have adopted modern conveniences such as cars and electricity. The 65,000 members of ultra-conservative groups, mostly Old Order Amish, do not allow cars and restrict technology; nearly all conduct their worship services in the German language in the homes of members, and limit education to the eighth grade. All Amish wear very plain, simple garb.

There are communities of plain people in Lancaster and Montgomery Counties, Pennsylvania; Holmes and Wayne Counties, Ohio; Elkhart and La-Grange Counties, Indiana; Arcola, Illinois; Bowling Green, Clark and Jamesport, Missouri; Kalona and Hazleton, Iowa; Harmony, Canton, and Mabel, Minnesota, and elsewhere.

Faceless Amish Dolls

The dolls of the Amish are faceless because of the Biblical reference to graven images. The Amish also refuse to allow photographs of people. Mennonites allow photographs. Certain groups of Mennonites wear attire similar to that of the Old Order Amish.

By Ruth Wile of Winesburg, Ohio

I started making dolls in 1986. At the time I was working in a factory to help out financially, but we felt my place was at home to take care of our four children (now 11, 14, 18, 19). After much prayer we stepped out in faith and I quit my job. I only made one size doll at that time, and never dreamed of a doll business. I only wanted to sell a few dolls a month so I could be home with the children.

Even today my aim is not to build a business but to help others in need. The ladies who work for me in their homes need an income, but have small children or poor health. They work at their pace, but take great pride in the piece of the doll they make. I cut and sew all the bodies and cut most of the clothes as well.

Most people think I am Amish, but I am really Mennonite. We have cars and electricity, but believe basically the same as the Amish. My grandparents were Amish and my parents were raised Amish but began attending a Mennonite church when I was 4 or 5, so I know what their rules and dress codes are. About half of the ladies who sew for me are Amish; the other half are Mennonites. The dolls are sold in Indiana, Illinois, Washington, California, Pennsylvania, Michigan, Wisconsin, and Florida, as well as all over Ohio.

Ohio

By *Dianne Stevens*

As America expanded her frontiers westward, German Americans sought to expand their opportunities beyond the East Coast. High birth rates in the established German communities in Pennsylvania, New York, Maryland, Virginia, and the Carolinas made good land scarce and expensive. With rich farm land and waterways, Ohio was a popular destination for German Americans.

Native-born and foreign-born Germans beat a path to the Buckeye State through Maryland and West Virginia. Many Pennsylvania Germans settled in Canton, Massillon, Alliance, Steubenville, and other communities farther west. German families from the Mohawk Valley and Hudson Valley followed New Englanders to Ohio along the borders of Lake Erie.

The German Americans honored their origins by calling their new towns Berlin, Hanover, Strasburg, Dresden, Frankfort, Potsdam, Freeburg, Winesburg, and other German names. Other Ohio names, such as Bethlehem, Nazareth, Goshen (two of these), and Canaan, bear witness to the religious roots of the German Americans. Farming was a popular profession for the Germans in Ohio but German laborers, craftsmen, and skilled professionals also flocked to Ohio. In 1841, Cincinnati's population was 28 percent German-American. By 1850 it was 50 percent. The hub of the German community was dubbed "Over-the-Rhine," an area across a canal from the main part of the city. The *Cincinnati Volksblatt* was published from 1836 until World War I.

Zoar

Just as Lot fled from evil Sodom to the refuge of biblical Zoar, 300 Separatists from Württemberg founded Zoar, Ohio in 1817. They had been persecuted after splintering from the Lutheran Church. After 1819 Zoar operated its 5,500 acres and buildings on a communal system with all resources pooled for the good of the community and with equal rights for men and women. Hard work, thrift, and the acute business sense of their leader, Joseph Baumeler, made Zoar prosper; by 1834 it was debt-free.

Christmas in Zoar was just another work day until one Christmas morning in the early years, the locally made earthenware horn, used to call the people to work, shattered when blown in bitter cold. The people took this as a sign from heaven that they should not work on Christmas. After that, Christmas was celebrated as a holiday.

Baumeler died in 1853. The coming of the railroad in the 1870s ended Zoar's isolation, and the nation's push toward industrialization and mass production hurt the village industries. In 1898 the society dissolved with each member receiving $200 and 50 acres.

Today Zoar is carefully restored to reflect its original simplicity and charm. A number of homes have been privately restored, and some house small shops or offer bed and breakfast. Buildings owned by the Ohio Historical Society and

Colleen Taylor and Susan Clouston are in front of the restored tin shop with its fachwerk (half-timbered) architecture, Zoar, Ohio. The Ohio Historical Society administers the site.

open to the public are wagon, blacksmith and tin shops; garden and greenhouse, Bimeler Museum, store, bakery, and Number One House. Events have included a Harvest Festival in August, a Christmas program early in December, art, quilt, and flower shows, and others.

Columbus

Sturdy brick houses, set close to the hand-laid brick streets, slate roofs, carved stone lintels, clay chimney pots, iron fences, neat walkways and heavy wooden doors make the German Village in Columbus a powerful reminder of the Germans who settled there.

Originally called South Columbus, the community was surveyed in 1814. Its residents founded St. Mary's Catholic Church, schools, a Lutheran seminary, Capital University, and many clubs and singing societies such as the Columbus *Maennerchor* which has been singing since 1848. World War I, the Depression, and World War II all caused decline of the village, but since 1959 restoration has been under way and houses are occupied.

The Village Valuables Sale is a huge yard sale held the first Saturday in May. The *Haus und Garten* tour is the last Sunday in June. The Backyards-by-Candlelight Tour is the second weekend in August, and the *Oktoberfest* is the second weekend in September. In December the village is decked out in holiday splendor with candles and wreaths. The German Village, six blocks south of the State Capitol, is listed in the National Register of Historic Places.

Holmes County

In Holmes County, about 50 miles northeast of Columbus, are settlements of Amish and Mennonites, with restaurants and craft shops. Adjoining Wayne county also has Amish and Mennonites, whose ancestors came west from Pennsylvania.

Frankenmuth, Michigan

By Dianne Stevens

Frankenmuth, Michigan is called Little Bavaria with good reason. A covered bridge, white stucco buildings with dark timbers, window boxes overflowing with flowers, a 35-bell carillon glockenspiel, a brewery, a Maypole, festivals, and lots of German food make visitors feel that they are just 90 miles north of Munich, not Detroit.

A band of 15 Lutheran settlers founded Frankenmuth in 1845 in an attempt to spread Christianity to the Chippewa Indians. Along with religion, the missionaries brought their German heritage, which has been preserved and is richly celebrated today.

Bavarian Fest is an eight-day German extravaganza in June featuring locally brewed beer, food, parades, folk dances, authentic Bavarian costumes, a marketplace and children's entertainment. For 10 days in August, Summer Music Fest features top polka and other bands, food, beer, and free polka lessons. The Twelve Days of Christmas celebration begins with a tree-lighting ceremony the day after Thanksgiving. Festivities continue until Christmas, with carols, home tours, shopping, thousands of lights around the town, and visits from traditional German Christmas characters. In May, hundreds of colorful kites fill the sky during Skyfest. In July, people put on their running shoes for *Volkslaufe* (people's race). Restaurants offer authentic Bavarian fare, and are noted for their chicken dinners.

The Frankenmuth Historical Museum documents four communities founded as Lutheran missions: Frankenmuth (1845), Frankentrost (1846), Frankenlust (1848), and Frankenhilf (1850, now Richville). The museum has 7,000 artifacts, including photographs, letters, and newspapers.

Nickless-Hubinger Flour Mill, Frankenmuth, Michigan

Life in Frankenmuth, Michigan

By Dr. Rudolph C. Block

*Dr. Block is Director of Curriculum Services for the Lutheran Church,
Missouri Synod, at St. Louis. He formerly was Academic Dean
at Concordia University, River Forest, Illinois.*

My great-grandfather Weber was among the first immigrants who settled in Frankenmuth Township, Saginaw County, Michigan. He and a small group of farmers and craftsmen were sent by Pastor Wilhelm Loehe of Neuendettelsau, Bavaria, Germany, to bring the Gospel to the heathen Indians. Of course, Indian conversions were few and far between. Why? The settlers insisted that the Indians had to learn German first because God "spoke only in German" to them. The colony was quite successful and grew rapidly.

The Franconian immigrants brought with them not only their Lutheran heritage but all their social and cultural customs and values as well. To effectively maintain their German culture, they built a church and simultaneously established a school. Reading, writing, arithmetic, and religion made up the curriculum, and everything was taught in the German language.

I knew little or no English until I started first grade. Church services in the 1930s were still conducted in *Hoch-deutsch* (Luther's German) and family conversation was all in *Bayrisch*, a dialect of southern Germany. *Die Fiebel* (a German reading primer) was as important to our early learning as were the Bobbs-Merrill readers.

At our farm home an important daily ritual involved morning and evening devotions led by my father. He would read a portion of Scripture and a lengthy selection from a devotional book, all in German, of course. We often would also sing a hymn, and always close with reciting the Lord's Prayer. And God help any one of us kids (there were four of us) if we should not be listening intently or make some kind of disturbance. Then as bedtime neared, mother took over. Mother made sure we had done our homework. We learned our first prayers at mother's knee or, should I say, on mother's lap. She went through a short prayer ritual expecting us to pray along as best we could. As soon as we were able, we recited our evening prayers and Ma just listened.

My frugal mother also taught me the value of a dollar. Like so many German *Frauen*, my mother was the pivotal member of the family. No decision of any consequence was ever made without her consent and blessing. She controlled the purse strings, keeping a tight rein on any expenditures. She was also generous with family contributions to our church, St. Lorenz.

All of our teachers at that time were men. This was neat because they would play ball with us at recess time. Families were so supportive of the teacher and his way of doing things that none of us would tattle on another. If a boy received a spanking, and if the parents found out about it, he would get twice as hard a spanking at home. Girls in our class wouldn't dream of getting into mischief. They worked overtime trying to please the teacher.

Parents had great love and respect for the teacher(s) of their children. In addition to a cash salary and living free in a teacherage, the teachers were showered with donations of food and clothing all year. I made frequent trips on Saturdays with my mother to bring the teacher and his family all sorts of produce. A bushel of potatoes, a crate full of carrots and all types of fruits and vegetables were brought to show our appreciation. My father was a butcher. He spent most of his winter days going from farm to farm all over the township butchering for relatives, friends, and neighbors. He slaughtered pigs, calves, and beef cattle, and made the best-tasting summer sausage and every type of sausage imaginable. We had our own smokehouse so my dad smoked bacon and ham, pork sausage and summer sausage. Thus the teachers in Frankenmuth, like our pastors, really were able to maintain a respectable standard of living even during the Great Depression.

All of the children from the Lutheran families in and around Frankenmuth attended a parochial school. After transferring to the Lutheran central school in uptown Frankenmuth, I was placed in the classroom of the principal, E. F. Rittmueller. He epitomized the true image of *der Herr Lehrer*. He was extremely strict, and there was no one who didn't fear him. Yet he was also fair, had a good sense of humor, was generous with deserved praise, and seemed to be an absolute authority on just about everything. Being selected by him to serve on the school's safety patrol squad was a coveted honor. Serving as lieutenant of the squad (with the captain, who was my best friend) during eighth grade was about as neat as being selected to play the Angel Gabriel in the all-school Christmas pageant. Needless to say, whatever doubts remained about my future were wiped out; I knew I wanted to be a teacher just like Mr. Rittmueller.

At our graduation, where I was the class speaker, my parents beamed with pride and joy as I publicly announced my decision to study for the teaching ministry. It was a tradition that religiously devout parents with more than one son would dedicate one of them for service to the Lord as a pastor or teacher. St. Lorenz of Frankenmuth contributed well over 500 of its sons (and recently daughters as well) to the ministry in its first 125 years.

My generation was the last to receive a bilingual education in Frankenmuth. My class was also the last to be confirmed in German. We had German readers that progressed from grade to grade parallel to the readers in English. As I look back now with fond and happy memories, I am saddened by what World War II did to the people of Frankenmuth. Five years after my graduation, German had been eliminated as a required part of the curriculum; it then was taught only as a foreign language. That did not stop the farm kids from using *Bayrisch*.

Among my earliest childhood memories of growing up in Frankenmuth is how we spent our Sundays. To begin with, we never failed to go to church on Sunday morning. Then came a fine noon meal, usually a great chicken dinner with all the trimmings. Next came an afternoon visit to the home of one of our many relatives. While our folks visited, we played elsewhere in the big house

32

or outside with our many cousins. It was really a form of the extended family.

A young couple contemplating marriage wouldn't dream of eloping or having a justice of the peace perform the ceremony. Marriage vows were spoken in church with one of the pastors performing the ceremony. Special friends of the family would be selected to supervise the gathering of all the delicious homemade bread, pies and cakes; the main course would generally be veal, chicken, or beef with mashed potatoes and gravy and home-grown vegetables.

The one fly in the ointment was having to do chores between the wedding ceremony and the dinner and reception later. The cows needed to be milked twice a day, seven days a week. The wedding I recall most vividly was that of my brother who was five years my senior. Not only was I his best man, I did not have to go home to do the chores. The wedding reception was quite typical of Frankenmuth weddings around the middle of the 20th century.

After the big dinner in the church grove, a lengthy program would be presented honoring the bride and groom and also embarrassing them some by digging out, or manufacturing, stories which would thoroughly amuse the gathered celebrants. The introduction of various family members and friends by the master of ceremonies would be interspersed with jokes and stories meant to amuse. At the appreciation hour the best man would lead the assembly with a loud and musical *Sie leben hoch!* Beer and wine flowed freely and dancing would start just as soon as the pastor(s) had found a convenient time to say good-bye to the happy couple.

No real wedding celebration was complete without a "shivaree." Friends of the groom who were not invited to the wedding would gather in a group of six to a dozen to interrupt the celebration by making a racket that would wake the dead. They clanged heavy hammers on various size heavy metal discs, started and ended at each round with a stick of dynamite. The object was to pretend to steal the bride or at least interrupt the festivities. After three or four rounds of this noise-making, the groom was expected to go out and dicker with them, offering them a keg of beer and some money to leave in peace.

Around midnight the bride would cut the first piece of a huge wedding cake and literally stuff it into the bridegroom's mouth. Each guest would then receive a piece of cake along with coffee, tea, or soda. Then several husky members of the bridal party would hoist high into the air the bride and groom, seated on chairs tied together with crepe paper—all this to the rousing cheers of three more *Sie leben hoch!*

Although Luther championed general education, the general attitude of the German farm families in Frankenmuth was that higher education was not to be "wasted on girls." Daughters were expected to learn how to clean, bake, and sew, as well as help with the chores on the farm. That would make them into fit wives for farm boys who had become men and were ready to get married.

The Franconians saw the necessity of a college education, however, and the importance of higher education spread beyond the professions. Yes, growing up German in America was quite an experience for those of us lucky enough to be born in Frankenmuth.

33

Iowa's Amana Colonies

The Amana Colonies, seven villages on 26,000 acres in eastern Iowa, are criss-crossed by highways 151 and 220, but retain the charm and nostalgia of earlier days, including homes of sandstone blocks shaped by ancestral hands, and locally fired brick . Forebears of these people joined together in 1714 in south-western Germany. They called their group the Community of True Inspiration, from their belief that inspired persons could receive God's wishes and commu-nicate them to the people as did the prophets of Biblical days.

The people rented estate lands in Hessen, a tolerant province, but rents kept rising until they were exorbitant, and in 1842 a committee was sent to America to buy land. The first villages, named Ebenezer, were near Buffalo, New York. Ahead was hard work, not utopia. Still, both richer and poorer had financed the Atlantic crossing and the land purchase. When the question of ownership arose, the leader, Christian Metz, said: "The church is the servant of God through which He gives His grace and blessing. Should not we give our all to Him by giving our all to the church?" Thus began an era of religious communal life which lasted until 1932, when it was voted out by the people.

With Buffalo's growth encroaching, the move to Iowa began in 1855. The Amana name was chosen from the Song of Solomon, Chapter 4, Verses 1-8. Persecuted in Europe, the people found religious freedom in America.

Today, visitors enjoy German cooking served family style at Amana Colo-nies restaurants, and find their way to the old Woolen Mill, Meat Shop, Furniture Factory, Museum of Amana History, General Store, Open Hearth Bakery, wineries, and other museums and attractions. One of the restaurants in Amana is named for the Ronneburg Castle where forebears of the Amana people found refuge in Germany.

The elders said "no" to photography, but enforcement was minimal. This picture of Sunday in Amana was taken in the early 20th century.

Back to Beginnings

By Madeline Roemig

Madeline Roemig and her husband Martin are lifelong residents of the Amana Colonies in Iowa (Seven villages, a religious communal society until 1932). Great-grandparents of both, and two of Martin's grandparents, were born in Germany. Martin is a former president of the Amana Society. Madeline is a founder and past director of the Amana Heritage Museum.

I have been to Germany three times. Somehow it seems we are linked closer than the spread of three generations, probably because so many of us live together in Amana and are able to practice the German language, and because our villages resemble the German villages our people left behind.

The language made the first impact on me. Arriving at the Frankfurt airport I could read the signs! Listening to the chatter around me I thought, "They all speak German. Even the little children speak so well." Using our Amana German is tremendous fun. Sometimes I am mistaken for a native, or asked which region I am originally from.

I looked for the familiar and found it. In one place we had *gefüllte Nudeln* (filled noodles) served with applesauce just like my mother makes. The soups with dumplings and the boiled potatoes, asparagus, and ham were like eating at Oma Schmieder's table again.

Familiar things abound: the locks and latches on doors, the lines on pieces of furniture, the flower gardens, the vegetable gardens planted in such neatly spaced patches and beds. I look at these things and realize why our gardens, furniture, and door locks are as they are.

In small villages, woodsheds with neatly stacked piles of kindling reminded me of that part of my home in Amana which years ago yielded itself up for a garage. The presence of large barns in our Amana villages is something I like very much.

A most pleasant experience on an early morning walk in Oberammergau occurred when I wandered into a dairy barn where a few cows were being milked by the farmer. I asked if I might watch and he nodded agreement. In addition to seeing this sight, the smells, clean and sweet, were transporting me back to our Amana dairy barns in the center of town where as children we were allowed to enter and observe when we felt like it. As was the one in Oberammergau, ours were immaculately clean.

The cleanliness and orderliness of Germany is seen everywhere and it struck me at once why we in Amana are that way. When apples fall from the trees they must be picked up and used. When the wind downs twigs and branches, out come containers and saws, and the cleanup begins as the wind ceases. That is why we air our quilts and carpets, sweep sidewalks clean, and scrub floors as compulsively as we do.

35

Amana people have made many pilgrimages to the castles and estates where our ancestors gathered before emigrating to America. These are located in Hessen near Budingen, all spaced a short distance apart. It is stirring to stand in courtyards and among ruins where our history began. It is as if the walls and ground should be able to speak to us. Most memorable is the moment when the Ronneburg castle comes into view. It sits on a hill, and the approach to it is as beautiful as the castle itself. It is unmistakable because pictures of that landmark are in almost every home in the seven Amana villages. The castle Engelthal, a cloister, has a hush and quietness befitting the spot, and invites one to imagine people living there with names such as Roemig, Dietrich, Marz, Moershel, Zimmerman, etc. At the Arnsburg the shadows cast by the walls of the ruins reminded me of the passage of time, and of the fact that no matter what the length of time, something draws us back to beginnings.

One of our Germany trips was with a group of Amana people that included my Aunt Magdalena Schuerer. One of my fondest recollections is that she (Magdalena Oehl Schuerer) and I (Madeline Oehl Roemig) stood together, silently, near the great Rhine Falls in Schaffhausen where our ancestor Magdalene Muller Roemig was born.

There is a *Freilichtmuseum* (open-air museum) named Hessenpark near Neu Anspach, which is near Frankfurt. It is an entire village reassembled to portray a typical Hessian village of the 19th century. One of the buildings is devoted to telling the stories of groups of people who emigrated from Hessen to other parts of the world, exploring where they went, how they fared, and what remains of these people today. I helped assemble material and objects for an Amana exhibit in the museum, and was present in 1983 at the dedication of the building and exhibit. Some of the things our forefathers brought from Hessen have thus returned home and are part of a story being told in Germany each day. Under the leadership of Professor Dr. Eugen Ernst, the museum continues to grow. It is a place in which farm animals, storks, and wild flowers live alongside wide buildings and objects of the past. Among attractions are an excellent restaurant, a hearth oven bakery, a performing stage, and a pottery and brick kiln.

Hessenpark, the Freilichtmuseum *near Neu Anspach, Germany.*

Some Family Names

(Mostly from the Milwaukee, Wisconsin phone book)

Historically, when family names were adopted, most were derived from occupations. German names reflect the range of occupations and titles from a medieval rural society in the villages, often built around the manor or "burg" of a feudal lord. Other surnames were taken from the place a person lived—a region, city or village. Some surnames are short sentences: *Traugott*—"trust in God."

German words often have the umlaut: ä, ö, ü. In the American version these letters become ae, oe, and ue, or the umlaut is simply dropped. The character ß is written in English as ss. Some German words have developed more modern spellings in the United States. For example, th has become a simple t; man is spelled *Mann* in German. Most American-German names have dropped the second n.

Abendroth, Abendrot
  (evening red)
Acker (field)
Ackerman, Ackermann (a
  man of the field, farmer)
Adler (eagle)
Ahrens
Albrecht
Amrhein (on the Rhine
  river)
Arndt
Arnold
Augustin
Bach (brook)
Bader (archaic for barber)
Baer, Bär (bear)
Bahr
Baier, Beyer, Bayer (some-
  one from Bavaria)
Ball (ball)
Bartz, Barz
Bauer (farmer)
Bauman, Baumann (con-
  struction worker)

Baumgartner, Baumgärtner
  (tree gardener)
Becker (baker)
Beckmann
Behrendt, Behrend
Benz
Berg (mountain)
Bergmann (miner)
Berlin
Berndt
Bernhardt, Bernhard
Bernstein (the mineral
  amber)
Biersack (beer sack)
Binder, Bender (binder)
Bischof (bishop)
Blau (blue)
Block (block, log)
Blumenfeld (field of
  flowers)
Blumental, Blumenthal
  (valley of flowers)
Boehm, Böhm
Boese, Böse (bad, evil)

Boettcher, Böttcher (cooper)
Bohlmann
Bohn, Bohne (bean)
Bohrer (gem borer)
Bonner (from Bonn,
  Germany)
Brand, Brandt (fire)
Brandenburg
  (a German region)
Braun (brown)
Bremer, Brehmer
  (from Bremen)
Brenner (distiller,
  brickmaker, burner)
Brunner (digs wells)
Bublitz
Buchholz (beechwood)
Buelow, Bülow
Buettner, Büttner (cooper)
Burger, Bürger (citizen,
  townsman)
Burgermeister,
  Bürgermeister (mayor)
Burkhard, Burkhardt

Busch (bush)
Cramer, Kramer, Kraemer, Krämer (shopkeeper)
Dahl
Dallmann
Decker (archaic for slater, thatcher)
Dietrich (picklock, skeleton key)
Doerr, Dorr, Dörr
Draeger, Dräger, Träger (carrier, porter)
Eberhard, Eberhardt
Ebert
Eiche (oak)
Eisenberg (iron mountain)
Engel (angel)
Erdmann (earth man)
Erhard, Ehrhardt
Ernst (earnestness)
Esche (ash—the tree)
Eschweiler (literally ash hamlet, a village with a dominant ash tree)
Esser (eater)
Fabian
Fassbinder (cooper)
Feldmann (man of the field, farmer)
Fiedler (fiddler)
Finger (finger)
Fischer (fisherman)
Fiske (fish)
Fleischmann (meat man, butcher)
Foerster, Förster (forester)
Frank, Franke (from the region Frankonia)
Freitag (Friday)
Friedmann (man of peace)
Friedrich (rich in peace)
Fritsche, Fritz
Fromm (pious)
Fuchs (fox)
Gaertner, Gartner (gardener)
Gebhardt, Gebhard
Gehrke
Geiger (violinist)

Gingerich
Goetz, Götz
Goldberg (golden mountain)
Gottlieb (approximately: lover of God)
Graf (count, earl)
Gross (tall, large)
Grossman (tall, large man)
Gruenwald, Gruenewald, Grünewald (green forest)
Guenther, Günther
Haberman, Habermann (rich)
Hahn (rooster)
Hartmann (strong or bold man)
Hase (hare)
Heidenreich (realm of the heathen)
Heil (salvation)
Heim (home)
Hein, Heine (corral)
Heinrich
Heinz
Held (hero)
Henkel (handle of a basket)
Herbst (autumn)
Herman, Herrman, Hermann
Herr (master, lord, gentleman, sir)
Herzog (duke)
Hess, Hesse (from the region Hesse)
Hildebrand, Hildebrandt
Hirsch (deer)
Hoffman, Hoffmann
Hofmeister (steward, literally master of the court)
Holzhauer (lumberjack)
Horn (horn, bugle)
Huebner, Hübner
Jaeger, Jäger (hunter)
Jahnke
Kahn (barge, boat)
Kaiser (emperor)

Karl
Kasper
Kastner, Kaestner, Kästner (builds small boxes)
Katz (cat)
Keller (cellar)
Kern (core, pit)
Kessler, Keßler (coppersmith)
Kirchner (sexton)
Kirschbaum (cherry tree)
Klein (small)
Kloss, Kloß (clod, lump, dumpling)
Klotz (block)
Klug (smart)
Knapp (scarce)
Koch (cook)
Koehler, Kohler, Köhler (makes charcoal)
Koepke, Köpke
Kohl (cabbage)
Kopp
Kraft (strength, power)
Kranz (wreath)
Krause
Krieger (warrior)
Kroeger, Krueger, Kröger, Krüger (makes jugs; also innkeeper)
Kuehl, Kühl (chilly, cool)
Kuehn, Kühn (courageous, bold)
Kurtz, Kurz (short)
Lamm (lamb)
Land (land)
Landgraf (count)
Lang, Lange (long)
Lauer (tanner)
Lehman, Lehmann (probably a vassal)
Lehrer (teacher)
Lembke
Lentz, Lenz (archaic for the season spring)
Leonard
Liebherr (dear master)
Lindeman (lived near linden tree)

Lorenz
Ludwig
Lueck, Lück (gap)
Luedtke, Lütke
Lustig (merry, jolly)
Lutz
Maier, Mayer, Meyer, Meier (dairy farmer)
Mandel (almond)
Mann (man)
Marks, Marx
Martin
Maurer (mason)
Meissner, Meißner (from the province Meißen)
Meister (master)
Metz
Metzger (butcher)
Michaels
Mielke
Mohr (moor)
Moll (moll)
Mueller, Muller, Müller (miller)
Nagel (nail)
Neff
Neubauer (young farmer)
Neuman, Neumann (new man)
Nieman, Niemann (probably: nobody)
Oldenburg (a town in Germany; literally: old castle)
Otto
Pfeiffer, Pfeifer, Peifer (piper)
Preuss, Preuß (Prussian)
Puetz, Pütz
Rauch (smoke)
Rausch (euphoria, drunkenness)
Rebholz (wood of the vine)
Reich (mighty or rich)
Reichert
Reimer
Reinhardt
Reinke

Reiter (rider)
Richter (judge)
Riedel
Riemer (makes leather straps)
Ritter (knight)
Rosenberg (rose mountain)
Roskopf, Rosskopf (head of the horse)
Ross, Roß (poetic for horse)
Roth, Rot (red)
Sattler (saddler, harness maker)
Sauer (sour)
Schaeffer,Schaffer,Schaefer, Schäfer (shepherd)
Schauer (shower)
Scheibe (slice, window pane)
Schiller (shield maker)
Schindler (shingle-maker)
Schlicht (simple)
Schlosser (locksmith)
Schmid, Schmidt, Schmied, Schmitz(smith)
Schneider (tailor)
Schoen, Schön (beautiful)
Schrank (cupboard, cabinet, wardrobe)
Schroeder, Schröder (van man, works in a mine)
Schubert (shoemaker)
Schueller,Schüller (related to Schüler, student)
Schuh (shoe)
Schulz, Schultz, Schultze, Schultheiß (village mayor)
Schumacher (shoemaker)
Schuster (shoemaker)
Schwab (from the province Swabia)
Schwan (swan)
Schwartz, Schwarz (black)
Schwartzendruber
Schweitzer (from Switzerland; dairy foreman)
Schwulst (swelling)

Seidel (pint)
Siegel (seal for letters)
Sommer, Sommers (summer)
Sonntag (Sunday)
Spitz (pointed, sharp)
Stahl (steel)
Stark (strong)
Stein (stone)
Stern (star)
Strauss, Strauß (floral bouquet)
Theisen, Thiessen
Thiel
Tisch (table)
Troyer
Ullrich, Ulrich
Unger
Viehmeister (master of livestock)
Vogel (bird)
Vogt (overseer, bailiff)
Volk (people)
Wagner, Wegner (makes wagons)
Wahl (choice)
Weidner (a pasture)
Weinberg (vineyard)
Weiss, Weiß (white)
Wendt
Wenzel
Werner
West (west)
Westphal (from Westphalia)
Wieland
Wiener (from Vienna)
Wiesner (lives near meadow)
Winkelman, Winkelmann
Winnike
Winter (winter)
Wolf (wolf)
Yoder
Zahn (tooth)
Zimmer (room)
Zimmerman, Zimmermann (carpenter)
Zook, Zug (train)

Irene Zirbel is shown with the hops bailer at the Koeopsell house, one of three pioneer German farmsteads in Old World Wisconsin outdoor museum near Eagle, Wisconsin.

America's first kindergarten met in this building, by the Octagon House in Watertown, Wisconsin. In front is Bill Jannke, president of the Watertown German Society. The Kindergarten House is on the National Register of Historic Places.

Walter Hammond
Oktoberfest
La Crosse, Wisconsin

Germans in Wisconsin

By Dianne Stevens

Germans were so thoroughly entrenched in Wisconsin that when it entered the Union in 1848, there was an unsuccessful attempt to make it a German-speaking state. In the proportion of German immigrants, Wisconsin led all states. The climate and soil were similar to those of Germany, and an immigrant could vote after living in Wisconsin one year. German churches, schools and societies kept the German language and culture alive.

Many Germans heard about Wisconsin from relatives already settled. There were glowing reports in books by Carl E. Hasse, Carl de Haas, and Ferdinand Goldman. The state printed pamphlets for distribution in New York and Germany. In 1852 Wisconsin sent a commissioner of emigration to New York to lure immigrants to Wisconsin. When Wisconsin was made a diocese in the 1840s with a German-speaking bishop, more German Catholics came. Most immigrants settled in the eastern and lakeshore regions.

Milwaukee was the most popular spot. About 8,000 Germans arrived in Milwaukee in the 1850s. In 1860, they were 16,000 of Milwaukee's 45,000 population. By 1900, 34 percent of Wisconsin's population claimed German descent.

Immigrants from Württemberg with names such as Schlitz, Pabst, and Blatz started breweries that made Milwaukee beer famous. Today, most Milwaukee breweries offer tours and samples. The Captain Frederick Pabst mansion, built in 1893 for the beer baron, is a popular site open to the public.

The House of Heileman was founded in 1853 at La Crosse, Wisconsin. Since 1960, among the nation's brewers, Heileman has moved from thirty-first to fourth in beer sales. It has breweries in 12 cities from Baltimore to Seattle, including Milwaukee, Wisconsin, St. Paul, Minnesota, and Frankenmuth, Michigan. Its brands include Heileman's Old Style, Blatz, Rainier, Black Label, Schmidt, Lone Star, Wiedemann, Tuborg, Heidelberg, and others, including 20 light beers.

Every July, Milwaukee reaffirms its German roots and lives up to the name "Munich of the Midwest." German Fest, on the Milwaukee lake front, is a huge celebration with everything German: music, food, beer, cultural exhibits, vendors selling German imports, a parade, and a church service.

Old World Wisconsin, an outdoor living history museum in Kettle Moraine State Forest southwest of Milwaukee, preserves the homes and buildings of 19th-century immigrants. The various farmsteads show the architectural and cultural heritage of the state, emphasizing the lifestyles of the ethnic groups of Wisconsin. The German area of the museum features three farms, meticulously restored. Visitors can walk or take a shuttle bus.

Margarethe, wife of the famed Carl Schurz, founded the first kindergarten in America in 1856 in Watertown. Originally downtown, it was restored and moved to the grounds of the Octagon House, a novel eight-sided home built in 1854. The Schurz farm, Karlshuegel, is near Watertown.

Germans in Minnesota

By Dianne Stevens

*Statue of Hermann
New Ulm, Minnesota*

Following the United States' expanding frontiers, thousands of Germans headed west to Minnesota and right into trouble.

Welsh and Irish were already settled in the Minnesota River Valley in the 1850s when 18,000 Germans and 12,000 Scandinavians arrived. The Sioux Indians were alarmed at the number of white men moving into their territory and were angry over the way they were treated by the intruders. In 1862 Little Crow, a militant chief, decided to seek revenge. The time was ripe: government troops were occupied with the Civil War and 5,000 white men from Minnesota were fighting for the Union. The warriors took an oath to kill every white person in the valley and to reclaim it.

Most of the white victims were German Americans. At one German settlement a few miles from New Ulm, Little Crow's warriors massacred a family, even ripping an unborn child from the mother's womb. A 14-year old girl was allowed to live, taken captive to Little Crow's teepee. Thirteen German families heading to Fort Ridgley crossed paths with the Indians who first promised protection, then murdered mercilessly. On one road near New Ulm, the Sioux massacred more than 50 settlers.

The warriors then turned to New Ulm, the heart of German settlement in Minnesota. The 900 residents were prepared for battle but most had never fired at another human. Literally fighting for their lives and their families, the New Ulm townsmen held off the Indians, winning the battle. Victory was not cheap. Nearly all the homes in the town were on fire and 26 men were killed.

Government troops soon recovered white captives, sent the Sioux to far-off reservations, convicted 307 chiefs and warriors of rape and murder, and executed 38 Sioux. A settler shot the starving fugitive, Little Crow, in a berry patch. Within months, New Ulm was being rebuilt and restored. Today, a monument on Center Street pays tribute to the New Ulm defenders. A statue on the highest hill in town honors an earlier hero, Hermann, who protected Germany in 9 A.D. from Roman legions.

Germans are Minnesota's most numerous ethnic group, and New Ulm is the state's most German city. According to a *National Geographic* writer, New Ulm is ethnically the least diverse town in the nation since most of its 13,755 residents are of German descent.

German immigrant Frederick Beinhorn, a day laborer in Chicago studying English at night school, founded New Ulm in 1854 as a settlement for hundreds of German immigrants flooding the cheap labor market. The carefully planned town attracted more German settlers who built churches, schools, stores and homes. Beer halls never closed, even on Sunday, making New Ulm famous for its festivities, a reputation it lives up to today. Heritagefest, the third weekend in July, features entertainment and a *Marktstrasse* with artists and crafts. *Octoberfest* is the second and third weekends in October. *Fasching*, New Ulm's version of Mardi Gras, is the weekend before Lent.

Music is a rich tradition. A 45-foot glockenspiel, a carillon clock, rings out its music three times a day. At Domeier's German Store (which claims to be "more German than stores in Germany"), a mechanical gnome from Germany, Heinz (Professor Wichtel), smiles from a heart-shaped window, playing an accordion.

Even in the 1860s New Ulm boasted a "Quintet of Singing Pioneers." They sang well-known folk songs of the late 18th century. Today, New Ulm's musical pride and joy are the Concord Singers, an acclaimed male chorus that has performed in Germany, Austria, and France, as well as in the United States, and has recorded four albums. Founded in 1931, the Concord Singers preserve the musical heritage of New Ulm with an extensive repertoire. As New Ulm's "Ambassadors of Good Will," the singers travel throughout the Upper Midwest.

The Concord Singers of New Ulm, Minnesota at the gazebo of the old Hauenstein Brewery. The brewery closed in 1970 after 106 years.

Photograph by Tate Stillwell, Meyer Studio.

German architecture is abundant in New Ulm. Turner Hall, completed in 1858 and destroyed in the Sioux War in 1862, had a gable facing the street, two turrets, and arched windows. Rebuilt in 1866, it served as a community center. The post office, built in 1910, now the home of the Brown County Historical Society, resembles the town hall in Ulm, Germany. The statue of Hermann is modeled after one in Detmold, Germany. Dr. Martin Luther College, founded in 1884, boasts an impressive German-style building. The brewery and home of August Schell are also representative of German architecture.

German immigrants settled heavily in the Twin Cities, more so in St. Paul, which has had more than 20 German-language newspapers over the years. The German love of beer is evident in St. Paul, where German Americans held 54 of the 57 brewers' licenses issued in a five-month period in 1878.

St. Cloud in Stearns County was another popular area. Many were attracted by the Catholic Church, which encouraged Germans to settle there. Today, large churches like St. Joseph show German influence.

No one had been able to grow alfalfa in the United States outside of California, but Wendelin Grimm, who came from Germany in 1857 with 20 pounds of alfalfa seed, did it in Minnesota. He experimented for six years. In 1863, a neighbor asked Grimm if he fed his thriving cattle corn. Grimm said his only feed was alfalfa. He began distributing seeds of his Minnesota Grimm alfalfa, the first winter-hardy strain in the United States. Today a monument marks the Grimm homestead in Carver County, west of the Twin Cities.

The Hans (Whoopee John) Wilfahrt Band, New Ulm, 1920, one of many Polka and "Oompah" bands. From left: Seated—Ed Stueber, John Wilfahrt, Eddie Wilfahrt. Standing—Emil Domeier, Otto Stueber, John Bauer. All were cousins except for Bauer.

German-American Folk Music

The Germans sailed for America with music in their souls and their instruments carefully packed. The Hinrichs family, for example, provided the music for the ship on which they sailed, and received a reduced fare for their passage. They came in the 1860s to escape German military conscription, and settled along the Mississippi River at Clinton, Iowa.

During the Civil War, German immigrant soldiers on both sides sang in the camps, sometimes within earshot of each other.

When they weren't singing, German Americans formed bands with brass, accordions and the concertina. When a farmer built a barn, the loft was used for dances. The floor was polished, and the invited neighbors and *Verwandten* (relatives) brought cakes and sandwiches for lunch. Music was furnished by the sons of neighbors, all of whom were of German extraction.

Music notes were often written down as the young listened to their parents singing around the supper table. Mothers often sang and yodeled as they did their daily household chores. Thus much of the music was German folk music with an American adaptation—polkas, waltzes, *Laendler,* and *Schottische.* Never mind whether it was folk music or "pop" folk music, or whether it was German or European. Definitions were not important; enjoyment was. Thus the polkas of Germany, Poland, and what is now Czechoslovakia, became intertwined.

Harold Loeffelmacher of New Ulm, Minnesota, founded his "Six Fat Dutchmen" band in 1936 and toured widely with never less than 11 players, all on the slender side, and none of totally German extraction. The Emil Domeier Dance Band's theme song was from a tune he had learned from his mother. At one time there were 21 New Ulm polka bands. Nearby Gibbon, Minnesota, has three polka festivals a year, drawing visitors from every state. Out of this tradition came concertina craftsman Christy Hengel of New Ulm, who was honored by the National Endowment for the Arts. German-American bands travel coast-to-coast today, and major festivals import bands from Germany and Austria.

At left: Besserer's "The Boys Band" of Austin, Texas. Photograph from the collection of the University of Texas Institute of Texan Cultures, San Antonio, Texas.

Lawrence Welk and His Band

By Julie McDonald

Born in the small German-American community of Strasburg, North Dakota, on March 11, 1903, Lawrence Welk once was too embarrassed by his heavy German accent to announce the next dance number, but he became one of the nation's all-time favorite band leaders. After his danceable "champagne music" became popular, Welk's preliminary "Uh-one-uh-two-uh-three" became as famous as the band's distinctive sound.

Welk was next to the youngest in a family of eight children. His father, Ludwig Welk, was a blacksmith who emigrated from Alsace-Lorraine in 1878. Young Lawrence's formal schooling ended in its fourth year, and he went to work in the fields. On winter evenings, members of the family entertained themselves by playing musical instruments. Lawrence learned the accordion from his father. By the time he was 13, Lawrence was playing his $15 instrument at weddings and community affairs. He couldn't read notes, but he made music well enough to collect as much as $150 by passing the hat at weddings.

On his 17th birthday his father gave him a $400 accordion with a piano keyboard. Lawrence embraced it with such enthusiasm that he lost jobs for playing so loud that he drowned out the other musicians. That's why he formed his own band, playing free broadcasts over station WNAX at Yankton, South Dakota, to advertise the group. By 1927 he had a six-piece band called "Lawrence Welk's Hotsy-Totsy Boys."

In 1930 he married a nurse, Fern Renner, and tried various business enterprises (hotel, restaurant, and music store management) that didn't work out. Then he joined comedian George T. Kelley, playing vaudeville houses in the Dakotas. After three years he had saved enough to start a 17-piece band that played at the Edgewater Beach Hotel in Chicago in 1939.

Fans called his music "sparkly" and "bubbly," giving rise to the "champagne music" idea and Welk's own composition, "Bubbles in the Wine." His music was a blend of dance rhythm and flowing melody that some sophisticates called "corny," but when he opened at New York's Capitol Theater, a critic wrote: "There's a touch of America in this genial, wholesome maestro's lilting, danceable music."

Welk played at dance halls small and large, rural and urban. Later, *The Lawrence Welk Show* and *Lawrence Welk's Top Tunes and New Talent* on national television won hearts from coast to coast. Welk's was the first dance band in television history to be signed for a full one-hour network program.

The Welks, Roman Catholics with wholesome interests, have three children, Shirley, Donna Lee and Lawrence Junior. Lawrence Welk became an American institution—a happy music man who says he's "square" and proud of it.

Growing Up in North Dakota

By Sister Bernardine Bichler, OSF

Sister Bernardine Bichler was born October 11, 1913. She became a Sister of St. Francis in 1935 at St. Francis Convent in Hankinson, North Dakota. She has been a nurse, a teacher, a director of nursing and a hospital administrator.

My parents were Germans from Russia. They came to this country in the early 1900s and settled on a farm in Pierce County, North Dakota. Their Catholic heritage was of utmost importance. When their ancestors fled from Germany to Russia, they built schools and churches. Here there was no church or priest for miles. Every Sunday the neighbors met at my grandparents' home to pray the Rosary and to read from the Scriptures. After a church was built, a priest came to offer Mass once every two months.

My uncle, a carpenter, built an altar to fit into the corner of our living room. It was painted white with gold trim. On the altar my mother kept a crucifix, statues of the Blessed Mother and the Sacred Heart of Jesus, two candles, and flowers. Every evening before bedtime the entire family, parents and ten children, gathered for night prayers before this altar. In summer I always enjoyed picking wild flowers to decorate the altar, especially for feast days.

All our prayers we learned at our mother's knee. By the time we were old enough to attend catechism classes, we knew all our prayers—in two languages.

My mother was an excellent cook and she began teaching us to make meals before we reached our teens. She had no recipes. She told me the taste and texture were her guides. From her I learned how to make borscht, a vegetable soup which was started with a beef soup bone. It is especially delicious when made with vegetables, including red beets, right out of the garden. The longer one cooks it, the better it tastes. She also made all kinds of pasta. I am happy that these ethnic foods are surfacing again and are being enjoyed by the present generation of the Germans from Russia.

Family celebrations were a vital part of our heritage. Weddings lasted three days. The most important part, of course, was the church service. I do not remember a wedding without a dance. Name days of father and mother were also a big treat for us children. All our neighbors and relatives would come together for a big dinner followed by a dance. The music was furnished by family members, relatives, or friends. I believe every German from Russia, young or old, automatically knew how to dance.

Sundays in our home were very special. The meat and dessert for the main meal were prepared on Saturday. During the week we could not afford any dessert, but on Sunday there was the best lemon pie! During the summertime, family reunions were special occasions, with outdoor picnics followed by games, usually a good baseball game. All these celebrations strengthened the family, keeping them faithful to family traditions.

My paternal grandmother was a midwife and delivered over 2,000 babies! She delivered nine of the ten children in our family. We were 23 miles from the nearest doctor. We had no cars in those days, no paved roads. Our only transportation was horse and buggy. Many years later I happened to meet the doctor who sort of supervised the work of my grandmother. He said, "I never worried when your grandmother took care of the deliveries within that locality." Whenever we saw our grandmother with her black bag, we knew she was on her way to help a mother deliver her baby.

My grandmother was a healer with herbs. Every summer I would see her going to the meadows to pick herbs, and sometimes I went along with her. She had something for a headache, a stomach ache, kidney problems, etc. Now I feel badly that when I began to study nursing I didn't question her about the remedies she used. One plant, the chamomile, was grown in her garden. From it she made tea which was a cure for everything. Even to this day I love to drink chamomile tea.

When one of my brothers fell and received a two-inch gash in his cheek, my parents and grandparents were gone for the week. I was only a teenager, but I remembered grandmother using chamomile tea to wash out wounds. That is exactly what I did, twice a day. I held the wound together with adhesive tape. The wound healed with hardly a scar.

I am deeply grateful to my parents for instilling in me a rich German-Russian heritage, especially the importance of our traditional Catholic religion.

Pictured below is a bobbin lace doily by Sister Rosalia of the St. Francis Convent at Hankinson, North Dakota. Born in Schönsee, Bavaria, and baptized as Maria Haberl, she attended the Royal Bobbin Lace School. She entered the Convent in 1917 and came to North Dakota in 1928. In retirement she resumed making lace.

Sister Rosalia incorporates birds, flowers, and butterflies into doilies, flower baskets, and other creations. Friends and relatives in Germany send new patterns to her. In 1988 she received a National Endowment for the Arts Heritage Fellowship award.

The Hutterites

Colonies in the Dakotas, East Coast States, and Canada

By Stephen Scott

There are Hutterites in nearly 50 separate communes in South Dakota, and others in North Dakota, Montana, and in Alberta, Saskatchewan, and Manitoba in Canada. A typical village of 140 people is surrounded by farmland of as much as 5,000 acres. A family lives in its own home, joining the group for meals at the community kitchen and dining hall, and for religious services. Children attend school until about age 14. High German, low German, and English are spoken.

Hutterites are descendants of 16th-century German-speaking Anabaptists who were forced to leave Switzerland, fleeing into southern Germany and the Tirol. They take their name from Jakob Hutter, who was tortured and burned as a heretic in 1536 at Innsbruck, Austria.

Invited to Moravia, now a part of Czechoslovakia, the Hutterites spent a peaceful century there in more than 100 communes, with others in Slovakia and Bohemia. As some of Europe's best physicians and craftsmen were Hutterites, the nobles resisted repeated orders by Emperor Ferdinand I to expel them. But troops of various armies took their stores, and at times there was a bounty on them. According to John A. Hostetler, in his book *Hutterite Society*, 87 Hutterites were killed and 238 were sent as slaves, mostly to Turkey. The *Hutterite Chronicle* lists 2,000 who were executed. A century in the Ukraine followed, until Russian pressure caused them to emigrate to the United States starting about 1874. Their first *Bruderhof* was and is in Bon Homme County, along the Missouri River in South Dakota.

The Hutterites drive cars and trucks. Modern farming methods and equipment are employed. Electricity finds many uses, including large walk-in freezers for the kitchens. Interaction between neighboring and distant communes is most common among young people of marriageable age.

Both the Harmonists and the Amana people helped financially in getting the Hutterites started in South Dakota. Their loans were all repaid. There have been contacts ever since between the Amana people and the Hutterites. One Hutterite youth visited Amana and married there; his descendants are among those who visit the Hutterites.

There are five Hutterite colonies in the northeastern United States. These people are descended from a communal group started by Eberhard Arnold in Germany in 1920. Arnold affiliated with the Hutterites in America in 1930. Because of persecution during World War II, these Hutterites went to England, then to Paraguay, and in the 1960s to the United States. Their colonies in New York, Connecticut, and Pennsylvania specialize in manufacturing wooden toys and equipment for the handicapped.

49

A Matter of Choice
In Georgia and Washington

Helen, Georgia

Helen, in the northeast Georgia mountains near the Chattahoochee River, was transformed from a dying mill town into a cheerful Alpine village. In 1968 three Helen businessmen decided to give their town a face-lift to attract tourists. They consulted an artist, John Kollock, who was in the army in Bavaria 18 years earlier. His watercolor sketches of Helen as an Alpine Village were followed. The downtown was remodeled and new buildings went up.

An 18-bell glockenspiel fills the town with popular and seasonal music several times a day. There are shops with crafts and European imports, and restaurants serving Bavarian fare.

Every month, Helen sponsors a festivity such as *Oktoberfest, Maifest,* the *Fasching* (a German Mardi-Gras celebration in February), July Fourth Tube Parade, Clogging Festival, Canoe Races and a Hot Air Balloon Festival. About two million tourists a year visit Helen, a town free of debt and growing.

Leavenworth, Washington

Leavenworth is a town that almost died. Founded in 1884, it prospered for years, then withered with the loss of railroad, sawmill and other payrolls. What to do? The town sought help from the University of Washington's Community Development Division. The residents were given choices. Did they want to become an Old West town, a New West town, a Danish theme town like successful Solvang, California, or an Alpine-German village? They chose the latter.

Today, this town of 1,400, nestled in the mountains east of Seattle, looks and acts truly Bavarian. Transplanted from Germany, edelweiss blooms. A 25-bell carillon serenades the valley each hour. Gingerbread buildings house cheese, clock, and gift shops. Colorful flowers spill from planters, hang from buildings and decorate window boxes. An all-bootstrap, no-public-aid rebirth! These days about a million tourists a year drop in. The *Maifest, Kinderfest,* Leaf Festival, Christmas lighting, and *Volksmärsch* are popular.

A bonus: Before the "rebirth," Leavenworth had no German-speakers, and a few new German immigrants have since chosen to live in Leavenworth.

Odessa, Washington

Odessa, Washington, was named by Germans from the Odessa region of Russia, who had grown wheat along the Black Sea and the Volga River. The town, 75 miles west of Spokane, has a population of 1,100. Wheat is the primary crop and lives still revolve around *Kinder, Kirche,* and *Küche* (children, church, and kitchen). The Odessa *Deutsches Fest* the third weekend in September features a German *Biergarten,* German music, a *Volksmärsch,* authentic German food, entertainment, and craft, art, and hobby shows.

Germans in Missouri

By Dianne Stevens

From nobility to peasants, thousands of Germans arrived in Missouri between 1830 and the mid-1850s. The greatest numbers were in St. Louis—one-third German in 1850—and the Lower Missouri River Valley, often called the Missouri Rhineland. The immigrants established newspapers, theaters, libraries, churches, and schools that kept their language and traditions alive. After the Civil War, the wine industry and new businesses thrived. In 1900 there were German-language newspapers in 20 towns. World War I brought an end to the celebration of German culture: German language was banned in churches, schools and public buildings, and newspapers switched to English.

Today, more than a million and a half Missourians claim German ancestry, and interest in German heritage is visible and acceptable. The flavor of Germany can be savored as towns with German roots celebrate their heritage with *Oktoberfests, Maifests* and traditional German Christmas festivities.

Bethel

In 1844, with Utopian goals, Wilhelm Keil, a German immigrant pastor, founded a religious communal society at Bethel, on the banks of the North River in northeast Missouri. Just 11 years later, with the commune off to a good start, Keil decided the location was "not isolated enough." Leaving 340 members behind, he took 198 in wagon trains to found Aurora, Oregon. Keil guessed wrong. Today Aurora has more than 500 population. It is close to expanding Portland, Oregon, and even closer to busy Interstate 5. Bethel, in contrast, enjoys the isolation of which he dreamed. It is 50 miles inland from Mark Twain's Hannibal on the Mississippi River, and has a population of something over 100.

In the beginning, each family in Bethel had a home with a large plot to raise fruit, vegetables, chickens, hogs, and a cow. Money made from selling the home-grown products could be kept by the family. Feed for the livestock came from colony farms, and goods from the colony store were delivered to every home.

Keil corresponded with people in Bethel, but never returned, and the society disbanded after his death in 1877. Members—nearly 300—divided the money and property.

People still seek out Bethel to learn of its fascinating history. In 1970 Bethel was declared a National Historic Site. Buildings erected by Keil and his followers are open to visitors. The Bair residence is the oldest home, built in 1845. Almost everything in the house was locally made. The white Victorian bandstand in the center of town is a stage for the 15-piece Bethel German Band, a proud tradition dating from colony days.

Bethel residents celebrate October and Christmas in grand style. Harvest Fest, the first weekend in October, features craft demonstrations, a flea market, house tours and authentic German food served at the Fest Hall, the Colony Restaurant.

The traditional Christmas celebrations include visits by St. Nicholas and the Black Santa, a dark figure wearing—over his head with "eyes" cut out—a cloth sack, topped with a flat, crowned hat. Also known as Knecht Ruprecht, the Black Santa arrives a few weeks before Christmas giving switches to bad children so they have time to mend their ways before St. Nicholas arrives with goodies.

Sheep Fest, on Labor Day weekend, is one of the largest sheep and wool shows in the country. There are sheep shearing contests, dog trials, weaving and spinning contests, and plenty of lamb to eat.

Washington

Washington, on the southern bank of the Missouri River, an hour west of St. Louis, has a distinct German flavor. It was just a landing in 1822 when a ferry began operating. By 1840 German Americans were about a third of the population. Many were Catholic Hanoverians from Osnabrück. St. Francis Borgia Church, the largest in town, was founded by Hanover immigrants.

The steamboat trade and the manufacturing of wagons, carriages, boots, shoes, tanned leather, pottery, bricks, furniture, wooden shoes, and beer spelled prosperity for Washington before the Civil War. With prosperity came impressive churches, shops, and homes built in German fashion of locally made brick. After the Civil War, zither and corn-cob pipe factories opened. The pipes are still being made and Washington is "the Corn Cob Pipe Capital of the World."

Washington celebrates its German heritage with a *Volksmärsch* through the town the second weekend in October and a Fine Arts Fair and Wine Festival the second weekend in May. Pork Sausage and Sauerkraut Festivals, sponsored by churches, are popular throughout the year, particularly in the fall. A famous dinner is at St. John's Gildehaus Church, Villa Ridge, on the fourth Sunday in October; the food is served family style.

The Busch Brewery and the J.B. Busch residence are open to the public. Founded by John B. Busch, Henry Busch and Fred Gersie, the brewery is older than the famous Busch brewery in St. Louis, started by John B. Busch's brother, Adolphus. The Spaunhorst House, built in 1869, is an excellent example of the brick houses of the early German settlers.

Hermann

Three times the people of Hermann, Missouri, have met adversity and won. The first time, these people—German immigrants—were in Philadelphia and decided things were getting too "Americanized." In 1837 they founded Hermann, about 70 miles west of St. Louis on the Missouri River. They named their town for the German hero who defeated the Romans in 9 A.D. Hermann didn't outgrow Philadelphia, which had been anticipated when they made Market Street 10 feet wider than Philadelphia's Market Street. Still, it prospered, and it took seriously its mission to preserve the German language and customs.

Adversity struck a second time in the form of World War I. Hermann sent its sons to war, but felt the sting of the nationwide aversion to anything German, especially the German language and customs.

Adversity's third strike knocked out the entire industry on which Hermann's prosperity depended—the wineries, plus some distilling and brewing. Prohibition was the law of the land from January 16, 1920 until 1934. To create jobs, the town attracted a shoe industry, but basically, Hermann felt the Great Depression 10 years earlier than other towns.

Gone were some valued Hermann traditions. For example, the city once offered to sell each resident from one to five lots at $50 each, to be paid within five years without interest—provided the lots were planted in grapes. About 600 lots were sold. The Stone Hill Winery, atop a high hill with storage cellars cut into the underground stone, was the third largest in the world, winner of gold medals in eight World Fairs.

The Stone Hill Winery, founded in 1847, did not resume wine-making until 1965. Its wines have won in state, national, and international competitions, and the winery has so many visitors it operates its famed "Vintage 1847 Restaurant." Stone Hill Winery, Hermannhof Winery, Puchta Winery, and Bias Winery are open daily for tours and tasting. Hermann restaurants proudly offer German sausages and traditional German dishes.

The Hermann National Historic District includes more than 100 structures built before 1870. The German School Building, used from 1870 to 1955, is a museum with artifacts, a handmade wooden wine press, pottery, a river room, locally made crafts, antique furniture, and the mechanism of the town clock. The Deutschheim State Historic Site is operated by the Missouri Department of Natural Resources.

Wurstfest, in March, is a tribute to sausage makers. *Maifest* features Show Boat Community Theatre, parades, food, and music. *Octoberfest* is a highlight.

"Here is to be found a most inviting countryside, in which exists more German sociability than perhaps anywhere else in America," a visitor to Hermann wrote in 1855. The observation holds true today.

The Stone Hill Winery in 1912

Office, Press Houses and Grape Crushing Plant. Storage Cellar No. 6. Capacity 175,000 Gallons.

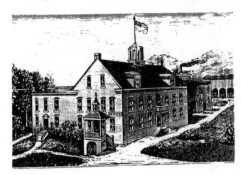 

Memories from St. Louis

By Paul L. Maier

*Paul L. Maier is a professor of history at Western Michigan
University, Kalamazoo, Michigan.*

Although my father's radio broadcasting career was an American success
story—he was Walter A. Maier, founding speaker of *The Lutheran Hour*—his
roots were totally Teutonic. A son of German immigrants who settled in Boston,
he married Hulda A. Eickhoff of Indianapolis in 1924, a union of total German
ethnicity, as the names easily suggest. Both, however, spoke English without a
trace of an accent—unlike *their* parents. But since they had been raised in
families where German was spoken before English, they attempted the same
with their own offspring, my brother Walter Jr. and me.

Brother Walt carried on with the German longer than I did, but his bilingual-
ism was quickly curtailed the first time he played with the neighbor boys and
asked them to throw him a ball by saying, *"Gib mir den Ball!"*

"So who's *that* foreigner?!" they shouted, derisively.

German was shunted aside after that, except in family devotions, where the
Lord's Prayer was uttered about half the time in the mode, *"Vater unser...."* Our
bedtime prayers, too, continued in German, a string of brief hymn verses and
Bible passages—the same series of German petitions we all recited together at
Father's bedside as he lay dying in January, 1950. By the 1930s both parochial
and Sunday school instruction were in English.

One of the earliest recollections of my childhood days was a conversation I
had with my mother—*in German*. When I was a toddler, she used to take me
sightseeing to various churches near our home in St. Louis County, but one day
she varied the routine by visiting a synagogue. I looked around inside, and then
asked, *"Aber wo ist der liebe Heiland?"* (Where is the dear Savior, Jesus?) When
mother explained that worship there did not involve Christ, I replied, *"Komm,
lass't uns gehen."* (Come, let's go).

In the spring of 1935, the Walter A. Maiers served as patrons of German art
for the city of St. Louis. The famed 700-year-old *Dresdner Kreuzchor*—the Boys'
Choir of Holy Cross College in Dresden, Germany—was planning its first
American tour with a debut at the Metropolitan Opera House in New York.
Father and Mother, with the help of interested friends, sponsored the St. Louis
appearance at a full Municipal Opera House, with prolonged ovations and en-
thusiastic reviews.

We housed two of the choristers overnight at our home on the grounds of
Concordia Seminary in St. Louis. En route to the concert, my brother tried to
restore the German *Sprachgefühl* we were both losing by asking them, *"Sprechen
sie Deutsch?"*

"Ah ... ja natürlich!!!" one responded, in disdain.

So much for small talk in a foreign language!

Mother also hosted German-speaking parties at our home, some of which were attended by the German consul and his wife, until the nefarious shadow of Adolf Hitler put an end to all that in the late 1930s.

Every Christmas the Maier family celebration began with Father at the piano playing (by ear) the German Yuletide folksong, *"Kling, Glöckchen, Kling-a-ling-a-ling!"* (Ring, Little Bell, etc.). The rest of the family sang the lyrics lustily while clanging bells and chimes of every description, as we all marched in festive procession throughout the house during endless choruses.

Grandmother Maier, whom we styled "Grossie" (for *Grossmutter*), often visited us at Christmastime. Born in picturesque Rothenburg in southern Germany, she never lost her German accent. With her, "faith" and "fate" received the same pronunciation. Before Christmas, *Grossie* filled the air with the fragrance of cookies baked from wondrous European recipes. We were convinced that her *Prügelkrapfen* would be "The Official Cookie" in heaven.

Whenever the Maier family embarked on a vacation, Father would lead us in prayer for a safe journey. The invocation always began, *"Unsern Ausgang segne Gott, unsern Eingang gleichermassen . . . ."* (May God bless our leaving, and our coming as well). As we were driving, however, if an automobile accident seemed imminent, Mother would cry out, *"Gott behütte uns!!!"* (God protect us!) We had not a few accidents on those narrow, twisting roads of the 1930s, and the younger Maiers grew to detest Mother's three-word shout, because it always seemed to herald disaster!

Mother's three sisters in Indianapolis were not our "aunts," but *"die Tanten,"* and whenever they visited us at our summer home along lake Ontario, morning table devotions often began with what Walt and I (now thoroughly Anglicized) irreverently called "Fang Song"—*"Fang dein Werk mit Jesu an"* (With the Lord begin thy task). At day's end, Father and Mother often stood arm-in-arm along the lakeshore and serenaded the setting sun with the song, *"Seh, wie die Sonne dort sinket . . . ."*

Although my mother was born and raised in Indiana, speaking and writing English perfectly, the German confirmation instruction she received and the German hymns she learned remained with her indelibly throughout life, especially toward its close. During the months before she passed away in 1986—on her 96th birthday—she would recite endless verses of German hymns from memory, finding extraordinary inspiration and comfort in them.

Christianity and music, then, served as the most reliable conduits for German culture in our family. I doubt that our experience is unique.

Virginia's German Farm Site

Museum of American Frontier Culture

By Karin Gottier

The Museum of American Frontier Culture is just off I-81 at Exit 57 in Staunton, Virginia. Nestled in the hilly countryside are three farms depicting the life in the homelands of Germany, Ireland, and England. At the fourth farm, all the buildings are from Virginia.

Because many Germans who settled in Virginia came from the Palatinate area (some by way of Pennsylvania), the German farmhouse comes from the village of Hoerdt in the district of Germersheim. A gift from the people of the state of Rheinland-Pfalz, the farm depicts life in the middle of the 18th century. Costumed interpreters reenact daily life as it was then.

Weinlesefest at the Museum of American Frontier Culture: "Vineyard worker" Paul Buckley (J.M.U. student) presenting the Grape-Harvest crown. —Karin Gottier photo

Together with members of the community and students from the Department of Dance and Theater at James Madison University and the Craigsville and Churchville elementary schools, the museum staff celebrates seasonal festivals of the Palatinate. Visitors can join in the historical *Kerwe (Kirchweih)* celebration. In Germany, this is still an annual celebration of the name-day of the saint for whom the Catholic or Lutheran church is named. Mostly secular today, *Kerwe* is celebrated with food, dancing, speeches, and drinking. The waltz and polka are gone and the young dance to contemporary rock and roll.

Museum visitors also can participate in the *Weinlesefest*—a wine harvest celebration.

In the spring, children can help drive out winter and welcome summer. In December, German Christmas customs are reenacted. Children try working at traditional crafts, and watch holiday preparations.

56

The Texas Germans

By Dianne Stevens

Mention Texas and colorful images come to mind: Stetson hats, cowboys, rompin' stompin' rodeos, tacos and tequila. But in central Texas Hill Country it is German territory, complete with *Biergartens*, sausage, and the German language. The Germans were the largest ethnic group from Europe to immigrate to Texas and today more than 750,000 Texans claim German descent.

The first German immigrants trickled into Texas during the Mexican period (1821-1836), lured by the Mexican government with promises of free land. In 1831, Friedrich Ernst and Charles Fordtran arrived in Texas, and Fordtran established the town of Industry, so named because of its quick early growth.

Ernst wrote to a friend in Oldenburg, Germany, that Texas had "enchanting scenery and delightful climate similar to that of Italy, the most fruitful soil, and republican government, with unbounded personal and political liberty, free from so many disadvantages and evils of old countries." Publication of the letter in a newspaper enticed more Germans to Texas.

Texas was not, however, an easy paradise. German immigrants fought in the Texas Revolution (1835-1836), battled Indians, and endured the hardships of settling in a raw country.

In 1842 the Society for the Protection of German Immigrants in Texas, or the *Mainzer Adelsverein*, was formed. Backed by noblemen and headed by Prince Carl of Solms-Braunfels, the *Adelsverein* encouraged immigration. In 1844 three shiploads of immigrants with the *Adelsverein* arrived in Galveston and traveled down the coast to Carlshafen (later named Indianola) only to discover that there were no living accommodations there. Camping on the wet, winter beach, hundreds of immigrants died; more perished on the long trek inland to New Braunfels on the Comal River. From 1844 to 1847 about 7,500 Germans arrived in Texas through the *Adelsverein*.

The society replaced Prince Carl with Baron Ottfried Hans von Meusebach, who arrived at Galveston in 1845. Dropping his title, he became John O. Meusebach. His fiancée, Elizabeth von Hardenberg, remained in Germany. They corresponded, but Elizabeth died. Meusebach later married a Texan, Agnes Coreth, from Austria. Their proud descendants cherish their lineage.

The fierce Comanches had been a constant threat to settlers. Realizing that a 3,000,000-acre area between the Llano and Colorado Rivers—the Fisher-Miller Land Grant—was claimed by Waco and Comanche Indians who called it home, Meusebach first settled with the less hostile Waco tribe, and then arranged with a Comanche chief, Ketemoczy, for a peace council.

In January 1847, Meusebach rode into the Comanche camp with 40 men. Several hundred warriors lined up on one side of the camp armed with guns, bows and arrows. Squaws and children were on the other side while the three head chiefs—Buffalo Hump, Santa Anna, and Mopechucope—sat in the middle on buffalo robes. Meusebach and his men rode up and down the aisle of warriors, emptying their rifles in the air to show they were peaceful and unafraid. Impressed by his bravery, the Indians named Meusebach *El Sol Colorado*, the Red Sun. For Meusebach's promise of $3,000 worth of presents, the Comanches agreed to allow the colonists to settle peacefully on the Fisher-Miller Land Grant. This became the only treaty between Europeans and Texas Indians under which both sides kept their promises.

Today some 150,000 Texans speak both German and English. Texas Hill Country, a 50- to 75-mile area near Austin, is "German Country." Festivals and organizations keep German traditions thriving. *Schuetzenfests* (literally, shooting festivals) are popular, as are the *Sängerbunds* (singing societies) which keep traditional German songs alive. *Turnvereine*, men's athletic social clubs dating from pioneer days, are active, and there are *Octoberfests* and *Maifests.*

The Order of the Sons of Hermann, with about 160 Texas lodges, is the oldest (1861) fraternal benefit society. Members participate in festivals, concerts, dances, and parades. The Grand Lodge is in San Antonio.

Exhibits at the University of Texas Institute of Texan Cultures at San Antonio tell of German Texans such as General and President Dwight D. Eisenhower, born in Denison, and Admiral Chester W. Nimitz, a native of Fredericksburg. The Texas Folklife Festival, sponsored by the Institute the first weekend in August, is a four-day celebration of the state's ethnic diversity. Nearly 6,000 people share their traditions with about 100,000 visitors through music, food, crafts, story-telling, and demonstrations.

German influence isn't limited to the Hill Country. Gainesville and Muenster, near the Oklahoma border, are German-American communities. Austin, San Antonio and Houston have sizable German-American populations. Some towns have German names, including New Braunfels, Fredericksburg, Solms, Hocheim, Westphalia, Oldenburg, Mecklenburg, New Berlin, Germania, Rhineland, New Baden, and Weimar. Others, such as Industry, Comfort, and Sisterdale, are German-American in all but name.

Fredericksburg

Founded in 1846, Fredericksburg was named for Prince Frederick of Prussia. Wide streets, homes with latticed windows, *willkommen* signs, and German restaurants confirm the German heritage.

Sunday houses are an attraction. Distances precluded one-day trips to town, so farm families built small "Sunday houses" and spent the weekend when they came to church. Some of these historic homes are bed and breakfast stops today. Fredericksburg's original *Vereins Kirche* is an eight-sided community church which also served as a school, town hall, and meeting place.

The *Kristkindl* (Christ Child) Market is an 800-year-old German Christmas tradition kept alive in Fredericksburg. Legend has it that the Christ Child, not Santa Claus, goes to the market to choose gifts for children. The *Kristkindl* Market features homemade goodies, handmade gifts, all the trimmings for a German Christmas, and carolers.

The Nimitz Museum, Fredericksburg, Texas

The Nimitz Museum is a treasure house of the memorabilia of Admiral Chester Nimitz, who commanded the Pacific Fleet in World War II, plus displays that thoroughly document that era. Nimitz was born in Fredericksburg. In 1905 he graduated with distinction from the U.S. Naval Academy. His grandfather, Captain Charles H. Nimitz, came to Fredericksburg in 1847, and built a series of hotels, each larger and more splendid than the last. The museum building was his last construction. It included a hotel, casino, saloon, general store, brewery, and stables, and was a stopping place on the road from San Antonio to El Paso. Its register contained the names of Robert E. Lee, Ulysses S. Grant, Rutherford B. Hayes, and a "Mr. Howard" (the notorious Jesse James).

The legendary Fredericksburg Easter Fires have been a tradition since 1847, when John O. Meusebach was negotiating a land treaty with the Comanche Indians. While Meusebach and his 40 men negotiated, fires blazed on the hills overlooking Fredericksburg as Indians signaled that all was peaceful. Children were frightened by the eerie fires until one mother spun a tale that calmed their fears and has delighted children to this day. With Easter still weeks away, she said it was only the Easter Bunny and his helpers who were cooking eggs in huge cauldrons, and coloring them with wildflowers from the hills so they could deliver them to children on Easter morning. Today the pageant of the fires still heralds Easter in Fredericksburg.

Karin Gottier, a native of Germany, writes: "In many regions of Germany, fires are burned at or around Easter. Some are huge piles of wood. Sometimes straw figures are burned in them. Some people wrap straw around wheels and roll them, burning, down hill. Some toss burning disks in the air. Sometimes young people will ignite torches on the bonfire and swing them in the air. Usually there are fires on top of hills, occasionally near water, or along the banks on both sides of a river. In southern Germany, Palms (elaborate structures of eggs and pussywillow) that hung under the roofs of barns are taken to a hill and

Easter in Fredericksburg, Texas

burned before new ones are put up on Palm Sunday. Whatever the Easter fire, it is always carried out by the young men in the town, assisted by the adolescent male population."

About 15 miles east of Fredericksburg, near Stonewall, the State of Texas has established the Lyndon B. Johnson State Historical Park, honoring the late United States President. Included in the park is the Sauer-Beckman farm, established by German immigrants. More than a century old, it is now a Living History Farm, operated as it would have been by a German family of the 1915-1918 period.

New Braunfels

Festivals, tree-lined streets, and beautifully preserved homes and buildings of the original settlers give historic presence to New Braunfels, founded in 1845 by Prince Carl. The Sophienburg Memorial Museum is on the site where Prince Carl erected his fortified headquarters. The original Sophienburg, named after his fiancée, Princess Sophia of Salm-Salm, was destroyed by a storm in 1866. Museum exhibits include a hand-crafted model of the Prince's castle in Braunfels, Germany. The Museum of Texas Handmade Furniture offers visitors an in-depth look at the art of furniture making.

Some restored historic homes are open to visitors. The Lindheimer Home was built by Ferdinand Lindheimer, editor of New Braunfels' first newspaper, the *Neu-Braunfelser Zeitung,* who is also known as the father of Texas botany. Lindheimer led the first colonists to the site that became New Braunfels.

The Baetge House, built in 1852, features hand-hewn timbers and cypress siding. Born in Germany, Carl Baetge built a railroad from St. Petersburg to Moscow to connect the Winter Palace to the Summer Palace. In New Braunfels he built his home near Canyon Lake. The original home has been dismantled and rebuilt on its present site, the Conservation Plaza.

New Braunfels' *Wurstfest* (sausage festival) the last 10 days in October features bands, dancing, tent shows, tours, demonstrations, and exhibits. It is one of Texas' most popular events.

The Wends of Texas

The Wends from Germany add to the cultural diversity of Texas. Also known as Sorbs or Lusatian Sorbs, most European Wends live near Bautzen and Cottbus in eastern Germany. Many of them are bi-lingual, speaking both German and Wendish, a Sorbian language.

Seeking religious freedom, a better way of life, and escape from agricultural disasters and poverty, the first Wends came to the Lone Star State in 1849, joining German settlers in the Hill Country. A hardy band of 35, sailing in 1853, all survived when their ship was wrecked off the coast of Cuba, but they were stranded until a German benevolent society in New Orleans bankrolled the rest of the journey to Galveston. The newcomers went to New Ulm and Industry. Descendants of these immigrants live in the area today.

The Texas Wendish Heritage Society, formed in 1971, seeks to preserve and represent the Wendish culture. The society participates in parades and festivals, sells cookbooks with authentic Wendish pioneer recipes, and converted the old Serbin schoolhouse into a museum.

Concordia College in Austin, which Wends help support, named the main building for Pastor Johann Kilian (1811-1884), leader of the nearly 600 conservative Lutheran Wends who landed at Galveston just before Christmas in 1854. Outside the chapel, the college displays the bell he brought over from Germany for his church.

Life With Indians

Herman Lehmann lived his first 11 years as the son of German immigrants in Texas and the next nine years as a wild Indian among Indians.

His family lived about 25 miles northwest of Fredericksburg. Herman was captured by hostile Apache Indians in 1870. His younger brother, Willie, also was captured, but escaped and made his way home in about nine days.

Herman was harshly treated and tortured until members of the tribe decided to raise him as one of them. He became thoroughly "Indianized," hunting, scalping, stealing, and fighting with the other warriors.

When an Apache medicine man murdered Lehmann's chief and tried to kill Lehmann, the boy killed the medicine man and, fearing for his own life, escaped into exile. He lived on his own for about a year before transferring his allegiance to the Comanche Indians.

When the Indians were rounded up and forced onto reservations, soldiers brought a reluctant Lehmann home to his family—nine years after being captured. He had a difficult time adjusting to wearing clothes, eating cooked meat, sleeping in a bed, and not stealing.

Eventually he was reconciled to civilized life. He relearned German, married, and had five children whose descendants live in Texas today. Lehmann always maintained his Comanche ties and was considered by the United States government to be a member of the tribe.

Lehmann said he was not the only paleface living among the Indians. He ran into several captives during his adventures. Some of them were restored to their families, and others chose to live among the Indians.

German Jews in America

By Harry Oster

*Dr. Oster is a professor of American Literature
and Folklore at the University of Iowa.*

After the downfall of Napoleon it was impossible for free Jewish life to thrive in Europe. The grudgingly granted equality Jews enjoyed during the dominance of Napoleon evaporated as a new wave of hate swept the continent. The Jews, as so often in history, served as convenient scapegoats. They were blamed for unemployment, social upheaval, and economic distress. The old anti-Jewish restrictions came to life again almost everywhere in Germany. Ghettos were reestablished and Jews were once more forced to live under the same oppressive rules as in earlier centuries. Lübeck and Bremen expelled most of their Jews and deprived others of civil and political rights. Professor Ruhs, a member of the faculty of the University of Berlin, proposed the restoration of the medieval badge "so that the German who could not recognize his Hebrew enemy by face, gait, or speech might do so by the doubtful badge of honor." An orgy of Jew-baiting began, and Jews were beaten and robbed. The 1815 Holy Alliance of Kings promised Christian conduct, but in Germany, just four years later, the medieval outrages of killing, pillaging, and burning were revived. In Heidelberg, the criminal rapist of a Jewish girl was freed by a howling mob. The world which was rebuilt by the Congress of Vienna (1814-1816) promised only new sorrows for Jews.

Many Jews allied themselves with Europe's revolutionary movement of 1848—on the barricades, in revolutionary parliaments, as student agitators, and as radical journalists. Political refugees coming to the United States after the collapse of this revolution were high in talent. Many of these had distinguished careers, including doctors Abraham Jacobi and Ernest Krackowizer, physician and chemist Joseph Goldmark, editor and journalist Michael Heilprin, and Rabbi Benjamin Szold.

In addition to the Jewish Forty-Eighters, thousands of other Jews in central Europe were drawn to a land where "the man comes first, then religion and the state and all else." Thus there occurred a dramatic rise in the number of American Jews—from 15,000 in 1840 to 50,000 in 1850 to 150,000 in 1860. There was a decline in the number from central Europe around 1870 when Jews finally won their rights in Germany and Austro-Hungary. German Jews in the United States worked as manual laborers, skilled artisans, small shopkeepers, and wealthy operators and owners. They were in all branches of the economy—trade and commerce, agriculture and related industries, mining, manufacturing, real estate, and banking. Their distribution, however, did not correspond to that of the general population, which had a preponderance of farmers, laborers, and craftsmen. The Jews, instead, gravitated toward the cities.

62

The average 19th-century German Jewish immigrant arrived with some capital. He saw that peddling supplied a chance for building up capital, which would in turn lead to retail and wholesale stores. Thus peddling attracted ambitious young men of a variety of backgrounds and education.

Unlike the pre-revolutionary Jews who clustered in five urban centers along the Atlantic seaboard, the immigrant peddlers spread out in many directions, planting the seeds of Jewish institutional life in most of the states and territories. Just before the Civil War, most of the 165,000 peddlers in the United States were Jews, following the footsteps of the Yankees, who had moved up the economic scale. The Jewish peddlers came through the major entry ports of New York, Philadelphia, Baltimore, and New Orleans, and through Midwestern centers such as St. Louis and Milwaukee. Many chose to stay close to the recent German settlement in the Cincinnati-Milwaukee-St. Louis triangle, where the ambience of a common language and origin was appealing. Some traveled to California to sell food and supplies to the mining camps of the Gold Rush. Others were attracted to the southwestern frontier, generally after service in the Mexican War and the Civil War or various Indian campaigns.

Storekeeping, like peddling, enabled the lucky ones to branch out into higher levels of economic achievement—wholesaling and the modern department store. Department store owners or "merchant princes" who advanced from the peddling-small store path included the Strausses (Macy's, Abraham & Strauss), Filenes, Gimbels, Rosenwalds (Sears and Roebuck), and Riches. Such roots led the Seligmans, the Lehmans, and Marcus Goldman (Goldman, Sachs) into banking and finance.

The first steps that led into the ready-to-wear industry were taken in the 1830s in Massachusetts and New York to supply clothing for the southern poor and slaves, sailors, miners, and frontiersmen. German Jews entered the field early. The invention of the sewing machine in 1846 helped. In the 1850s Levi Strauss developed tough, copper-riveted canvas pants for laborers. Today jeans connote a curious mixture of earthiness, casual sportiness, and fashion.

The Civil War opened new markets for the clothing industry to produce uniforms. In Milwaukee one Jewish firm had a contract for 12,000 uniforms; in Cleveland another produced 500 officers' uniforms in one month. Seligmans, who had started as peddlers in 1837, opened a small store.

The next important wave of German Jewish immigrants came with Hitler's rise to power in 1933. *Der Fuehrer* shocked the world by firing the titans of German scholarship, most of whom were Jewish. The infamous book burning on May 10, 1933 was an expression of Hitler's belief that writing and thinking were forms of political behavior. He lumped together university professors, free-lance critics, and vanguard artists as though they were one breed. Eighty percent of the 30,000 radicals exiled between 1933 and 1939 were Jewish. In 1935 the Nuremberg Laws deprived all Jews of their citizenship and their rights, but there was no danger of extermination until after the 1938 *Kristallnacht* rioting (the breaking of windows of Jewish shops) when being a Jew or even a quarter Jewish was grounds for extinction.

Of the refugees, 132,000 came to the United States. As a result of the demographics of German Jewish society, they were more prepared for urban life than earlier immigrants had been. Required by the U.S. government to show evidence that they were financially solvent, they tended to be richer and better educated than earlier waves of immigrants—a fertile stream of doctors, lawyers, businessmen, scientists, artists, and writers who would greatly enrich the culture and science of their new homeland.

The greatest scientist of our time, Albert Einstein (1879-1955), was born in Ulm, grew up in Munich, became a Swiss citizen at age 21, and in 1905 published *Toward the Electrodynamics of Moving Bodies*, the first statement of his theory of relativity. He taught at the University of Zürich and Zürich's Federal Institute of Technology until 1914, when he went to the University of Berlin to concentrate on research. He was awarded the 1921 Nobel Prize for his work in photoelectricity and theoretical physics. In the early 1930s, as a visiting professor at Oxford University, Einstein vigorously promoted pacifism, and helped found the Einstein War Resisters' International Fund. In 1933, both because he was Jewish and had taken a strong stand against National Socialism (Naziism), the German government expelled Einstein from the Prussian Academy of Science, revoked his citizenship, confiscated his property, and put a price on his head. Einstein was in Belgium on a lecture tour at the time, and never returned. He accepted a professorship at the Institute for Advanced Study in Princeton, New Jersey, becoming a United States citizen in 1940. Thus the mind which produced the theory of relativity, and whose findings were precursors of automation systems and even television, became a major asset of the United States. Kept fully informed by his friends in Europe of progress in atom-splitting in Denmark and Germany, Einstein, in August 1939, wrote a letter to President Franklin D. Roosevelt, warning that unless the United States produced the atomic bomb the Germans would develop it first and have us at their mercy. In this way the pacifist Einstein played a central role in initiating the Manhattan atomic bomb project. A great number of German Jewish scientists worked on this project. It makes one wonder whether without Hitler's murderous anti-Semitism, Germany might have won World War II.

- •In Germany, they came first for the communists,
  and I didn't speak up because I wasn't a communist.
- •Then they came for the Jews, and I didn't speak up
  because I wasn't a Jew.
- •Then they came for the trade unionists,
  and I didn't speak up because I wasn't a trade unionist.
- •Then they came for the Catholics,
  and I didn't speak up because I was a Protestant.
- •Then they came for me, and by that time
  no one was left to speak up.
—*Pastor Martin Niemöller, arrested in 1939 by the Gestapo*

Names to Remember

By Julie McDonald

The accomplishments of German Americans are woven so tightly into the fabric of our national life that we tend to take them for granted. The names of these energetic contributors have become household words.

Dr. Franz Daniel Pastorius, born in Franconia on September 26, 1651, led the first German emigration to the United States in 1683. Arriving with 13 families on the *Concord*, later known as "the German Mayflower," he founded Germantown, Pennsylvania, now a part of Philadelphia.

Baron Friedrich Wilhelm von Steuben, an army officer under Frederick II the Great, came to America in 1777, trained soldiers at Valley Forge, Pennsylvania, and wrote the training manual that was used by all the American forces. He was a division commander in the siege of Yorktown. Johann Paul Schott, who came to America in 1776, also had served with Frederick the Great. He recruited an independent troop of German dragoons, was captured by the British, and refused to be a turncoat, saying, "I have chosen America as my fatherland." Johann de Kalb, a Revolutionary War general, helped recruit the Marquis de Lafayette for America, and lost his own life in the battle of Camden, South Carolina.

Carl Schurz, an exile from the 1848 revolution, was nominated for lieutenant governor of Wisconsin before he became an American citizen, but was defeated. Schurz was editor of *The Westliche Post* in St. Louis, *The New York Evening Post*, and *The Nation*. He authored biographies of Abraham Lincoln and Henry Clay. A general in the Civil War, he also served as U. S. Senator from Missouri, Secretary of the Interior, and Ambassador to Spain.

Robert Wagner, born in Germany in 1877, was the architect of the American Social Security system and the National Labor Relations Act of 1935, known as the Wagner Act. He served as a Senator from New York.

Two United States presidents were descended from German Swiss immigrants. Herbert Hoover, the 30th President, traced his roots to Andreas Huber, who arrived in America in 1739. The Hoover birthplace, presidential library and tomb in West Branch, Iowa, show the progression from a tiny house where the future president slept in a space-saving trundle bed, to the Oval Office, and finally to the peaceful hillside where Herbert Hoover is buried.

Dwight D. Eisenhower, the 33rd President, descended from a German Swiss ancestor who arrived in 1741. Eisenhower distinguished himself as Supreme Allied Commander in World War II and was president of Columbia University before his 1952 campaign for the presidency. The life story of this American leader in war and peace is memorialized at the Eisenhower Presidential Library, Abilene, Kansas.

General John J. (Black Jack) Pershing commanded the American Expeditionary Force in World War I, and "Stormin' Norman" Schwarzkopf led the American and Allied forces that drove Iraq's troops from Kuwait in 1991.

During the Civil War, General Franz Sigel held Missouri in the Union with the help of German groups in St. Louis. General George Armstrong Custer (1839-1876), a German American who distinguished himself in Civil War battles, was killed by Indians with all 266 of his men in the Battle of the Little Bighorn in Montana. Custer State Park and the town of Custer in western South Dakota are named for him.

Heinz Alfred (Henry) Kissinger was the first German-born U.S. Secretary of State. Born in Bavaria in 1923, he came to New York with his family in 1938. He served on the Harvard University faculty, becoming an adviser to three presidents (Eisenhower, Kennedy and Johnson) before being appointed Secretary of State in 1973, the year he won the Nobel Peace Prize.

Many of America's legendary fortunes were amassed by German Americans. John Jacob Astor arrived in New York in 1784 with seven flutes to sell, hoping to open a musical instruments shop. He died in 1848, a fur trader and the richest man in America. He distributed much of his fortune philanthropically.

The Steinway pianos preferred by many keyboard artists are made by a family that changed its name from Steinweg to Steinway. The Steinways arrived in 1850, and father and sons went to work in a piano factory. They started Steinway & Sons three years later, developed the upright piano, and prospered.

Charles Spreckels from Hannover became the "Sugar King" of California. Other royalty of the world of commerce included Frederick Weyerhauser, the "Lumber King" who owned more timberland than any other American, and H. John Heinz, the "Pickle King" of Pittsburgh.

The beer barons of America included Eberhard Anheuser, the owner of a Bavarian brewery who teamed in the 1870s with Adolphus Busch, a wine merchant's son from Mainz, to produce Budweiser in St. Louis. Names like Pabst, Schlitz and Best were firm proof of German quality, and countless smaller breweries employed German-American brewmasters.

How could American teens live without the blue jeans of Levi Strauss? This Bavarian immigrant became a supplier to the gold-hungry hordes bound for California in 1850. Discovering a need for "tough pants" among the prospectors, he asked a tailor to make some from canvas and rivet the pockets to make them strong enough to hold gold nuggets. The word "jeans" comes from the Italian city, Genoa, where the tough fabric was first made. Strauss hated the word. He called his product "overalls."

Henry Villard, born in Germany in 1835, helped open up the American continent through railroad construction. First noted as a journalist, he owned *The Nation* and *The New York Evening Post*. He also raised money for constructing the Northern Pacific Railroad. He was the first president of Edison General Electric, which became the General Electric Company. His philanthropy set an example for the Rockefellers.

Dr. Abraham Jacobi, born in Hartum, Westphalia in 1830, is known as the father of American pediatrics. The city hospital in the Bronx was named for him, and he established the first children's wards at Lenox Hill and Mount Sinai hospitals in New York.

Julius Robert Oppenheimer (1904-1967) headed the Manhattan Project laboratory that developed the nuclear bomb, and later was head of the Institute for Advanced Study at Princeton University. Oppenheimer's father had emigrated from Germany at the age of 14.

After World War II, Wernher von Braun and other German rocket specialists came to Huntsville, Alabama, to work on development of American spacecraft. Their neighborhood was affectionately known as Sauerkraut Hill. Wernher von Braun received 20 honorary degrees and knows how to turn a phrase. Of the space program, he quipped that "your tax dollar will go further."

Engineers and builders of German origin included Johann Augustus Roebling, who designed and started to build the Brooklyn Bridge. After his death in 1869 from an injury on the job, his son, Washington A. Roebling, completed the construction. The bridge was dedicated in 1883.

Charles Proteus Steinmetz, born in Breslau in 1865, came to the United States in 1889 and became a pioneer inventor for General Electric. He worked with Thomas Edison, and his inventions, based on complex mathematics, involved alternating current.

Count Ferdinand Zeppelin, who came to the United States as a military observer in the Civil War period, gave his name to the giant dirigibles that appeared in the skies above New York in 1928. The last dirigible seen outside Germany was the Hindenburg, which exploded and burned at Lakehurst, New Jersey in 1937.

American journalism owes much to the Germans. John Peter Zenger, born in the Palatinate in 1697, opened a print shop in New York in 1726. In 1734, he was jailed for writing and printing articles on nepotism and corruption in government. His wife talked to him through a peephole at the jail and continued his crusade. Zenger's successful defense by Andrew Hamilton established the principle of freedom of the press.

Ottmar Mergenthaler, who came to the United States in 1872, invented the linotype, a machine to stamp letters and cast them in hot metal, which produced American newspapers for many decades. Adolph Ochs of the *New York Times* dynasty arrived in the United States in the early 1850s.

Thomas Nast, the cartoonist who created the beloved image of Santa Claus and the symbolic elephant and donkey of the nation's major political parties, is remembered for his effective attacks on Tammany Hall. This nest of corrupt politicians was led by William Marcy (Boss) Tweed, director of the New York Commission of Public Works, and Nast's cartoons roused the electorate to throw the rascals out. Nast was born in Landau in 1840 and came to the United States when he was six years old. He was the father of American political cartooning.

Manfred George, born in Berlin in 1893, founded the German-Jewish weekly, *Aufbau*, published in New York. An immigrant newsletter in the beginning (1939), the publication became a newspaper with world-wide circulation. It was noted as a forum for those who had fled Hitler and for its support of the infant off-Broadway theater.

The early optical industry was predominently German. Lens-grinders John J. Bausch from Württemberg and Henry Lomb from Hesse-Kassel opened their optical firm in Rochester, New York, in 1855.

Henry Clay Frick and Charles Schwab, who worked with Andrew Carnegie in Pittsburgh, were noted iron manufacturers of the 19th century.

Kindergarten, still known by its German name, was brought to America by two students of Friedrich Froebel, who believed children should grow like flowers in a garden of creative play. They were Margarethe Meyer Schurz, whose husband was the multi-talented Carl Schurz, and Caroline Louise Frankenberg. Mrs. Schurz opened a kindergarten in Watertown, Wisconsin, and Miss Frankenberg started one in Columbus, Ohio.

American education benefited from the mass immigration of scholars from Germany in the 1930s. Sixty of them were teaching in1940 at the New School for Social Research in New York, better known as "Little Heidelberg on 12th Street."

Among sports greats, none stands higher than Lou Gehrig (1903-1941). He joined the New York Yankees in 1925 and played in a record 2,130 consecutive games. He had a batting average of .340, with 493 home runs and 1,990 runs batted in. On June 3, 1932, he hit home runs in four consecutive at-bats. He played in seven World Series, batting .361, hitting 10 home runs, and driving in 35 runs. Gehrig's death at age 38 was from a rare paralysis, amyotrophic lateral sclerosis, better known as "Lou Gehrig's disease."

Another Yankee hitter, Babe Ruth, was a German American, as were such celebrities as Clark Gable, Grace Kelly, and Doris Day.

This is a birth certificate in modern fraktur by Sukey Harris of Annville, Pennsylvania. For more information about fraktur see page 128.

68

A Sampling of Names for Babies

Girls

Adele
Anna
Annegret
Anneliese
Annemarie
Annette
Barbara
Bettina
Birgit
Brigitte
Brunhilda
Carlotta
Caroline
Catarina
Catherine
Claudia
Dorthe
Dorthea

Edith
Elisabeth
Elise
Else
Emilie
Erika
Erma
Ermtraud
Erna
Eva
Frieda
Gabriele
Gerta
Gisela
Greta
Gretchen
Gretel
Hannelore

Heidi
Heike
Helene
Helga
Henrietta
Henriette
Hilda
Hildegard
Hildegund
Ida
Inga
Ingeborg
Ingrid
Irma
Johanna
Julia
Jutta
Karen

Karin
Katharina
Käthe
Krista
Kristiana
Kristina
Liese
Liesel
Lili
Lina
Lisa
Loretta
Louise
Lydia
Magdalena
Margarethe
Maria
Marlene

Marianne
Marion
Milda
Monika
Renate
Rosina
Rosemarie
Sabine
Sigrid
Sophia
Susanne
Ursula
Ute
Wilhelmine
Zensi

Boys

Adam
Adolph
Albrecht
Alfred
Arnim
Arnold
Arthur
August
Bernard
Bernfried
Bernhard
Bertolt
Blasius
Caspar
Christ
Christian
Christoph
Conrad

Dieter
Eberhard
Erich
Ernst
Franz
Franz-Josef
Friedrich
Fritz
Georg
Gerhard
Gerd
Giesebart
Gottfried
Gottlieb
Günther
Gustav
Hans
Hansjürgen

Heinrich
Heinz
Heiko
Helmut
Hermann
Horst
Ivan
Jakob
Joachim
Johann
Johannes
Josef
Jörg
Jürgen
Karl
Klaus
Kurt
Leo

Lothar
Louis
Ludwig
Manfred
Markus
Martin
Matthias
Max
Michel
Nicolas
Niklaus
Oskar
Oswald
Otto
Peter
Petrus
Phillip
Reiner

Reinhold
Richard
Rudolf
Siegfried
Stefan
Theobald
Ude
Ulf
Ulrich
Valentin
Walter
Walther
Werner
Wilfried
Wilhelm
Wolfdietrich
Wolfgang
Wolfram

The Lure of Literature

By Julie McDonald

*Mrs. McDonald, a novelist, is a journalism lecturer
at St. Ambrose University, Davenport, Iowa.*

German-American writers are seldom singled out in the United States, where they have been a fact of life since Franz Daniel Pastorius helped found Germantown, Pennsylvania, in 1683 and wrote the primer that was the first schoolbook ever printed in Pennsylvania.

Pearl Buck (1892-1973) wrote about the Chinese, but her maiden name was Sydenstricker. Born in West Virginia, she grew up in China, where her parents were missionaries. Her novels and short stories included *A House Divided* and *The Good Earth*. She was awarded the Nobel Prize for Literature in 1938.

John Steinbeck (1902-1968) was awarded the Nobel Prize for Literature in 1962 for his *The Grapes of Wrath*, depicting the plight of an Oklahoma farm family forced by the Great Depression to seek a new life in California, and other novels portraying life among migratory farm workers and other laborers.

Threatened with jail for his *Austria as It Is, or Sketches of Continental Courts, by an Eyewitness*, Karl Postl, a clergyman, came to America in 1823. He changed his name to Charles Sealsfield (1793-1864) and wrote *The United States as They Are, in Their Political, Religious, and Social Bearings*. His *Tokeah, or the White Rose*, a love story, involved the Comanche and Creek Indians and early Americans including Andrew Jackson. Sealsfield's *Nathan. . .the First American in Texas*, and his *Das Kajutenbuch oder National Charakteristiken* (1841) were historical novels that incidentally helped lure new immigrants from Germany to Texas, including liberals disturbed by the revolution of 1848.

Theodore Dreiser (1871-1945) won acclaim for *An American Tragedy, Jennie Gerhardt*, a novel about the German-American experience, and others. He drifted out of literature, and joined the American Communist party.

Joyce Kilmer (1886-1918) is known for his poem *Trees*. He wrote other poems and books, was killed in action in World War I, and was posthumously awarded the Croix de Guerre.

Gertrude Stein (1874-1946), born in Allegheny, Pennsylvania, was a writer and art collector who lived in Paris after 1903. Some of her writing was in unusual style, as in "a rose is a rose is a rose." She was an early adviser of author Ernest Hemingway and a friend of artist Pablo Picasso.

Born in Germany, Erich Maria Remarque (1898-1970) served in the German army in World War I, and came to America in 1939, becoming a citizen in 1947. His *All Quiet on the Western Front* was the most powerful novel to come out of World War I. His second wife was Paulette Goddard, the American film star.

A title more American than *Breakfast of Champions* would be hard to find, but the novel's author, Kurt Vonnegut Jr., shaped his views from a long heritage of German and German-American free thinkers who rejected authority and tradition in forming their opinions. A prisoner of war in Germany in World War II, Vonnegut survived the fire-bombing of Dresden and memorialized it with mordant humor in a novel (later a film), *Slaughterhouse Five*.

H. L. Mencken (1880-1956) was a German-American editor whose wit was sharper than his pen. He wrote for the *Baltimore Sun,* was co-editor of *The Smart Set,* and editor of *American Mercury.* His caustic writings jabbed at the middle class, organized religion, business, American culture, and what he called the Bible Belt. He remained the darling of American liberals until the late 1980s when his diary was made public, revealing racist comments.

Thomas Mann (1875-1955), who fled Hitler's Germany to live in Switzerland and came to the United States in 1938, is known for his *Joseph* series, *Buddenbrooks* (a family name), and *The Magic Mountain.* The latter, set in a Swiss tuberculosis sanatorium, had a suggestible generation of American students worried about their lungs. Mann was awarded the Nobel Prize for Literature in 1929.

After 1933, writers made a mass exodus from Germany to the United States. They included Stefan Zweig, Franz Werfel, Lion Feuchtwanger, and Thomas Mann's brother Heinrich, who wrote the novel that became the famous film, "The Blue Angel," starring Marlene Dietrich. Paul Tillich and Reinhold Niebuhr, theologians known for their writings, also came to America.

Fritz von Unruh (1885-1970), whose play *Bonaparte* (1928) foretold the Hitler dictatorship, left Germany in 1932 for France and the United States, and did not return for 30 years. His novels and poems stressed the responsibility of each individual, as opposed to authoritarian societal models.

Some of the best-known themes of American literature are of German origin. The Tristan and Isolde legend—of the fatal love affair of an Irish princess and the knight who escorts her to the king she is to marry—first appeared in 1210 in a poem by Gottfried von Strassburg. Parsifal, the perfect knight who devotes himself to heroic exploits, chivalrous love, serving God, and helping mankind, was born from the pen of Wolfram von Eschenbach in the same year.

Johann Wolfgang von Goethe (1749-1832) gave us an enduring version of Faust, the tale of a man who sells his soul to the devil in return for youth, knowledge, and magic powers. In the 16th century, the real Faust was Germany's foremost magician. As a child, Goethe was impressed by a puppet show about Faust, and his own full version of the story was published in 1833, the year after his death. The American musical *Damn Yankees*, which won the Tony award for the best musical of 1955, is based on the Faust theme.

Most American children know and love the stories of *Hansel and Gretel, Rumpelstiltskin* and *Tom Thumb,* first put in writing by the brothers Grimm, Jakob (1785-1863) and Wilhelm (1786-1859).

The earliest Germanic writing to survive was a translation of the Bible by Ulfilas (311-383), bishop of the Visigoths. But Bible reading did not deter these people from sacking Rome in 410.

In the Fatherland, German literature got its recorded start at the time of Charlemagne (742-814). The great work of that early period was a harmony of the gospels. Soon after came Otfried's *Evangelienharmonic*, the first attempt in German poetry to replace alliteration with rhyme.

The interest in epic poetry extended to the old German sagas presented by wandering minstrels. The outstanding lyric poet of the Middle Ages was Walther von der Vogelweide (c. 1170-1228), who wrote both love songs and poems. His poetry is still memorized today:

> *Who slays the lion*
> *Who slays the giant*
> *It is he who overcomes*
> *Himself.*

Johannes Gutenberg (1398-1468) invented the method of printing from movable type that survived with little change well into the 20th century. He is credited with most of the work that went into the printing of the Latin Bible of 1456. The first book ever printed, it brought the Bible and the printed word into lay hands for the first time.

The Reformation and Counter Reformation period brought *Epistolae obscurorum vivorum*, a satire by Johannes Reuchlin (1455-1522), supporting the struggle against the papacy. Martin Luther translated the Bible into German and achieved poetic quality in his church hymns. The defender of Catholicism was Thomas Murner, who wrote a satire, *Von dem grossen Lutherischen Narren* (By The Great Lutheran Jester), in 1522.

A notable literary work of the 17th century was the introduction of R.E. Raspe's *The Adventures of Baron Munchhausen* to the German public by Gottfried Burger (1747-1794), relating and expanding on the exploits of Baron Karl Friedrich von Munchausen, who was famous for his tall tales.

Christoph Martin Wieland (1733-1813) published his classic novel, *Agathon*, in 1766. It was the beginning of the German psychological novel.

Johann Friedrich von Schiller (1759-1805), like Goethe, was inspired by the Greek ideal of human and artistic perfection. His *Don Carlos* showed his development as a dramatic poet, but his fame rests on plays written in his last years, *Wallenstein, Die Jungfrau von Orleans* (The Maid of Orleans), and *Wilhelm Tell* (William Tell).

E. T. A. Hoffmann (1776-1822) wrote stories of the supernatural and the fantastic which became the basis of the opera *The Tales of Hoffmann* by Jacques Offenbach and *The Nutcracker* ballet by Peter Ilich Tchaikovsky.

A creative genius of the 19th century was Heinrich Heine (1797-1856), who wrote poetry, prose, and literary criticism. Jewish and anti-Prussian, he emigrated to Paris in 1831. No German classical author is more widely read. The poetic cycle *Nordseebilder* (North Sea Image) is one of his works.

Rainer Maria Rilke (1875-1926) is well known in the United States. His poetry, expressing the plight of man in search of positive, eternal values, has stood the test of time.

The novels *Damian* and *Steppenwolf* (Wolf of the Steppes) by Hermann Hesse (1877-1962) were cherished by American Flower Children of the 1960s for their indictment of bourgeois society.

Most famous of the German literary Expressionists, who tried to grasp and recreate intuitively and find new modes of artistic expression, was Franz Kafka (1883-1924), who was born in Prague but wrote in German. His best-known work is the mesmerizing tale of a man turning into a cockroach, *The Metamorphosis*. Other works included *Das Schloss* (The Castle) and *Amerika*.

Franz Werfel (1890-1945), the author of *The Song of Bernadette* (a nun's story that became a Hollywood film) and *The Forty Days of Musa Dagh*, was well known in America.

Günter Grass, born in 1927, wrote *The Tin Drum*, set before, during, and after World War II. The film was widely shown in the United States.

Heinrich Böll (1917-1985) received the Nobel Prize for Literature in 1972. The role of Catholicism in society was the theme of his work. His books included *Gruppenbild mit Dame* (Group Portrait With Lady) and *Ansichten eines Clowns* (A Clown's View). Other German winners of the Nobel Prize for Literature include Theodor Mommsen (1817-1903), historian, in 1902; Rudolf Eucken (1846-1926), philosopher, in 1908; Paul von Heyse (1830-1914) in 1910; Gerhart Hauptmann (1862-1946), dramatist, poet and novelist, in 1912; Carl Spitteler (1845-1924), German-Swiss epic poet, in 1918, and Hermann Hesse (1877-1962) in 1946.

Woodcarvings by Georg Keilhofer of Frankenmuth, Michigan

Snow White   *Hansel and Gretel*

The German Influence In Musical America

By Arthur Canter

A professor emeritus at the University of Iowa, Dr. Canter writes and lectures about music and musicians.

The contribution to the musical world of America and Europe made by composers and musicians of German origin is without challenge. Concert-going audiences today are familiar with the musical idiom of Bach and Handel, Haydn and Mozart, Beethoven, Brahms, and Wagner. If we add to the list the rest of the Bach family, Dittersdorf, Spohr, Weber, Gluck, from the 18th century; Berg, Bruch, Bruckner, Flotow, Hindemith, Humperdinck, Mahler, Mendelssohn, Offenbach, Reger, Schubert, Schumann, Richard Strauss, Webern, and Wolf, born in the 19th century, we have only touched a fraction of the list of composers without covering those born in the 20th century. Throughout the last two hundred years or more the composers from Germany dominated the style, form and content of music.

If we go back before the time of the Renaissance, we find that music was a vital part of the life of the German people. The peasants had their folk songs and folk dances, the burghers had town bands. They and the clergy had their church music and organists, and the nobility fostered the various courtly musical activities. The post-Renaissance period saw a flowering in the development of the German song, exemplified by the great Nuremberg Song Collection (1539-1556) of Georg Forster (c.1510-1568). The Reformation saw the impetus by Martin Luther to incorporate song in Christian worship, inspiring the chorale, which in turn became the basis of organ compositions and the cultivation of various kinds of church music.

To what can we ascribe the great numbers of German composers that appeared in the 17th and 18th centuries? Perhaps it was something in the spirit of the people that allowed musical talent and genius to be recognized and nurtured, as happened with Bach, Haydn, and Mozart. In any event, the talent residing in the people was given outlets by the extensive patronage system that existed in Germany during the 200-year period. Composers and musicians alike were supported by the 300 states making up the land of Germany. From these composers, and the musicians who played their music, came the development and refinement of all forms of musical expression, in particular the symphony, the quartet, and keyboard music. The rise of German romantic poetry in the late 18th and early 19th centuries inspired a fresh blossoming of vocal melodies. It was natural that Romanticism in German literature be expressed in the music of German composers during the 19th century. Robert Schumann, Johannes Brahms, and Richard Wagner were particularly notable in this movement.

74

By mid-19th century, Germany was unquestionably in ascendancy in the world of music. Coincidentally, this was the time when large numbers of Germans immigrated to America. The new immigrants brought with them a love of music, willingness to listen, to play, to sing, and to take instruction. Thus the first wave of German Americans provided the core of musical interest and activities in the major cities and towns of the United States that attracted professional musicians to America when faced with troubled times in Germany. A group of 23 young musicians, discontented with conditions in the revolutionary Germany of 1848, banded together in Berlin to form the Germania Society and emigrate to America. The Germania Society toured the United States for several years before disbanding to provide cadres that helped spawn other orchestras across the country. Many of these new orchestras were known as Germania Orchestras. They played the music of the greater German composers and helped bring about inclusion of their works into the standard repertory. Gottlieb Graupner (1767-1836), who came from Germany at the end of the 18th century, founded the Handel and Haydn Society in Boston (1815). Carl Zerrahn (1826-1909) led the orchestra of this society, which developed into the Boston Symphony Orchestra. In 1839 Charles Grobe (1817-1880) moved to the United States, and became known for his "parlor music" piano compositions. The Saxonia Band, introduced into America from Germany in 1848 and led by its organizer Herman Kotzschmar (1829-1909), had its impact upon the development of town band musical organizations and instruction in the playing of brass instruments. Kotzschmar was the first teacher of John Knowles Paine, who in 1875 became the first professor of music in the United States, at Harvard.

The conductors of the newly formed symphony orchestras across America were for the most part German-trained in the traditions of Berlin, Leipzig, Munich, and Vienna. The ultimate in fine music during the latter half of the 19th century was considered to be written by ethnic German composers. In 1871 Leopold Damrosch (1832-1885) came to New York, where he founded the Oratoria Society and New York Symphony Society. He introduced German opera into the repertory of the newly founded Metropolitan Opera, which he directed. His son Walter (1862-1950) took over his post at the Metropolitan and directed the New York Philharmonic Society and the New York Symphony. The German American Theodore Thomas (1835-1905) played a prominent role in the development of several musical organizations across the United States, including the Brooklyn Philharmonic Society, which merged with the New York Symphony and later became the New York Philharmonic Orchestra. He helped organize the Cincinnati Musical College, which became the Cincinnati Conservatory. Thomas is best known for founding the Chicago Symphony Orchestra, which he developed out of his own Theodore Thomas Orchestra, a popular touring group in the style of the Germania orchestras.

Among noteworthy German-American conductors who have led major orchestras in the United States are: George Henschel (1850-1934), the first director of the Boston Symphony Orchestra; Alfred Hertz (1872-1942), who conducted German opera at the Metropolitan for many years; Frederick Stock (1872-1942), who conducted the Chicago Symphony from 1905 until his death; Emil Oberhoffer (1867-1933), an organist in Minneapolis who helped found the Minneapolis Orchestra; Fritz Scheel (1852-1907), co-founder and first conductor of the Philadelphia Orchestra; Bruno Walter (Schlesinger) (1876-1962), the conductor of the New York Philharmonic and the CBS Orchestra, and well-known interpreter of the music of Mahler, who had to flee the Nazi regime; William Steinberg (Hans Wilhelm) (1899-1978), who directed both the Pittsburgh and Boston Symphony Orchestras and also had to leave Nazi Germany; Arthur Fiedler (1894-1979), the celebrated conductor of the Boston Pops, Lucas Foss (Fuchs), the composer-conductor of many U.S. orchestras, including the Buffalo Philharmonic, who was a child refugee from Hitler's Germany.

Opera in America had its course influenced by German Americans. A German opera company was the first to occupy the then-new Metropolitan Opera House in the late 1800s. Many of the conductors of leading opera houses in the United States were ethnic Germans. Their numbers were increased by refugees from the Nazi Germany of the 1930s.

Operetta and musical theater in America were also nurtured by composers of German origin. Victor Herbert (1859-1924), although born in Dublin, was half German and had trained in Stuttgart as a cellist. Edward Kuennecke (1888-1953) was known in the United States of the 1920s for his operetta *Caroline*, a resetting of his *Der Vetter aus Dingsda*. Kurt Weill (1900-1950), a refugee from the Nazis, became well-known in America for his operettas and musical comedies based on jazz, blues and cabaret music. These include *The Three Penny Opera, Lady in the Dark, Street Scene* and *Mahagonny*. Frederick Loewe (1904-1988), who completed classical training in Germany before immigrating to the United States, is known for his work with Alan Jay Lerner on a number of Broadway hits (*Brigadoon, Paint Your Wagon, My Fair Lady*, and *Camelot*). Oscar Hammerstein (1846-1919) was an impresario who brought many fine singers to the United States. His grandson, Oscar Hammerstein II (1895-1960), a lyricist, collaborated with Rudolf Friml, Jerome Kern, Vincent Youmans, and others on operettas and musical comedies, including *Oklahoma* with Richard Rodgers.

Hollywood film music was also influenced by German Americans. Paul Dessau (1894-1979) was a pioneer in composing background music for movies, opening opportunities for other composers such as Erich Korngold, Max Steiner and Ernst Toch. "Bix" Leo Bismarck Beiderbecke (1903-1931), the son of German immigrants, was a popular jazz cornetist and composer in the late 1920s. In his honor an annual festival is held in Davenport, Iowa, on the banks of the Mississippi River.

Sometime in the early 1900s, around the time of World War I and its aftermath, German influence upon the music of America passed its peak, and since the turn of the century it has been slowly but surely melding with the musical heritage of other cultures.

Art and Tradition

A Fusion of Soul and Energy

By Julie McDonald

What could be more American than prefabricated buildings and skyscrapers? It was Walter Adolph Gropius (1883-1969) who designed many ultra-American rectangular towers with a skin of glass. Gropius had advocated prefabricated construction before World War I. In 1919 he founded the Bauhaus School of Design by combining three schools of arts and crafts in Weimar. The school was moved to Dessau in 1925, and Gropius resigned in 1928 to reenter private practice. He moved to England in 1934, became a professor of architecture at Harvard in 1937 and was chairman of the Harvard School of Architecture from 1938 to 1952. He became a United States citizen in 1944. In a distinguished career in Europe and America, Gropius brought an end to historically imitative architecture in favor of modern design. A purist, he taught students both art and craftsmanship as fundamental to architecture.

Ludwig Mies van der Rohe (1886-1969) was director of the Bauhaus from 1930 until he closed it in 1933 rather than see Hitler shut it down. He came to the United States in 1937, and became head of the school of architecture at the Armour Institute in Chicago, which became the Illinois Institute of Technology. He designed its campus. Mies insisted that "less is more." His functional designs include the Seagram building in New York City; apartment buildings at 860 and 880 Lake Shore Drive, Chicago; Convention Hall, Chicago; the Cantor Drive-in Restaurant, Indianapolis; Farnsworth House, a weekend retreat in Plano, Illinois; the Foster City apartments in San Mateo, California; the Museum of Art at Houston, Texas; the Public Library in Washington, D.C.; One Charles Center in Baltimore; and the Gallery of the Twentieth Century in Berlin.

Josef Albers (1888-1976) is noted for geometric studies in color relationships. He taught at the Bauhaus from 1923 until its closing in 1933. He then headed the fine arts department at Black Mountain College in North Carolina for 10 years, and served 10 years as chairman of the art department at Yale University.

Emanuel Leutze (1816-1868), born in Germany and brought to America as a child, spent 20 years in Germany painting historical pictures, including *Washington Crossing the Delaware*. He returned to the United States in 1859.

German-American artists created some of the most dramatic images of the American West, cowboys, and Indians, capturing on canvas a rapidly disappearing way of life. Among them were John Hauser (1859-1908), Charles Schreyvogel (1861-1912), Walter Ufer (1876-1936), a charter member of the Taos Society of Artists in New Mexico, and Fritz Reiss (1888-1953).

Americans recognize themselves in the paintings of Norman Rockwell (1894-1978), who was inspired by Joseph Leyendecker (1874-1951), the German-American artist who created the handsome Arrow Collar man for magazine advertisements.

German-American painters included Charles Frederic Ulrich (1858-1908) who painted Pennsylvania Dutch scenes; William Ritschel (1864-1949) and Anton Otto Fischer (1882-1962), who did marine paintings; Jean Mannheim (1863-1945), a painter of the coast of California, and Franz Arthur Bischoff (1864-1929), who did impressionistic studies of California scenery. Carl Rungius (1869-1959) portrayed big game animals in their habitats. Walt Kuhn (1877-1949) did clown paintings. Max Ernst (1891-1976) is remembered for his "anti-art" combination of objects in their natural state. George Grosz (1893-1959) created harsh images of war profiteers, and Adolph Dehn (1895-1968) created poetic landscapes and satires of art lovers. Hans Hofmann (1880-1966) was a major abstract painter. Ad Reinhardt (1913-1967) and Franz Kline (1910-1962), were abstract expressionists. Abstract expressionism seeks to reflect subjective emotions and responses of the artist with images not found in reality or nature. Daniel Garber (1880-1958) and Walter Emerson Baum (1884-1956) were members of the New Hope School of painting, a group of impressionists who sought to capture light and atmosphere in their works. Max Kuehne (1880-1968) was a German-born painter influenced by the Impressionists, and Walter Koeniger (1881-1943) was known for his winter landscapes. Poor blacks were the subject of Julius Bloch (1888-1966), a social-realist painter.

The art movements Americans have embraced most enthusiastically have their roots in the German soul. Albert Bierstadt (1830-1902), the famous landscape painter of the Hudson River School, immortalized the American wilderness in two large canvases for the nation's Capitol in Washington, D.C. Bierstadt's inspiration stemmed from an earlier era when Albrecht Altorfer (1480-1538), in his landscapes of the forest, expressed the Germans' mystic union with nature. His were the first German paintings that existed for the landscape itself.

German art is Gothic with ornamental line, complex composition, and an upward surge as opposed to the classic tradition of the Latins with its simplicity, regularity and restraint. The Gothic spirit created forms of unrest and suffering, and Germany was the only European country where the Gothic tradition remained pure through the Renaissance, the flowering of culture that divided medieval and modern times.

Germany's first contact with the Renaissance opened the great period remembered for Albrecht Dürer (1471-1528) and others. Durer started the vogue for the self-portrait and is responsible for the prominence of German drawings, engravings and woodcuts. As a youth he worked in the studio of Michael Wohlgemuth during the creation of *The Nuremberg Chronicle* of 1493, and woodcuts in this "account of the world to our time" have been attributed to him. This was the second book ever printed. The Bible was first.

After the Germans recovered from the Thirty Years' War (1618-1648), the Gothic spirit became the Baroque (curved forms with lavish ornamentation) and Rococo (elaborate ornamentation combining shellwork, scrolls and foliage).

The architect Karl Friedrich Schinkel (1781-1841) gave Berlin its distinctive style, classical grandeur with buildings of heroic scale and wide boulevards. Romantic fairy tales and folklore subjects were favored by Moritz von Schwind

(1804-1871), known as the "German Fra Angelico." Like the Italian painter, he filled his work with a spontaneous piety and gladness of spirit.

Both the Expressionists and the Surrealists (artists who find their images in dreams and the subconscious mind) claim Arnold Bocklin (1837-1901), whose work exhibited a vigorous naturalism. His best-known painting is "Self-Portrait with Death Playing the Violin."

The first German exhibit of works by Vincent van Gogh, the Dutch artist, in 1905, inspired the founding of a group of artists who called themselves *Die Brucke* (The Bridge). They were more concerned with content than with form.

Next came *Der Blaue Reiter* (The Blue Rider) founded in Munich in 1910 by the Russian-born Wassily Kandinsky (1866-1944), who left Germany for Paris in 1934, and Franz Marc (1880-1916), who died at Verdun in World War I. Ernst Ludwig Kirchner (1880-1938) was a painter of the modern city, and Erich Heckel (1883-1970) painted the sick and the dead. Austrian Oskar Kokoschka did portraits that signaled the imminent decay of the subjects.

Lyonel Feininger (1871-1956), the creator of airy cityscapes suffused with light, is among the artists recognized by most Americans, as are Swiss-born Paul Klee (1879-1940), who painted fantasy and enchantment, taught at the Bauhaus, and left Germany in 1933, and Max Beckmann (1884-1950), known for monumental carnival figures and expressive lithographs.

When the Nazis denounced certain works as "degenerate," the famous "Degenerate Art Show" was mounted in Munich in 1937 and went on tour. The day after the opening, Max Beckmann went into exile. In 1939, Goebbels and other high Nazis took the "degenerate" works they wanted and burned the rest of the exhibit in the yard of the Berlin Fire Brigade.

Otto Dix (1891-1969) practiced the New Objectivity, a severe and uncompromising realism. The Nazis condemned his work as degenerate. Emil Nolde (1867-1956) brought glowing color to Expressionism. Paula Modersohn-Becker (1876-1907) painted mothers and children. Longing to have a child of her own, she died in childbirth.

The most famous woman artist in the German annals is Kathe Kollwitz (1867-1945), known for her drawings, woodcuts and sculpture. Her subjects were working people suffering from hunger, cold, poverty, and war. She created many lithographs and etchings of mothers and children and death. In 1919 she became the first woman to be elected to the Berlin Academy. The Nazis expelled her from it in 1933.

Well-known in the United States today is Anselm Kiefer, born in 1945. His emotional canvases have been blasted by German art critics for reviving World War II memories people want to forget. Huge, turbulent and semi-abstract with heavy impasto, they evoke the ravages of war.

German and German-American art have had a profound effect on the New World. Its practitioners have done everything from preserving our vanishing scenes and traditions to catapulting us into the challenges of futuristic designs.

Stage, Screen, and Marlene

By Julie McDonald

From F. H. Ehmcke's
Graphic Trade Symbols
by German Designers, *1907*

When it comes to actors and actresses, Marlene Dietrich, called "the Kraut" by novelist Ernest Hemingway, is the magic name and face that comes to mind. A Berliner with a laconic and languorous but electric manner, she didn't act, she sizzled. In her own inimitable style, she played everything from the sleazy cabaret girl in *The Blue Angel* to the dancehall girl in *Destry Rides Again.* Jean Cocteau wrote, "In her voice we hear the voice of the Lorelei." Marlene Dietrich introduced slacks to American women (for better or for worse), and she won the French Legion of Honor and the Medal of Freedom for making more than 500 appearances before Allied troops during World War II. All of this was a long but fabulous journey for the daughter of a German army officer, born in 1904 and growing up as Maria Magdalene von Losch.

Ernest Lubitsch (1892-1947), one of the great film directors in American movie history, was born in Berlin and studied acting with Max Reinhardt, the noted German stage director. Lubitsch's earliest major features were made for Pola Negri, and he became the master of the film spectacle. He was brought to Hollywood in 1923 to direct Mary Pickford in *Rosita,* a picture that never was made. His films were noted for sophisticated and witty comedy. He directed *Lady Windermere's Fan* and *The Student Prince in Old Heidelberg* with Ramon Navarro, *To Be or Not to Be, Heaven Can Wait,* and others. He was the first to use songs as a part of the plot, in films starring Maurice Chevalier and Jeanette MacDonald.

Erich von Stroheim, son of a Prussian soldier, directed his first American picture, *Blind Husbands,* in 1918. He worked with Irving Thalberg at Universal Studios, and his talent for creating atmosphere was notable. His masterpiece, *Greed,* was severely cut by Thalberg, but it remains a powerful reflection of life.

Josef von Sternberg, another great director, was an American who hid his identity in a labyrinth of legend. Like Erich von Stroheim, he was of the tough whip-and-jodhpurs school of directing. His first film was a disaster, but he found commercial success with *Underworld* in 1927. This was a preview of the gangster films of the 1930s. Von Sternberg survived the talkie revolution and directed Marlene Dietrich in *Morocco* (1930), *Dishonored* (1931), *Blonde Venus* (1932), and *The Devil is a Woman* (1935). His most famous work was *An American Tragedy* (1931). Paramount Studios separated von Sternberg and Dietrich in 1936, and the hot love affair between them also came to an end, which he said destroyed his talent.

Billy Wilder was among the first of the film directors Hitler chased to our shores in the 1930s. He came from Vienna and made frothy pictures until public taste demanded something else. *Hold Back The Dawn* (1941) was more serious, and Wilder went on to make *Double Indemnity* (1943) and *The Lost Weekend* (1945). He also directed Gloria Swanson in *Sunset Boulevard* (1950).

Fritz Lang, the German director Joseph Goebbels tried to recruit for the Nazi propaganda machine, came to America in 1934. He made *The Woman in the Window* with Edward G. Robinson and Joan Bennett, and *The Big Heat* (1953).

Other refugees who directed films were Edgar Ulmer; John Brahm, who created Gothic films like *The Lodger* (1944); Douglas Sirk, *Thunder on the Hill* (1951), and Fred Zinnemann, *High Noon* (1952).

Carl Zuckmayer wrote *The Devil's General* in the United States. It was the first play to come to grips with the Nazi evil, and it was enthusiastically received.

Bertolt Brecht, born in 1898 in Bavaria, left Germany in 1933 and, with composer Kurt Weill, created *The Three Penny Opera*, which ran for nearly a decade off-Broadway in the 1950s and 1960s. *Mother Courage, The Good Woman of Setzuan*, and *Caucasian Chalk Circle* are other Brecht productions.

The German influence on motion pictures began with Athanasius Kircher, a German Jesuit and mathematician in Rome. In 1640 he invented the magic lantern, a device for projecting images. Early in the 19th century, Baron Franz von Uchatius, an Austrian artilleryman, used a zoetrope, an instrument for creating illusions with a series of hand-drawn pictures, to demonstrate the performance of a cannon ball. Some of the earliest film strips included footage of Kaiser Wilhelm reviewing his troops.

The earliest German theater was religious drama, which survives in the famous *Passion Play*, performed every 10 years at Oberammergau, and which also has been transplanted to the Black Hills of South Dakota.

Contemporary German cities have their own repertory theaters, a custom dating from feudal times, when every prince had his own theater, no matter how small his domain. The idea of "putting the show on the road" has never taken root in Germany.

Few German plays are produced in the United States because of the language barrier and because German drama is heavier and more intellectual than the "tired businessman's special" popular in this country.

Opera is the best-loved German performing art, a taste that influences all other forms of public presentations. Ballet exists as an adjunct to the numerous opera houses. Companies in Stuttgart and Dusseldorf have achieved a distinctive style and repertoire.

Organizations and Events

By Karin Gottier

Where there are German Americans there are German-American societies. And the German Americans are in all 50 states. California and Pennsylvania have more than 4 million each. Ohio and Illinois have more than 3 million. New York, Michigan, Wisconsin and Texas have more than 2 million. There are more than a million in Indiana, Minnesota, Florida, Missouri, New Jersey, Iowa, Washington, and Maryland; more than a half-million in Colorado, Virginia, Kansas, Oregon, North Carolina, Nebraska, Arizona, and Oklahoma.

In World War I there were feelings against German Americans and a rise in the "100% American" thinking. Use of the German language in educational facilities was banned, and many German books were removed from libraries. In World War II such feelings were much weaker. Many organizations date from much earlier times and are strong and healthy today. German-American groups are devoted to many pursuits, such as music, theater, physical culture, sports, language, culture, genealogy, stamp collecting, and others.

Turnvereine: Gymnastic Clubs

Many German immigrants brought with them the philosophies of *"Turnvater Jahn"* (Friedrich Ludwig Jahn, 1778-1852). Jahn held that strong, healthy bodies produce strong, healthy people who would be disciplined enough to create a liberal, free, and united country. He hoped to instill love of fatherland and to bring about political reforms through personal reform of the individual. His means of achieving this was through physical training. In accordance with his beliefs he founded the first *Turnverein* (gymnastic society) in 1811 and in 1816 wrote a book on physical training, outlining his methods. Jahn had fought in campaigns against Napoleon and had called for democracy and German unity. His liberal ideas earned him five years incarceration.

Immigrants of the mid-19th century were political refugees, intellectuals rather than farmers, whose revolutionary activities and calls for freedoms and political reforms made it impossible for them to remain in Germany after the 1848 revolution failed. Thousands were men who had fought in the wars of liberation from Napoleon's rule.

Inspired by the teachings of Jahn, the new immigrants founded *Turnvereine* in German communities of the United States. Both men and women pursued the ideals of a healthy body through physical training. Clubs joined together to organize state competitions *(Staats-Turnfeste)* as well as regional events.

Turner societies, as they were called, also advocated social reforms. They spoke for women's suffrage, social welfare, and direct elections. They opposed slavery. During the Civil War entire Turner clubs enlisted as groups in support of their new homeland. In Milwaukee a *Turnlehrer* seminar was founded to prepare students to become physical education teachers.

Photo: Archives of the Vernon, Connecticut, Historical Society.

Turnfest *of the Connecticut Gymnastic District, July 3-4-5, 1909,*
Holyoke, Massachusetts.

Today there are *Turnhallen* (Turner halls) in large and small towns all over the United States. Some are still used by gymnastic organizations. Others have become social clubs, soccer clubs, or singing societies such as the *Turnverein* of Meriden, Connecticut. Although emphasis has shifted, the principles advocated by Friedrich Ludwig Jahn have left their mark on American social history and have had a profound impact on physical education in American schools.

Singing Societies

Wherever and whenever Germans gather, they sing. As soon as there was a large enough group of people, German immigrants founded a *Sängerbund* or singing society, and Germans are singing still. Although the primary activity is choral singing, a *Sängerbund* is also a social center where the community gathers for dances and other cultural activities.

In some states, individual singing societies joined together to form a statewide *Sängerbund*. Some of the larger ones, like the Pacific *Sängerbund*, German-Texans *Sängerbund*, New York State *Sängerbund*, and the super-regional North-American Singers Union, can look back on a long history of cultivating German song. The Connecticut State *Sängerbund*, which is by no means the oldest, was founded in 1882 by a number of singing societies, some of which were in existence as early as 1858. During its 108 years of existence the Connecticut State *Sängerbund* has been joined by singing societies of Massachusetts and Rhode Island. Under the auspices of the state organization, the *Staats-Sängerfest*, a singing competition, is held annually. According to strict rules, each chorus competes in several categories for a panel of judges who cannot see the chorus.

83

There are prizes for men's, ladies' and mixed choruses: a trophy, a plaque, a chalice or a small work of art. A committee selects the prize-songs, determines the rules by which the competitions are judged, and arranges for the judges. Each year the *Sängerfest* is hosted by a different member club, which finds suitable facilities for the competition and for the festivities that follow.

After the competitions are held, and while clubs are anxiously awaiting the results of the judging, there is music, food, drink, dancing and, of course, more singing. After the winners are announced and the prizes are awarded, the festivities begin in earnest. Larger singing societies hold state-wide concerts and compete in the prize-singing at the national *Sängerfest* in Germany.

Not all organizations have large choruses or belong to state organizations. Some often call themselves "Quartette" clubs, cultivating small-group or "Quartette" singing. There are also groups that concentrate only on sea-chanties or who sing more informally. Although the societies cultivate German song, most groups also sing in English and welcome anyone who likes to sing.

Schützen Vereine

Shooting societies or *Schützen Vereine* evolved out of the tradesmen's guilds during the Middle Ages. Since all able-bodied male residents were required to defend the town during siege or attack, they met in loosely structured associations to practice target-shooting. Later these groups acquired structure, statutes, ritual, and ceremonial paraphernalia.

During the middle of the 19th century, German immigrants in America founded *Schützen Vereine* as target-shooting clubs, some of which exist today. The early shooting clubs in America purchased land on which to build their clubhouses and for shooting ranges to hold their practice sessions. In times of war and national crisis, these shooting ranges were used by the military for training purposes. Many have become public parks or golf courses, with only the name indicating their earlier function.

For the members of *Schützen Vereine*, the highlight of the year is the *Schützenfest*. Central to this often three-day celebration is the Kingshoot—a competition to determine the *Schützenkönig*—champion marksman or "king."

With ceremony, speeches, music, drink, food, and conviviality, he is crowned *Schützenkönig* and presented a medal engraved with his name and date of the event. The "king" wears it as badge of office until a new "king" is determined. The medal is then added to the club chain, a silver necklace containing the medals of all previous champions.

Because the honor of being *Schützenkönig* carries with it the obligation to host a dinner for the entire company, some crack shots are known to have missed deliberately by a minute fraction of an inch to avoid both the honor and the obligation. The champion also receives other prizes, perhaps a decorative target, a beer stein, a commemorative plate, or money.

Schützen clubs are by no means for men only. As early as the turn of the century, women's teams were formed. They hold their own competitions. Instead of a dinner, the champion hosts a luncheon.

Members of *Schützen* societies often wear identifying items of clothing such as a jacket or a hat, vaguely reminiscent of the forest-green clothing of the hunters and foresters in Germany. Medals, prizes, and decorations further underline the themes of hunting and marksmanship: oak leaves, stag horns, targets, crossed rifles, and hunting horns. A more glamorous note is introduced by depictions of *Schützenliesl*, a pretty young woman carrying a prodigious number of full beer steins. In Bavaria she was an actual person who worked as a waitress in a beer garden where *Schützen* clubs met. Her face appears on targets, posters, steins, and other items.

Fasnacht—Fasching—Karneval
Mardi Gras celebrations among the German Americans

In the yearly events calendar of German-American organizations the pre-Lenten period is given over to various celebrations of Mardi Gras. In Germany and in Catholic countries, this period is celebrated with parades, masks, costuming, food, drink, dance, and all kinds of tomfoolery. It is the time of the "fool" who, from behind his mask, can say and do outrageous things with impunity.

The capital of German *Karneval* is Cologne. Officially, the carnival season begins on the eleventh day of the eleventh month at 11 o'clock and 11 minutes with the first meeting of the "Council of Eleven." Together with other "Fools Guilds" they plan the carnival festivities, which reach their climax in a huge Rose Monday parade with floats representing satirical, political, and traditional topics. Also marching in this parade are the *Koelsche Funke*—the "Cologne Sparks." Dressed in 18th-century uniforms with red coats, white wigs and three-cornered hats, this drill team/band carries out some irreverent maneuvers, occasionally bending over and wagging their posteriors at authority. With them marches *Funken Mariechen*—"Marie of the Sparks," a high-stepping, majorette-like dancing girl in similar uniform. The parade, as well as the entire carnival season, is presided over by the Triumverate, the *Dreigestirn*. It consists of *Prinz Karneval*, the "Maiden" (symbolizing the city of Cologne and always portrayed by a man), the "Farmer," and their court. All over town people don costumes, and shouts of *Koele Alaaf* are heard everywhere.

Other large cities, most notably Munich, celebrate *Fasching* in much the same style, with masked balls, parties, and parades. The market women of the *Viktualienmarkt* (an open-air market) dance in comical costumes, and every seven years the Coopers Guild performs its traditional hoop dance.

In the small villages of southern Germany, people celebrate *Fasnacht*. Here too, masks are worn and much feasting takes place. However, while choice of costume is individual in the carnival celebration of the large cities, here each town has one, two, or more stock characters with specific attributes, who carry out a specific ritual.

85

The "Hemdgloncker" *Brigade, Hartford, Connecticut* Sängerbund *dancers,* Fasching, *1988. Members masquerade as carnival characters. The* "Hemdgloncker" *always appears in a nightshirt along with a number of others dressed in nightshirts.*

Typical of the southern German *Fasnacht* is the use of beautifully and elaborately carved wooden masks. Recurring over and over again are figures of "Wise Fools" with smooth, pale faces, scary witches with grotesque features, and animal masks of all kinds. There are even masks representing fruits and vegetables.

Commonly the beginning of *Fasnacht* is announced before dawn by members of the local Fools Guild, who then march to the town hall, depose local authority for the duration of the celebration, and assume the government. In many towns the Fools Guilds publicly criticize the doings of the local prominents, the town council and the politicians, but always in rhyme and with humor. After several days of much drinking and general merry-making, the *Fasnacht* is symbolically buried with much moaning and groaning, to be born again next year.

German-American organizations celebrate this period of the year on larger or smaller scale, depending on their size and resources. Almost all clubs organize a *Maskenball* (masquerade ball). People come in costume and masked to dance incognito until late in the evening, when there is a costume parade, prizes are awarded, and everyone takes off the mask. This often leads to some surprises; the lovely lady with whom you danced all evening might turn out to be a man. In larger organizations there may be a "Council of Eleven" which organizes entertaining evenings with funny speeches, skits, songs and, of course, much food and drink.

Some clubs, like the *Koellsche Funke rut-wiess* of New York, which were founded as carnival societies, go all-out in re-creating the carnival celebrations of Germany. With groups of marching Red Sparks and high-stepping *Funken Mariechens, Prinz Karneval* and his court, they stage glittering gala events that are the social highlight of the year.

Still other groups content themselves with a performance by a group of characters in traditional *Fasnacht* costumes, such as the *Hemdgloncker* of the Hartford, Connecticut *Sängerbund*. In nightshirts, stocking caps, and wooden washtubs, they enliven the carnival program. Whether *Fasnacht, Fasching,* or *Karneval*, German-American groups celebrate the pre-Lenten season with the same joy and abandon as their European relatives.

Schlachtfest

In the old country this was a butchering festival which brought the butcher to the farm to butcher the animals and process the meat. Neighbors were invited to join in festive dinners.

In the festivals of German clubs the pig is dressed and brought in ceremoniously on a bier to the music of a funeral march, preceded by a pseudo-clergyman and followed by "mourners" carrying menus as prayer books. The individual cuts of meat are raffled off, and from the kitchen is served a *Schlachtplatte*—a platter with fresh liverwurst, blood sausage, potato salad, and sauerkraut.

This is a Schlachtfest *at the Hartford* Sängerbund *in Newington, Connecticut. Founded in 1858 in Hartford, Connecticut, as a singing society, the organization also has a golf team, skat club, dance group, and a curling team. Members are from all areas of Germany, with a large portion having come after World War II from German settlements in the Carpathian mountains of Slovakia, from Hungary and Lithuania, and from the former German territories of Pomerania, Silesia, and East and West Prussia.*

Volkssports

In the 1960s in Southern Germany, clubs called *Volkslauf* began offering non-competitive events that appeal to the young, old, individuals, and families. *Volkssports* appeared in America in 1976. Today, with 60 chapters, the American *Volkssport* Association sponsors non-competitive organized athletic events.

Perhaps the most popular, *Volksmärsches* promote activity and physical fitness. Hikers can choose from, say, a 10- or 20-mile trek, or shorter distances. Participants can walk, run, or jog at their own pace. It's relaxing, fun, and a way of socializing.

Volksswims allow participants to tackle the 200-, 500- or 1,000-meter distances, using strokes they find comfortable. Several breaks are permitted.

For snow-lovers, cross-country skiing over 10 or 20 kilometers combines exercise, savoring the outdoors, and making friends. It's called ski-wandering.

Bicycling events are also offered.

Bauernball

At a *Bauernball* (farmers' ball) a folk-dance group on stage reenacts a shotgun wedding with role reversal (men are played by women and vice versa) and humorous, satirical speeches. There are variations. Short and fat may "wed" tall and thin, or a "lady" with baby may enter, claiming that "he" promised her first.

Bierfest

There are tents, music, dancing, beer, and food. The *Oktoberfests* are *Bierfests*.

Straussball

In a hall ornate and Victorian, people wearing historical uniforms, hoop skirts, or other clothing suggesting the Strauss era dance to a non-amplified band playing music of Johann Strauss the Elder and the Younger and their contemporaries. A *Straussball* might also be a debutante ball.

Christkindlmarkt

German clubs plan elaborate Christmas programs. If a *Christkindlmarkt* is held, it will offer handicrafts, baked goods, food, possibly a reenactment of Christmas customs of different German regions, and music and singing.

Maifests

German Americans popularize the *Maifests*. The Amana Colonies in Iowa begin the tourist season with a *Maifest* for which shops and streets are decorated with geraniums and other flowers, and the end of winter is celebrated.

Sommertag

In the Palatinate, on a Sunday in March, children carry *Sommertagsstecken* (summerday wands). In the entourage of Spring marches *"Hansel Fingerhut"* in a multicolored suit with blackened face. He tries to catch the girls and blacken their faces also. In the Winter group marches the *Nudelgret*, a young man dressed as a fat and funny lady, carrying a stick and tossing pretzels to the crowd.

The procession leads to a meadow. Children surround Spring in a circle. Winter stands outside the circle, and the two debate the merits of one and the shortcomings of the other. Winter tries to catch Spring, fails, and is driven away, disappearing over the hill. In America, this is celebrated at the German farm site at the Museum of American Frontier Culture in Virginia (see page 56).

The Language Village

By Dianne Stevens

Just as if they were in Germany, excited villagers clear customs and exchange dollars for *marks*. But these villagers aren't in Germany. They are at *Waldsee*, the German Language Village on Turtle River Lake east of Bemidji, Minnesota.

Waldsee, German for "lake of the woods," is one of 10 language villages sponsored each summer by Concordia College of Moorhead, Minnesota. Par-

ticipants range from 7 to 18 years old and come from all over the world to immerse themselves in German language and customs.

They live in a *Haus* reflecting German architecture. One residence hall looks like it belongs in the Black Forest while the other is Austrian in style. Villagers eat common foods from German-speaking countries: *Muesli*, *Brötchen* (hard rolls), or *Weichgekochte Eier* (soft-boiled eggs) for breakfast. Small-group sessions, sports, crafts, games, and a carnival, all in German of course, make learning the language fun.

By the third or fourth day, villagers are likely to wake up and say *"Guten Morgen"* instead of "Good morning."

Nearby, in other Corcordia Language Villages, young people are learning in the same way to speak Chinese, Danish, Finnish, French, Japanese, Norwegian, Russian, Spanish, and Swedish. For information, write to Concordia Language Villages, 901 South 8th Street, Moorhead, Minnesota 56560.

Laura Spires, 12, of Lake Forest, Illinois, at the German Language Village sponsored by Concordia College of Moorhead, Minnesota.

Merry Old Santa Claus, by Thomas Nast in Harper's Weekly, *December 25, 1886*

Merry Christmas!

Fröhliche Weinachten!

Santa Claus illustrations by Thomas Nast in Harper's Weekly, *1886*

By Julie McDonald

Most ingredients of "an old-fashioned American Christmas" came from Germany: St. Nicholas (Santa Claus), "The Messiah" by George Frederick Handel, and the Christmas tree (Tannenbaum), to name a few.

One of the most enchanting German Christmas traditions is St. Nicholas. The patron saint of sailors and students, St. Nicholas has been venerated in Germany since the 12th century. St. Nicholas statues stand guard in towns along the Rhine, and churches bear his name.

St. Nicholas was a 4th century Bishop of Myra in Asia Minor, revered for his generosity and worshiped by sailors for miracles at sea and in harbor. He also helped poor girls by providing their dowries. Hung by the fire to dry, stockings were miraculously filled with gold so the girls could marry.

St. Nicholas is said to have brought back to life three children who had been murdered and stored as pickled meat in the house of a wicked butcher. The children carried out church duties thereafter and were rewarded with small gifts on December 6.

The custom of a gift-giver representing a bishop took root, and the question, "Have you been good?" preceded the presentation. St. Nicholas was accompanied by a dark figure wrapped in old clothes or fur who carried the sack of presents and dealt with bad children. He was called Knecht Ruprecht.

Thomas Nast (1840-1902), who came to America from Germany as a child, created the white-bearded Santa Claus with a pack on his back, combining St.

Nicholas and Knecht Ruprecht. Nast's Santa, introduced during the American Civil War, also was a self-portrait—as rotund and cheery as the artist who created him.

The Christmas carol "Silent Night" was composed on Christmas Eve in 1818 by Franz Gruber, the son of an Austrian linen weaver. From 1816 to 1829 he was soloist and organist at the Roman Catholic Church in Oberndorf near Salzburg. The words were written by the priest, Father Josef Mohr.

For many Americans, the Christmas season truly arrives with the performance of *The Messiah,* the oratorio composed in 24 days of 1741 by George Frederick Handel. Even though the premiere of the work was in April (1742), the arias concerning the birth of Christ have linked the oratorio to Christmas. *The Messiah* was written long after Handel became a British subject, but the country of his birth is responsible for the intensity of its inspiration.

The origin of Christmas tree customs is hidden in the mists of the past, but we do know we must give up the pleasant image of Martin Luther and his family in front of a candle-lit tree. The combination of the festive evergreen and lights didn't happen that soon.

The tradition of creating a Christmas pyramid of pine boughs and decorations, and later of decorating an entire tree, started in Germany. In 1708 Duchess Elisabeth Charlotte of Orleans wrote to her daughter describing "box bushes on tables with a candle fixed to every branch. This looks absolutely charming." A 1605 manuscript in Strasbourg described "fir trees with roses cut from multicolored paper, apples, cakes, tinsel, and sugar hanging from the branches."

German settlers introduced the Christmas tree in America, but its wide popularity came after England's Prince Albert installed one in the royal palace in 1841 and magazines began to feature beautifully decorated trees. Placing a star at the top of the tree became a common practice in the last half of the 18th century.

In some parts of Germany trees were decorated with edibles: apples, nuts, and raisins. Fancy cookie molds were brought out at Christmas to make *matzebaum,* almond cakes with raised images. Most were eaten when the tree came down, but some were put away and used year after year. After slow-baking at a low temperature, *matzebaum* were painted with homemade vegetable dyes and dated. Thicker shapes made from almond-flavored dough were called *marzipan.* Miniature fruits and vegetables were favorite shapes for these sweets, popular in Germany since the Middle Ages.

Another decorating favorite was the white *springerle* made of egg dough seasoned with anise seeds. The finest *springerle* molds were made by woodcarvers. Other treasures brought from the homeland were cookie cutters made by tinsmiths in the shape of the moon, stars, hearts, trees, and flowers.

In Pennsylvania Dutch country, white cookies were sprinkled with red sugar "for pretty," and a washbasketful of cookies was not enough for Christmas! Included were *Christbäume* (pretzel-shaped to represent praying hands) and paper-thin sandtarts.

Around 1880, the glass-makers of Thuringia discovered a new method of blowing glass bells, balls and animals and silver-coating the inside. In 1800 a merchant named Woolworth brought to the United States the first colorful glass-ball ornaments, called *kugels*. The *kugels* lasted season after season and became a traditional ornament. Tinsel strips to hang on the branches became popular, and angels' hair, spangles, and silver stars were made from glass fiber.

Some of the loveliest ornaments ever devised were the small silver and gold embossed cardboard Dresden Christmas tree ornaments. Shaped like dogs, cats, suns, moons, frogs, turtles, alligators, exotic animals, sea life, bicycles, skates, cars, boats, pianos and musical instruments, they were remarkably detailed. Other German ornaments were made from shiny wire twisted and tied into stars, butterflies and rosettes. Germany contributed the custom of the *putz*, a fence-enclosed scene of figures and toys or a nativity scene beneath the tree.

The Germans always have unveiled the Christmas tree on Christmas Eve in a theatrical moment of sudden radiance. German Americans are more likely to put the tree up sooner and enjoy its beauty longer. The earliest record of a Christmas tree in the United States is the diary of Matthew Zahm, who wrote about his family going into the woods to cut the tree on December 20, 1821. An 1825 issue of the *Philadelphia Saturday Evening Post* described "trees visible through the windows, whose green boughs are laden with fruits richer than the golden apples of the Hesperides."

Among the Pennsylvania Dutch, carefully prepared baskets were set out on Christmas Eve for the Christ child to fill with cookies, candies, nuts, and raisins. The baskets were made of rye straw to represent the manger and lined with a clean white napkin to symbolize the swaddling clothes of Jesus.

Germans were in the forefront of Christmas tree stand design. In 1877 Johannes Eckardt of Stuttgart applied for an American patent for a revolving musical tree stand. Four more men with German names received patents for their stands, and in 1899 Alfred Wagner of St. Louis patented a stand that held water for the tree, and rotated the tree with an electric motor. Those who could not afford the metal stands put their Christmas trees in buckets of coal, and enjoyed them to the fullest. The poor farmers of Pennsylvania got double use from each tree, removing the dry needles and, for the next year, making a "snow tree" by covering the bare branches with cotton.

Christmas among the Moravians of Pennsylvania has always had a special flavor. Each home had a corner set aside for a nativity scene. People went to the woods in September to dig moss; they tended it carefully in the cellar until it became the green grass of the Christmas *putz*. Frequently, a winding road was built of sawdust or sand to accommodate several hundred small wooden animals making their way to Noah's ark. These traditions continue today.

In contrast to the simple and devout celebration of Christmas, "General" Johann August Sutter, the flamboyant German whose California land was the center of the Gold Rush, celebrated December 25, 1847, lavishly just before his property was overrun by gold-crazed prospectors. The menu that day at the Rancheria de Hoch included soup, salmon, pigs' feet and pepper, frijoles and beef, veal, and all manner of game, with champagne and wine. Music and dancing went on until dawn.

Through every age and political circumstance, the Germans have celebrated the festival of Christmas with warm and rich profundity. The United States, a young nation yearning for the glow of tradition, has embraced the German customs of Christmas with joy.

Christmas Pyramids

By Helen Kraus

If your ancestors were from Germany, the word "pyramids" would not conjure up visions of Egyptian monuments, but of wooden structures which were called pyramids and were brought out at Christmastime.

The tree which is associated with Christmas was banned in many German provinces because it was considered a waste to cut down a tree merely for ornamentation. In part of Alsace, an ordinance stated that no person "shall have for Christmas more than one bush of more than eight shoe lengths." In 1531, that meant a tree or bush less than 4 feet tall. In many other provinces cutting down a tree without permission could mean a fine or imprisonment. Because of fear of imprisonment or the fact that the church considered the Christmas tree a form of pagan worship, people looked for new ideas.

In Saxony, which is known for its delicate glass Christmas ornaments, men would fashion left-over wood into little fences. These would surround wooden animals, often sheep with wool batting glued to their sides, presenting a pastoral scene and reminding the pious Saxos of the shepherds who were told of Christ's birth. In a crib or manger scene in Bavaria, religious cards would represent the holy family. In all provinces the wooden pyramid, made of materials such as wood, paper, or tin, came into use as a "Christmas tree."

Paddles on the apex of the pyramid were propelled by a steady current of warm air rising from the candles placed under and somewhat to the sides of the paddles. At first, paddles were made from paper and had a small circular piece of paper connected to them from which hung paper angels. When the heat of the candles made the paddle turn it would appear as though the angels were flying above the Baby Jesus' crib.

Since the paper burned easily, tin was substituted, and then wood. Because tin and wood were more substantial than paper a new innovation took place: the one-story pyramid became two, three, four, and even five stories tall. All were connected firmly to, and turned with, the same dowel that was turned by the paddles. The dowel ran through the middle of each story of the pyramid.

Candles were used because they are symbolic of Christ—the Light of the World. Because wax candles were expensive, candles of tallow were used, or candles were lit for only a short time. The pyramids were, and still are, often decorated with pine boughs, and often the pyramid is painted a deep green so that any bare spots are not so noticeable. Pyramids are popular today in the Amana Colonies of Iowa and among other German Americans who are interested in preserving their culture.

Christmas in Germany
Notes by Lynn Hattery-Beyer

At Christmastime almost every German household displays some kind of carving. The most well-known carvings come from the area of the Erz Mountains in Saxony. In the evenings and during winter the miners had time to carve and paint figures. After mining was no longer profitable the production of these figures became their main source of income. Many different figures were carved. Most famous are the nutcrackers, with their jaws open wide to receive nuts, and the *Räuchermmännchen*, the "Incense Men" painted to look like miners. Much more complicated are the revolving pyramids.

Christmas Markets

Sometimes called the Christ Child's Market, Christmas Markets begin with Advent. Booths offer all the trappings of a German Christmas—gingerbread, trees, candles, decorations and presents. The most famous market is Nuremberg's, founded 300 years ago by craftsmen and merchants. The Christ Child Market in Munich is more than 600 years old.

Christmas Cribs

Many households display Christmas Cribs which are nativity scenes. Complete with animals, angels, Wise Men, shepherds, the Christ Child, Joseph, and Mary, the Cribs can be elaborate or simple and are made from a variety of materials such as straw, clay, wood or plaster of Paris.

Advent Wreaths

The German Christmas season is officially opened on the first Advent Sunday, four Sundays before Christmas Eve. Advent wreaths, artistically bound of pine boughs and adorned with dried berries, nuts, pine cones, ribbons, and four candles, appear in homes and offices, sometimes hanging from the ceiling. On each of the Advent Sundays a new candle is lighted; by the week before Christmas all the candles are burning. Many families make the lighting of each new candle a festivity; they sing Christmas carols by candlelight and enjoy scrumptious cookies that are baked only during the Christmas season.

Advent Calendars

On the first day of December, wherever there are children, Advent calendars appear. The traditional calendar depicts a scene and has 24 doors which open, one each day until Christmas, to reveal a small detail of the scene. The doors of many modern Advent calendars also hide small pieces of chocolate.

St. Nicholas Day

Ever since the Middle Ages, St. Nicholas Day, December 6, has been an important part of the Christmas celebration. In rural southern Germany, St. Nicholas, dressed in a red bishop's robe and miter and carrying a staff, pays personal visits to children. His servant, Ruprecht, shoulders the sack of goodies and threatens children who have not behaved themselves. After St. Nicholas has talked with the children and they have sung carols for him, he gives them presents from his sack, usually oranges, apples and nuts. Then he wishes them a Merry Christmas and leaves to visit other homes. In northern Germany and in urban areas, St. Nicholas does not visit homes. Instead, children put well-polished shoes in front of their doors before going to bed on December 5 and awake the next morning to find them filled with treats—or coal!

Christmas Eve

For those celebrating a traditional Christmas, the afternoon is full of secrecy and anxious waiting. Behind closed doors, parents, sometimes only the father, set up and decorate the Christmas tree and get the presents ready. After everyone dresses in their best clothes, the celebration begins. Before everyone enters the "Christmas Room" the mother usually peeks in to make sure everything is ready. She then rings a bell and the family enters. At first, everyone just stands and admires the tree. Sometimes carols are sung. Then it is time for presents. After the presents have been opened, the children often recite poems, play carols on their instruments, or sing. An important part of a German Christmas Eve is to attend church.

Christmas

Christmas Eve is followed by two days of celebration. Both December 25 and 26 are official holidays. Whereas Christmas Eve is usually reserved for the small, nuclear family, the first and second days of Christmas are dedicated to visiting relatives, enjoying big meals and going on extended walks.

The Christmas Tree

Greenery has always been used in German households to add cheer during the colorless winter. The use of light at Christmas symbolizes Christ. The first trees introduced were small—table-sized. At the same time it became popular to wrap evergreen boughs around pyramid-shaped wooden frames. These pyramids and trees were always decorated with real candles, even by those too poor to afford real candles at any other time of the year.

Epiphany

The Christmas season does not end until January 6, Epiphany. This is the 12th day of Christmas, the day of the Three Wise Men or the Three Holy Kings. In Catholic parts of Germany, groups of three boys dressed as the Wise Men go from house to house, reciting Bible verses and blessing each house by writing the Wise Men's initials on the front door in chalk:

19—C † M † B—91

(Casper, Melchior, Balthasar, two crosses, and the current year.)
This day marks the end of the Christmas season in Germany.

Below: Illustrating Christmas
From F. H. Ehmcke's Graphic Trade Symbols by German Designers, 1907.

Right: Harvey Jeck made this Christmas pyramid in the collection of the Museum of Amana History, Amana, Iowa. Pyramids with nativity scenes and with collections of small Christmas objects have been a German tradition for centuries.
Below: A beautiful gingerbread house by Carol Schuerer Zuber of Amana, Iowa, whose recipe is on page 207.

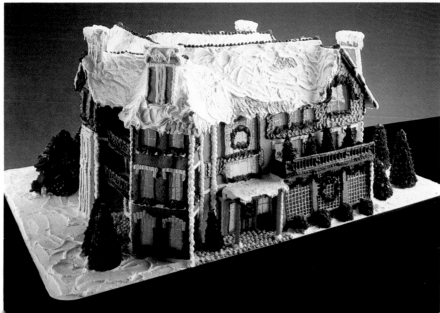

Above: Dolls in traditional German costumes are in the collection of Karin Gottier, Vernon, Connecticut. Front row, from left: a Protestant woman, Marburg, Hessia; a single girl, Schwalm district, Hessia; a bride, married woman, and single girl, Gutach Valley of the Black Forest; and a woman in festival dress and bride from Schaumburg-Lippe, Westfalia. Back row from left: Catholic woman, Mardof, Hessia; woman from the Island of Föhr; Danube-Swabian woman; Transylvania-Saxon girl, Romania; Karpathian-German girl, Topporz, Slovakia.

Bottom, left: A shelf in the bookcase of the Gottier home. The painting is by the late Alfred Ludwig, a folk artist in Rockville, Connecticut. The shelf holds Karin's collection of miners and angels. In the Ore mountain region, it was a Christmas custom to place in the window a miner for each boy and an angel for each girl.

Top, left: Dining room scene in the folk-art-decorated home of Nelson and Karin Gottier of Vernon, Connecticut includes a pyramid typical of those produced in the Ore mountains of Germany. The first tier shows figures of the Biblical Christmas story, while the second and third show figures of the popular Christmas celebration. Karin's Aunt Helen's bundt cake (recipe page 190) is next to a tea service typically used in Friesland. The porcelain is hand-painted with the Friesian rose design. The tea is kept warm by placing the pot on the "Stövchen," a small brass candle warmer. The Amish quilt comes from Intercourse, Pennsylvania. Standing guard (at right) are nutcrackers. The one at left in bottom row is from Tirol, Austria. All others are from the Ore mountains.

German-American Steuben Parade

With appropriate pomp and color, the annual New York City parade honors Baron Frederick William von Steuben, who fought for Frederick II the Great in Germany, and for American independence under George Washington (See page 65). Musical groups from Germany join in this parade. Queen and attendants wear blue to symbolize the cornflower (bachelor button), symbol of German Americans. Geese came from a Long Island farm.

Photos by Karin Gottier

BMW OF NORTH AMERICA

AUTOBAHN ACROSS THE ATLANTIC
35 YEARS Lufthansa

LEIPZIG   BERLIN   MÜNCHEN   FRANKFURT   STUTTGART   KÖLN   HAMBURG

GERMAN NATIONAL TOURIS

Milwaukee's German Fest

Over 100,000 people attend this annual weekend summer event on the Lake Michigan waterfront. The German Fest revitalized German-American clubs in the area. Brats, kraut, and beer, with musical groups from America, Germany, and Austria are featured attractions. Volunteers and staff work all year for this spectacular event.

Photos courtesy of the Milwaukee German Fest

Pommersche Tanzdeel Freistadt *of Freistadt, Wisconsin, is a folk dance group preserving a rich heritage. The Pomeranian language* Plattdeutsch *of Lowland German was spoken there until World War II. At left are Mrs. Gretchen Mauritz and Daniel Boehlke, sister and brother. Gretchen teaches the children. Daniel is president of the group and of the United Pomeranian Societies of America. In 1989 he won the Pomeranian Culture Prize awarded by the* Pommersche Landsmannschaft *of Germany. Right: Gail and Craig Tews. He is a dance instructor.*

An entire building on Main Street in Frankenmuth, Michigan, was constructed as a working cuckoo clock with a giant cuckoo and colorful figurines that come out each half-hour to the music of Edelweiss, Blue Danube, and Lara's Theme. The building was completed in 1986 by Jack Boening and his late father John for their Boening's Bavarian Clock Haus and its display of Black Forest cuckoo clocks, Swiss watches, music boxes, and jewelry.

The German Pavilion, EPCOT Center, Walt Disney World Vacation Kingdom, Lake Buena Vista, Florida

Gems from the world of sculpture delight visitors at the World Showcase in EPCOT Center, the unique international experience created by Walt Disney World in Florida. The German pavilion, one of many circling the 40-acre World Showcase Lagoon, has a Glockenspiel with sculpture of two doll-like whimsical children, a contrast to the three solemn Hapsburg emperors gazing down on visitors from 18 feet up. Nearby a statue of St. George and the Dragon stands in the center of the plaza-like entrance area.

Traditional German architecture lends charm to the displays of crafts and products of Germany, including fine porcelain and Hummel figurines. The restaurant is staffed with young people from Germany and offers dishes typical of all regions of Germany from cold wurst and potato dumplings to pork in aspic and fresh-baked pretzels. A typical German cookie shop features baked goods, cookies, and gift tins.

The many imports from Germany include German beers and wines from the famed Mosel region, plus imported drinking steins and fine German crystal wine glasses. Musical entertainment brings the *Biergarten* to life.

Marlene Domeier is shown in front of her store in New Ulm, Minnesota, holding Heinz, Professor Wichtel. Marlene explains: "A Wichtel is a Gnome—a little person who brings good luck. Our Heinz was born back in 1630, on October 6, but don't let that shock you for the life span of a Wichtel is around 400 years. Once a Wichtel reaches the age of 350 years, he begins to get wanderlust and he wants to expand his horizons beyond the forests and ravines of Germany. His godfather, a Pate, in Germany, found him wandering in the hills of the Taunus Mountains near Frankfurt. He picked up the little fellow, arranged for a work permit in the United States, and shipped him via commerical airlines to Domeiers where he plays his accordian daily in the shop window."

Gretel in der Butten (a Gretel in the bucket) is a traditional character in Mardi Gras festivals and parades. The origin of the Gretel character with an attached basket containing a "man" took place in Nuremberg in the 16th century. This photograph shows Karin Gottier of Vernon, Connecticut in costume as a Gretel.

In 1933, to celebrate the first bottle of beer brewed after the repeal of Prohibition, August A. Busch Jr. gave his father a Clydesdale hitch of the Scottish horses pulling a red beer wagon. In early days, brewers put emphasis on how far their draft horses could pull a load of beer in a day. Today the Budweiser Clydesdales travel world-wide. The 70-block Anheuser-Busch, Inc. Brewery in St. Louis offers free tours daily.

Left: Harold Graves of Milwaukee flies his hot air balloon, the Augsburger, sponsored by the Augsburger Brewing Company, over the Mississippi River at McGregor, Iowa. The German-styled Augsburger beer is named for the Augsburg region in Germany. Once brewed in Monroe, Wisconsin by the Joseph Huber Brewing Company, Augsburger now is brewed in St. Paul, Minnesota.

*Above right: the **Burgermeister** of the Busch Gardens, The Old Country. The Busch Gardens in Williamsburg, Virginia is a family theme park developed by Anheuser-Busch. It features the **Rhinefeld** and **Oktoberfest** of Germany and other countries. Das Festhaus is a 2,000-seat festival hall with an oompah band, German dancers, and the **Burgermeister.** There is **Der Autobahn,** bumper cars, and the Big Bad Wolf, a suspended roller coaster traveling through Bavarian villages before dropping 80 feet to the Rhine River below.*

Fredericksburg, Texas

Above left: Replica of the historic eight-sided church and community center.

Right: Ingrid Haas, German immigrant, shows rugs utilizing wool from sheep in the Texas Hill Country.

Left: Loretta Schmidt and daughter Heidi cook cheese (recipe page 148) to serve on bread (recipe page 165). The Schmidt family operates Gästehaus Schmidt.

San Antonio, Texas

The Steves Homestead in the King William Historic District of San Antonio is open to the public. Owned by the San Antonio Conservation Society, this Victorian mansion reflects the elegance of a gracious residential section settled by German businessmen.

New Braunfels, Texas

Top left: Barron Schlameus, whose German ancestors came to Texas in 1850, is at the Conservation Plaza, a project of the New Braunfels Conservation Society. Early buildings are relocated in the plaza.

Top Right: Ethel Canion, volunteer for the Conservation Society, stands by the home of Ferdinand Lindheimer (1801-1879). He served as a guide to lead German colonists to New Braunfels. The Comanche Indians thought he was a medicine man. He also edited a German language newspaper. The home is made of Fachwerk adapted to Texas limestone and cedar.

Below: Virginia Grona, who has German ancestry, is making noodles and feeding the chickens at the Sauer-Beckmann living history farm, part of the Lyndon B. Johnson State Historical Park near Fredericksburg, Texas. Sauer's daughter was the midwife who delivered the late President Johnson.

Above: This German-American farmstead of 19th-century Wisconsin is one of three at the 576-acre outdoor museum of the Wisconsin State Historical Society at Kettle Moraine State Forest near Eagle, which is southwest of Milwaukee. Tram services take visitors to the sites.

Below left: At the German farm at the Museum of American Frontier Culture near Staunton, Virginia, "Mayor" Bob Flippen (museum staff) welcomes visitors to the Weinlesefest. Below right: Bringing the bush to the inn are Frank Strassler and Philip Barry of the museum staff. It's part of the annual Kerwe celebration. Story on page 56.

America's Bavarian-style villages include Helen, Georgia (above) and Leavenworth, Washington (below). Both villages were updated into the Bavarian style after World War II and today are leading tourist attractions in their states. The bandstand in Leavenworth is used daily during festivals by a band and choral groups in costumes, featuring German music. An article about each village is on page 50.

Crocheted animals in the collection of Ruth Schmieder are by the late Louise Rettig. The Museum of Amana History displays work by Mrs. Rettig. Coloring mixed with glue from the furniture factory creates the shiny dye for Easter eggs created every spring in the Amana Colonies (Recipe page 198). Basket holding the eggs is from the collection of Terry Roemig. Jo Schanz has revived the tradition of making willow baskets in the Amana Colonies. Ham baked in bread by Jack Hahn at the Open Hearth Bakery in Middle Amana is shown at the home of Carol and David Heusinkveld in Amana. Recipe on page 173.

Easter in Germany

by F. E. Corne.

From St. Nicholas Magazine, April 1878.

"THE HARES LAY THE COLORED EGGS."

"Oh, look! Look! All those pretty little Easter things in the window already!" exclaimed my little sister one day, as we passed one of the largest confectionery stores in Stuttgart; and, true enough, though Lent was but half over, there they were, a pretty show. Eggs, of course, in quantities and of all sizes, from that of an ostrich to a humming bird's made of chocolate or of sugar, and gayly decorated with little ribbons and pictures. Then there were fat little unfledged chickens, some just emerging from their shells, some not an inch long, and others large as life; pure white lambs, with ribbons and bells round their necks; paste-eggs, with holes at the ends, and, looking through, behold, a panorama inside! And eggs with roses on one side, which, when blown upon, emit a musical sound.

But odder than all these were the goats playing on guitars, or dragging behind them fairy-like egg-shaped carriages, with little hares gravely driving; and in others of these carriages were reclining one or two (generally two) baby hares, or a hare mother rocking her little one in an egg cradle; there were sugar balloons, in the baskets of which hares watched over their nests full of eggs; wheelbarrows full of eggs, and trundled by a hare; and dainty baskets of flowers, with birds perched upon each handle, peering down into nests of eggs half hidden amidst the blossoms. When one knows that each nest comes out, and forms the cover to a box of *bonbons* neatly concealed underneath, this pretty structure certainly loses none of its attractiveness.

In all directions signs of the approaching season begin to appear. Every old woman in the market places offers for sale a store of hard-boiled eggs, smeared over with some highly colored varnish, besides candy chickens, hares, etc., in abundance. All the various shop windows display pretty emblematic articles. Besides the sugar and chocolate eggs, there are eggs of soap and of glass; egg-shaped baskets and reticules; leather eggs, which really are ladies companions, and filled with sewing implements; wooden eggs and porcelain eggs, and even egg-shaped lockets made of solid gold.

It would be difficult to explain why these things appear at Easter, and what they all mean. The eggs, as everyone knows, we have at home, and where they are in such abundance chickens will not be very far away. For the lamb and the goat we can find scriptural interpretations, but the rabbit and the hare—what can they have to do with Easter? Nine persons out of ten can only answer, "The hares lay the Easter eggs." Queer hares they must be, indeed, but the children here believe it as devoutly as they do that the "Christkind" brings their Christmas presents, or as our own little ones do in Santa Claus. No one knows exactly whence came this myth. Many think it a relic of heathen worship; but a writer named Christoph von Schmid, in an interesting story for children, suggests this much prettier origin:

Many hundred years ago, a good and noble lady, Duchess Rosilinda von Lindenburg, at a time when a cruel war was devastating the land, was obliged to fly from her beautiful home accompanied by her two little children and one old man-servant.

They found refuge in a small mining village in the mountains, where the simple but contented and happy inhabitants did what they could for their comfort, and placed the best of all they had at the disposal of the wanderers. Nevertheless, their fare was miserable; no meat was ever to be found, seldom fish, and not even an egg; this last for the very good reason that there was not a single hen in the village! These useful domestic fowls, now so common everywhere, were originally brought from the East, and had not yet found their way to this secluded place. The people had not even heard of such "strange birds." This troubled the kind duchess, who well knew the great help they are in housekeeping, and she determined that the women who had been so kind to her should no longer be without them.

Accordingly, the next time she sent forth her faithful old servant to try and

gather news of his master and of the progress of the war, she commissioned him to bring back with him a coop full of fowls. This he did, to the great surprise of the simple natives, and the village children were greatly excited a few weeks later at the appearance of a brood of young chickens. They were so pretty and bright, were covered with such a soft down, were

THE OLD SERVANT BRINGS A COOP FULL OF CHICKENS.

so open-eyed, and could run about after their mother to pick up food the very first day, and were altogether such a contrast to the blind, bald, unfledged, helpless, ugly little birds they sometimes saw in nests in the hedges, that they could not find words enough to express their admiration.

114

The good lady now saved up eggs for some time, then invited all the housewives of the village to a feast, when she set before them eggs cooked in a variety of ways. She then taught them how to prepare them for themselves, and, distributing a number of fowls among them, sent the dames home grateful and happy.

When Easter approached, she was anxious to arrange some pleasure for the village children, but had nothing to give them, "not even an apple or a nut," only some eggs; but that, she concluded, was, after all, an appropriate offering, "as an egg is the first gift of the reviving spring." And then it occurred to her to boil them with mosses and roots that would give them a variety of brilliant colors, "as the earth," said she, "has just laid aside her white mantle, and decorated herself with many colors; for the dear God makes the fruit and berries not only good to eat, but also pleasant to look upon," and the children's pleasure would be all the greater.

Accordingly, on Easter Sunday, after the church service, all the little ones of about the age of her own, met together in a garden; and, when their kind hostess had talked to them a while, she led then into a small neighboring wood. There she told them to make nests of moss, and advised each to mark well his or her own. All then returned to the garden, where a feast of milk-soup with eggs and egg-cakes had been prepared. Afterward they went back to the wood, and found to their great joy in each nest five beautiful colored eggs, and on one of these a short rhyme was written.

The surprise and delight of the little ones when they discovered a nest of the gayly colored treasures, was very great, and one of them exclaimed:

"How wonderful the hens must be that can lay such pretty eggs! How I should like to see them!"

"Oh! No hens could lay such beautiful eggs," answered a little girl. "I think it must have been the little hare that sprang out of the juniper bush when I wanted to build my nest there."

Then all the children laughed together, and said "The hares lay the colored eggs. Yes, yes! the dear little hares lay the beautiful eggs!" And they kept repeating it till they began really to believe it.

Not long afterward the war ended, and Duke Arno von Lindenburg took his wife and children back to their own palace; but, before leaving, the Duchess set apart a sum of money to be expended on giving the village children every Easter a feast of eggs. She instituted the custom also in her own duchy, and by degrees it spread over the whole country, the eggs being considered a symbol of redemption or deliverance from sin. The custom has found its way even to America, but nowhere out of the *Vaterland* are the eggs laid by the timid hare.

To this day children living in the country go to the woods just before Easter, and return with their arms full of twigs and moss, out of which they build nests and houses, each child carefully marking his own with his name. They are then hidden behind stones and bushes in the garden, or if the weather be cold, in

corners, or under furniture in the house. And on Easter morning what an excitement there is to see what the good little hare has brought! Not only real eggs boiled and colored, but sugar ones too, and often wooden ones that open like boxes, disclosing, perhaps, a pair of new gloves or a bright ribbon. He even sometimes brings hoops and skipping-ropes, and generally his own effigy in dough or candy is found trying to scamper away behind the nest.

Then what fun they have playing with the eggs, throwing them in the air and catching them again, rolling them on the floor, exchanging with each other, and *knocking* them! This game is played by two, each child holding an egg firmly in his hand so that only the small end appears between the thumb and forefinger, or under the little finger. The two eggs then are knocked smartly against each other until one cracks, when it becomes the property of the victorious party, who adds it to his stock. Those who have never tried to break an egg in this way will be astonished to find how many hard taps it is able to stand. But, as the game called "picking eggs" is played in some parts of the United States during the Easter holidays, it may be that many of our readers know all about this matter, and understand very well how to select the eggs that shall prove strong and victorious.

In Germany, presents are frequently bestowed upon servants at this season, and exchanged between friends; and on Easter morning the churches are crowded by many who scarcely ever think of entering at any other time. On Good Friday only, considered here the holiest day in the whole year, are they still more largely attended. The music is usually fine, but one misses the beautiful flowers which adorn our home altars.

Easter Monday is looked upon as a grand holiday by the peasantry in many parts of the country. Weddings are often deferred to this day, and many village games are reserved for this season. The lads and lassies all appear in their gala costumes; the girls with short, dark skirts, braided with gold or silver, snowy aprons and full white sleeves, bright colored bodices and odd little caps; the boys with knee-breeches, white stockings, low shoes, and scarlet or yellow vests, the solid gold or silver buttons on which are often their whole inheritance. But when they are dancing gayly together on the green, they look a good deal happier than if they were little kings and queens.

Games vary in different villages throughout the country, but one example will give some idea of what they are like.

Two of the leading young men of the place take entire charge of the day's amusements, selecting for the purpose, as the scene of festivities, some inn or *Wirtschaft*, to which is attached a large garden or meadow.

For several preceding evenings, when work is over, they go about from

116

house to house, dressed in their best, and carrying large baskets on their arms. Everywhere they are kindly received, and bread with wine or cider is placed before them. While they eat and drink, the baskets are quietly slipped away by some member of the family, a generous donation of eggs is placed within them, and they are secretly returned to their places. The eggs are not asked for, neither are they alluded to in any way; but the object of the visit is well understood and prepared for long beforehand.

When Monday morning dawns, the inn is found to have been gayly decorated with garlands of green and flowers, and fluttering ribbons of many colors. The tree nearest the house is ornamented in like manner, and on it the prize to be contended for, conspicuously hangs. On the smooth grass hard by, a strip, a few feet wide and perhaps a hundred long, has been roped in, and at either end of this narrow plot a large, shallow, round-bottomed basket, called a *Wanne*, is placed, one filled with chaff and the other with eggs, dozens upon dozens, cooked and raw, white and colored.

The plan of the peculiar game which follows is that one player is pitted to run a given distance, while another safely throws the eggs from one basket to the other, he who first completes his task being, of course,  the winner. Accordingly, when the young men and maidens have arrived, two leaders draw lots to determine who shall run and who shall throw. That decided, the contestants are gayly decked with ribbons, a band strikes up a lively air, a capering clown clears the way and the game begins. He who throws takes the eggs, and one after another swiftly whirls them the length of the course, and into the chaff-filled basket, which is held in the hands of an assistant. Occasionally he makes a diversion by pitching a hard one to be scrambled for by the crowds of children who have assembled to see the

sport. Meantime (while wagers are laid as to who will likely win) the other contestant speeds the distance of a mile or two to an appointed goal, marks it as proof of his having touched it, and if he succeeds in returning before all the eggs are thrown, the victory and the prize are his, otherwise they belong to his opponent. The game finished, the prize is presented to the victor with due ceremony and amid the cheers of the crowd; the hard eggs are distributed among the company, and the raw ones carried uproariously into the neighboring inn, there to be cooked in various ways and eaten.

The remainder of the day is spent in dancing and merry-making, and if a wedding can possibly be arranged to take place on that afternoon the fun is wilder than ever.

117

My Story

From Germany to America

By Karin Gottier

As long as I can remember, folk dance has captured my imagination. On warm summer evenings I would stand by the fence in the corner of our garden and watch as the "big" boys and girls left to go folk dancing. Because they always came back singing and laughing, I decided that as soon as I was old enough, I would go folk dancing, too.

When I was six, I was a flower girl at a rural wedding in East Prussia. After a long train ride we traveled by horse and wagon through dark pine forests to the farm. The following evening was *Polterabend:* neighbors came to break dishes and glass in front of the bride's door. She had to sweep away the shards and invite people in for coffee and cake and stronger refreshments. The next morning, on the wedding day, the doors of the farmhouse were wreathed in pine garlands, and the draft oxen's horns were decorated with paper flowers and ribbons. The threshing floor was cleared and large boards were placed over sawhorses, then covered with linen bedsheets to serve as banquet tables. The posts of the barn were also garlanded and a space was set aside for the musicians. There was coming and going all day as neighbors brought piles of cakes and helped with the cooking.

Almost everyone in the village took part in the bridal procession, which went on foot from the farm to the old Lutheran village church. The church was very dark. The only bright touches were the pink and white floral crowns in glass cases, hanging on the walls. It was the custom to place a bridal crown on the coffin of a young man or woman who died before being married.

After the ceremony, which was performed by a woman pastor (the first German woman minister was ordained in 1932; this wedding was in 1943), the procession was waylaid by the village children, who had stretched a green rope across the street. The bridegroom was obliged to buy our passage by tossing coins and candy into the crowd of children. Then, after a long and ample meal, several guests and children presented small sketches and poems appropriate to the occasion. Later there was dancing. People danced the usual dances that were popular in the 1940s—fox trot, two-step, with a waltz or a polka thrown in. As the party went on, older people began to do dances with figures, dances that looked like much more fun than what had been danced earlier. They also sang as they danced. For me it was a revelation: "So that is what folk dance looks like." Later the women who had cooked all day came out of the kitchen and danced while holding out their aprons, into which the guests tossed small coins.

We children were supposed to sleep under the roof in a very small room with sloping sides that was reached only by a very precarious structure, more ladder than stair. That night I woke up with a start to discover that the bride was hiding among us. The married women were looking for her, intent on tearing her veil at midnight, but they had to catch her first. Of course they found her, and with much clamor, took her back to the party.

These were the war years. When the war finally ended, on a radiantly beautiful May day with clear blue skies, birds singing, flowers blooming, and bees buzzing, the entire man-made world was a smoking heap of rubble. Burned war equipment, dead soldiers of both armies, burning and smoking houses, and downed power lines were everywhere.

The following day my mom sent me on an errand into the village, which was on the outskirts of greater Berlin. The path I had to take cut through a field where the last battle had been waged. Without looking left or right, in order not to see the dead soldiers, I stared straight ahead and ran as fast as I could. Coming through the center of the village on my way back home, I saw a Russian army truck parked in the shade of a large chestnut tree along the street. One soldier sat on the hood playing his accordion, a second one stood clapping in rhythm, and the third danced one of those vigorous male dances so typical of Russian dance traditions. I looked around to see for whom they were performing, and seeing no one, I realized that they were playing and dancing for their own enjoyment. As I watched, I began to wonder why we humans all dance so differently. Looking back, I am convinced that this was one of the precious moments that set me on my life's path.

As May turned into June, a notice was posted in town that all children were to report to school. When we gathered, those of us who had gone to school here before were outnumbered by strange faces and dialects. The school had lost its windows and roof shingles, all of its doors, and most of its desks. A young man, himself barely out of the teens, who was to bring order into this chaos, resorted to a quick method of sorting us out: "How old are you? . . . what can you read? . . . read this paragraph . . . O.K., third grade . . . next!"

I found myself in third grade together with 60 other children, some of whose German was so strange that we could hardly talk to each other. They were children who had to leave their homes in East and West Prussia, Silesia, Slovakia, Hungary, and elsewhere. Many didn't know where their parents were. Others had become orphans on their wintertime trek across Northern Europe, and ended up in Berlin at war's end. None of us had much clothing. Arms and legs stuck out too far from sleeves and pant legs. Shoes had their toe caps cut to allow for growth, or we wore sandals made of old rubber tires. But we natives had homes and a place where we belonged. These other children were without even that.

This, then, was the make-up of the class that our young teacher was supposed to teach. We had no paper and no books. Chalk was a precious commodity which the teacher carefully carried around with her in an empty Band-Aid box. But we all coped valiantly and soon winter approached.

By now it became apparent to the occupation forces that it would be extremely difficult to supply Berlin with food and fuel during the winter months. Consequently the British military authorities organized a program called *Aktion Storch* (Action Stork). The objective was to remove as many children as possible from Berlin and to ship them to the British zone, an area of Germany that had seen little of bombing and fighting.

We left by train at 5:00 a.m. on a gray, foggy November 1st. After hours of traveling through flat countryside, we transferred to army trucks and spent the night in a British military camp after first being deloused by huge syringes, which sprayed yellow powder down our necks and sleeves. We spent the night on army cots in tents, and were taken further in the trucks. I had never been so far away from home alone in all of my nine years. I had no idea where we were.

Still, it was a grand adventure. The land continued to become flatter. Huge brick, straw-thatched houses seemed to duck into the landscape or huddle in a cluster of old trees. Fat cows were grazing everywhere. It seemed that we had driven for hours in a cold drizzle when suddenly the truck made a sharp turn, came to a stop, and there—in front of me—was the vast gray expanse of the Atlantic Ocean. I had heard about oceans, especially the Baltic, from my father who came from there, but I was unprepared for such a sudden confrontation with this overwhelming endlessness. My immediate reaction was to cover my face with both hands and to duck. When nothing happened I cautiously moved my fingers, one at a time, and peeked out. We were at a pier, so we surely must have arrived, since there was nowhere else to go. Soon we were bundled into a resort steamer that served as ferry, and headed out to sea. Most of us got caught up in the excitement and didn't notice that the sea was running high with large white foam crests. While the adult companions of this transport were slowly turning green below deck, we were roaming around topside, cheering the seagulls that followed the steamer.

After a relatively short time the ship docked and we children huddled together in the center of the cobblestone harbor. The mayor, our welcoming committee, informed us that we were on the island of Norderney and that there was no more room for refugees, but since we were here he would have to put us up somehow. While he made his speech I crept away from the group and hid behind two young men who happened to be watching the scene.

In my best Berlin slang I said "I ain't goin' where they don't want me."

The young men turned around and smiled, and one said, "What have we here? A genuine Berlin big mouth, eh?"

Ultimately some of us were settled in a Lutheran Children's Home for the night. The sisters were totally unprepared for a sudden invasion of such a large group in the middle of winter. There was no food, no heat, and no light, but they rose to the occasion.

Early the next morning I crept out of the garden and followed the sound of the surf, which led me to the beach at low tide. What a discovery! There was a whole world in those tide pools on the breakwater: starfish, shells, and assorted creepy-crawlies which were promptly gathered into my handkerchief. When I found my way back to the home with my treasures, the Sister told me of a family with a toddler who would like a girl to look after her and to play with her. She took me to meet them, and we liked each other immediately. So I became part of a family that consisted of parents, several young adult sons, a daughter-in-law, and a baby. While the young men were seafaring, the rest of the family operated a store that occupied the front of the house. The house, like all houses on the island, featured a large glassed-in veranda and rooms for summer guests.

The first evening I sat in awe of the large blue-and-white tiled kitchen and marveled at the sausages and bacon sides threaded on rods along the ceiling.

While the housemother was busy frying flounders for supper, the door opened and two young men walked in. We looked at each other and laughed. They were the same young men behind whom I had hidden in the harbor the day before. Now I really felt at home. We children from Berlin went to school in the afternoon, double shift with the local children, and again the teacher had to cope with 60 students of various levels, without any educational materials.

As time went on I learned to understand the Low-German dialect and to appreciate the 4:00 p.m. tea time. I explored the town, roamed the dunes and the beaches, and fell totally in love with the island and its culture. Especially when I discovered people here who wore native dress and folk-danced.

Every week a group of young men and women wearing their folk costumes came to the house to pick up one of the sons. They were all members of the local "Homeland Guild" who met to cultivate their songs, dances, and traditions. They went folk dancing! Despite all my pleading to go along and watch, I was told once again "You aren't old enough." By now I was more determined than ever to become a folk dancer. A slightly older neighbor girl, who knew some of the local dances, finally took me down to the beach at low tide and showed me some simple dances, which we danced over and over again.

In due time it became spring. On May 1 we all boarded the white steamer again, this time in bright sunshine, to return to Berlin. As the steamer pulled away there were tears on both sides of the dock, because we had become fond of our foster families and they of us. Even now, some of the Action Stork children still communicate with their foster parents and siblings.

A Red Cross train took us back to Berlin where the lilacs were blooming, and a place in the ballet school was waiting for me. That summer my father died. After that, my mother and I got along as best we could. I was the only child of their marriage. Then came the blockade of Berlin with its food shortages, power, and fuel rationing. These were very cold and very hungry days. The whole world seemed gray and the adults very hopeless and discouraged.

Because the ballet school was affiliated with an operetta theater, I had the opportunity to participate in some of their productions and was very wrapped up in ballet. One day a classmate told me that there was folk dancing in our gym after school. But by now I had become a snob: "Folk dancing was for people who couldn't dance any better." Nevertheless, I did go to the dance in school. It was absolute, passionate, unconditional love at first step. This was what I had been looking for all my life. Everything else fell by the wayside while I went folk dancing and, because the dances were organized by the Tourist Club of Nature Friends, also hiking and youth hosteling.

Finally I was old enough to go folk dancing! By now I was 15 and my mother had become very ill. Because there were no other relatives and all her sisters and brothers were in America, they invited me to come and live with them. The first six years in Connecticut were spent pining for folk dancing and for my friends at home. There was an all-girl folk dance group in high school with a repertoire of exactly three dances, but it just wasn't the same. In order not to forget the dances from home, I went alone into the back yard to dance, without music, each part as it came up in the dance.

On graduation from high school I went to work in a department store while going to college in the evening. After having been buyer for a number of years I became youth coordinator assigned to develop merchandising programs addressed to teenagers. What an opportunity to start an informal folk dance group with the store's Teen Board!

One day, while in New York on business, I happened to walk past a red door over which was written in large letters "FOLK DANCE HOUSE". I opened the door, walked in, and was home. Folk Dance House, under the direction of Michael and Maryanne Herman, also directs a folk dance camp in Maine, dedicated to the dance and folklore of all nations. The vacation that I spent there was the beginning of a new direction in my life.

After marriage and a child, I did graduate work in German studies. With encouragement from the Hermans I began to teach German folk dance and folklore.

It is now 40 years that I have been in America, yet each time that I give a workshop in the dances and folk culture of the different German regions my homeland is here with me through its dances and traditions. When I return to Germany to dance and research, it feels as though I had never left. Dance has been the bridge between my old homeland and my new home.

Karin Gottier's costume is a Schalk, *the gala dress of married women in and around Miesbach in Upper Bavaria. The* Schalk *is made for her wedding, but usually a bride has a second, plainer jacket to be worn at funerals and other solemn occasions, at which time the gold cord on the hat is removed. Karin's Christmas tree holds handmade ornaments from her folk dance friends in many countries.*

Costumes

By Karin Gottier

When Americans seek to go back to their roots, they often reach for the colorful clothes of their immigrant ancestors as a quick and visible symbol of ethnic affiliation. Native dress has its historical roots in rural communities of the 17th century and later. At first dictated by the local authorities, clothing styles changed slowly over the decades. Native dress evolved in highly structured, conforming village societies and demanded total integration of the wearer into the group.

The industrial revolution increased social and political freedoms and brought wider availability of materials. As a result, native dress experienced its fullest flower in the middle of the 19th century. It dwindled during the first decades of the 20th, although in some German areas it is still possible to see older women wearing the traditional clothing styles of their communities.

In most European countries at the turn of the century there was a trend toward the creation of a "national" dress. It was intended for those who were not part of rural society but who wanted to show their national affiliation. Young Germans adapted the traditional dress forms of the Alpine areas and the dirndl dress was born. The dirndl was comfortable and becoming, it was easy to care for, and for its wearers it epitomized the simple, wholesome country life.

Because the dirndl dress is not native dress but folklore fashion, it is subject to fashion changes and spawned a whole fashion industry. It can be a jumper-blouse-apron combination, a two-piece dress with apron, or even a one-piece dress with apron. In each case it always has a full skirt and an apron. The hemline may rise or fall, the color palette may change, certain details may be emphasized (depending on which native dress served as inspiration for the designer) but it always has the unmistakable look of ethnic clothes, even though interpreted through the current taste in fashion. A favorite dirndl dress is usually worn with white, or sometimes colored, lace-knit knee socks together with buckled shoes, and jewelry based on traditional pieces.

Native dress prescribes exactly who wears what, when and how, and what colors and combinations of accessories are appropriate on a given occasion according to the wearer's age and marital status. Dirndl dresses place no such restriction on the wearer. Each woman can choose the style her taste and pocketbook allows. Current folklore fashions show elegant evening dirndls, long or tea length, made of sumptuous iridescent silks and luxurious brocades. One can also purchase Alpine-looking sportswear, suits, and coats. Although little girls sometimes wear a wreath with their dirndl dresses, floral wreaths with ribbons, as are proper for certain Ukrainian and Polish costumes, are not customary with German folk dress. None of the traditional costumes use floral wreaths of that type, although tall crown-like structures of artificial flowers and tinsel are worn by brides, bridesmaids, and young women walking in religious processions. The wreath has traditionally been a symbol of maidenhood, and married women consider it inappropriate to put wreaths on their heads. Color choice is individual when choosing dirndl fashions; however, one never sees the national colors featured. To wear one's flag is considered in poor taste.

Women adapted the dirndl dress in the pre-World War I period, while men gave up their stiff collars and tight vests and reached for the short leather pant— the *Lederhose*—which originally was a traditional garment of the Alpine lumber worker. Shortened from knee-length to mid-thigh, it became a comfortable and durable item of clothing for hiking and leisure activities. Many a man cherishes the by-now shiny and greasy *Lederhose* of his youth.

Since those early days the dirndl dress and the *Lederhose* have become, for German Americans, the means of identifying with their roots. During the last 30 years, there seems to have evolved a form of dirndl dress that is preferred by Americans of German descent. It is usually a jumper with a very low-cut bodice; in bright colors, featuring bands of profuse and elaborate embroidery on skirt and bodice. Blouse and apron are trimmed with much lace, lace inserts, and ornamental braiding. The bodice is decorated with buttons or chains and sometimes even both. Often manufactured in this country, this type of dirndl is readily available through catalogs and in stores that specialize in German imports and gift items.

Although any German-American festival is an opportunity to see dirndl fashions in all their variety, it is the dance groups that illustrate the multitude of traditional costumes. Predominant among them are the Bavarian-style groups. Often these groups wear the native dress of Miesbach, a small town in Bavaria, or other forms of Bavarian Alpine dress. Characteristic are the ladies' bodices laced with silver chains and hooks. The full-flying skirts, fringed shawls and aprons are as familiar as the *Lederhosen,* green vests, embroidered suspenders, and green hats of the men.

Even though *Lederhosen* have become symbolic of German costume, they are actually worn in only a very small area of Bavaria. Much more common are the *Kniebundhosen* or knickers. Universally worn until the French Revolution when it was replaced by long pants, it remains an integral part of German male native dress. Made of dark or yellow leather, knickers are worn by many dance groups in America, together with a colored vest, either solid or striped, depending on the region the group represents.

Other dance groups appear in costumes from North Germany and Friesland and wear wooden shoes (wooden shoes are indigenous in all of Germany, varying in form from region to region). The men wear blue and white striped shirts, bell-bottomed sailor pants and fishermen's caps; the ladies wear neat, brocaded bonnets with long embroidered ribbons, long skirts, fitted jackets, aprons, and embroidered shawls. Men in the Hessian groups wear fur caps and blue smocks; ladies favor embroidered, knitted shoulder scarfs and embroidered stockings.

Most conscious of their native dress are the groups of displaced Germans from Hungary, Transylvania, Czechoslovakia, and Yugoslavia who have found new homes in America. Because the people in most of these German communities were still wearing native dress at the time of their dispersal, there are still many women today who grew up in native dress. They have the skills necessary to create costume pieces and the knowledge to assemble authentic replicas for their dance groups.

Most spectacular among these groups are the costumes of the Transylvanian-Saxons and Danube-Swabians. Because of their settlement history the Transylvanian-Saxons' costume retains many medieval elements. It features lavish embroideries both of colored satin stitch and black-and-white cross-stitch. Aprons, blouses, and headscarfs are creations of sheerest gossamer tulle, embroidered in white or black, contrasting in their airiness with the heavy silver belts, huge ornamental chest pins, and the jeweled hairpins of the married women. The men appear in high black boots, pants, white shirts embroidered in black cross-stitch, velvet ties with colored floral embroideries showing the initials of the wearer and the date on which the tie was made. In winter, both sexes wear heavy white sheepskin coats, fur side in, that have been profusely trimmed with colored embroidery and leather appliqué.

The Danube-Swabians stand out with their large, bell-shaped pleated skirts, either white or in floral patterns, worn over layers of starched white petticoats. Their shoulder scarfs are masterpieces of colored embroidery on black with lavish widths of hand-knotted fringe. The shawl is artfully draped in a neat pattern across the wearer's back and pinned into place to give it the proper shape. Aprons are often black and trimmed with soutache or lace. They appear rather stiff and shield-like without many gathers at the waist. Danube-Swabian girls and women usually wear their hair in braids wrapped around the head, set off by a black velvet ribbon. The costume of the men is rather dark. Black trousers tucked into black boots, black vest with silver buttons, white shirt and black hat. Men as well as women wear a sprig of rosemary pinned to their clothes as was customary for special festivals and dances.

Although the costumes worn by German-American dance groups and by others are as diverse as the places from which their ancestors emigrated, the universal dirndl fashion, together with the *Lederhose*, has become to German Americans the accepted and favorite form of German costume.

The Story of Folk Dance

By Karin Gottier

All over the United States, in cities and towns, there are German dance groups, both large and small, which cultivate the dances of all German regions. Some are sponsored by German-American societies, some are international folk dancers who have formed performance ensembles, some are made up of German language students in high school or college. Others still simply dance recreationally for the social interaction and to learn more about German culture. Members of these groups are of all ages, from children to senior citizens. Some are native-born Germans, some are of German descent, and many aren't German at all. What unites them is the joy of dancing and the determination to preserve the German heritage.

The seeds of the contemporary folk dance movement were planted in the early decades of the 20th century. Folk dance pioneers, who had come into contact with the English and Scandinavian folk dance movements, began to comb the countryside, notating and collecting the dances they found. Inspired by the idealism of the youth movement, they perceived a need to provide for young adults' activities to promote physical and emotional well-being, and to foster a sense of community. Because of these early contacts with Britain and Scandinavia, many English and Swedish dances have become a permanent part of the German folk dance repertoire. From these early days, too, date the *Jugend und Gemeinschaftstänze* (youth and community dances). These were dances in the folk idiom, created by talented dance leaders to fill the need for group dances that would appeal to young people. Several of these dances have truly become folk dances and are beloved by German and American folk dancers alike.

In the United States the German folk dance scene is as diverse as in Europe. The most visible groups are the Bavarian *Schuhplattl* clubs. Organized into a North American Federation—*the Nord-Amerikanische Gau Verband*—these groups cultivate a repertoire that is traditional in the context of the *Schuhplattl* movement. They hold dance competitions, encourage the correct wearing of the Bavarian costumes, publish a newsletter, and hold national and international conferences.

Besides the numerous Bavarian *Schuhplattl* clubs, there are the dance groups founded by the displaced Germans from Silesia, Pomerania, East and West Prussia, Romania, Slovakia, the Sudeten and Egerland, and Hungary. These groups wear their costumes, sing their songs, and dance their dances as a link with a homeland which is no longer theirs, and to pass on their cultural heritage to their children.

German folk dancing as well as German music, dialect, costumes, and customs can be divided into two areas—the mountainous, predominantly Catholic South and the flat, predominantly Protestant North. The Alpine culture of the South extends across national borders into Austria and in some cases into Alemanic Switzerland.

Dances of the mountain areas fall into several categories:

1. The traditional social dances of one or two figures.
2. The turning-couple dances such as the *Ländler*—a smooth, stepped dance in 3/4 time in which dancers continuously intertwine their arms into intricate positions.
3. The *Dreher*, which uses pivot steps in 2/4 time.
4. The *Zwiefacher*, which alternates in irregular sequences between waltz and pivot steps.

The show-off dancing so unique to the Alpine area, the *Schuhplattler*, a vigorous men's dance consisting of various stomps and slaps, appears to have been described in the 13th century in the poetry of Neidhart von Reuental, a Minnesinger. While in its pure form it is danced spontaneously and free-style, it experienced its greatest development with the establishment of organizations dedicated to the preservation of Alpine dance, costume, and custom during the last decades of the 19th century. Because of the demands made by group performance, there developed uniform slapping patterns within the various *Schuhplattl* clubs. Today a *Schuhplattler* is made up of the following parts: The entry march; the actual *Plattler* in which the men show off with stomping and slapping while the women spin around their own axis in place or travel around the circle; the chase, in which the men stalk their partners; and finally, after catching them, the waltz.

Another major group of dances is ritual in nature and is tied to specific seasons, festivals, and customs. They are always group dances, very often men's dances. Included in this group are the dances of the various guilds. One of the most famous examples is the *Schäfflertanz* of Munich's coopers guild, which is performed every seven years by members of the guild carrying green hoops. The various sword dances, such as the *Unterwössner* and *Überlinger* sword dance, can be classed in this category as well.

The dance traditions of North Germany are mostly survivals of 18th and 19th century ballroom dances. Here we find quadrilles, long-way sets—variously called *Anglaise*, *Ecossaise*, or *Francaise*, according to their formation—as well as couple dances. There is also a greater variety of steps. Waltz, polka, mazurka, and *schottisch* steps as well as step-hops, step-swings, skipping, and running steps all appear in North German dances. These dances require larger areas and move somewhat more quickly than southern dances.

Few ritual dances are still performed in the northern areas even though at one time these, too, were practiced. In 1747 Anton Viethen described a sword dance performed by men decorated with bells and ribbons, which culminated in the interlocking of the swords and lifting their leader over their heads on the lock. The sword dance tradition is common in all of Europe and the British Isles.

Folk Art and Collectibles

By Dianne Stevens

From barns to birth certificates, German Americans enhanced everyday objects from implements to tombstones with extraordinary art. Hinges had tulip forms, guns were carved and inlaid with brass and copper, and barns were decorated with colorful hex signs. Today, folk arts abound in many states.

German-American folk art is characterized by bright colors and simple motifs borrowed from religion, nature, and myth. The lily of the field design, often called a tulip, and the tree of life motif are both religious symbols. The *distelfink* is the legendary bird of good luck. A unicorn harks back to medieval legend as the guardian of maidenhood. The thistle represents hard work and perseverance. Love birds represent love, marriage, and romance.

In Pennsylvania Dutch country, *fraktur*, hex signs, painted furniture, and redware pottery are created and enjoyed today.

Fraktur

Fraktur is a striking combination of text in *fraktur* lettering (an angular, 16th-century Gothic typeface) and design, rooted in the medieval art of manuscript illumination. A revival of the art began in mid-18th century at the Ephrata Cloister and spread to the rest of Pennsylvania, Maryland and Virginia.

Originally drawn on parchment or paper with a finely cut tail feather from a crow or pheasant and India or drawing ink, *fraktur* mixed words and vivid watercolors. Fanciful symbols used in *fraktur* were borrowed from nature (birds, tulips), design (hearts), religion (angels, devils), and mythology (mermaids, unicorns).

Many *fraktur* artists were ministers in Lutheran or Reformed churches, or schoolmasters in church schools. Children were taught the art in school. *Fraktur* became so popular that in the mid-19th century it was preprinted.

Fraktur was a personal art to the owners because it decorated items like baptismal records, confirmation records, marriage and death certificates, house blessings, hymns, inscription pages on gift books, Bibles, church records, birthday greetings, and school awards. Since it was private and tucked away in Bibles and books or pasted onto blanket chest lids, *fraktur* was an acceptable art form to sects like the Mennonites and Amish who frowned on public art.

Today, handmade 18th- and 19th-century *fraktur* is one of the most sought-after Pennsylvania Dutch arts, sometimes worth thousands of dollars. If you can't find *fraktur* in your old family Bible, don't despair. Artists today still practice the art and offer custom pieces at reasonable prices.

More than 160 examples of fraktur are in the collection of the Henry Francis du Pont Winterthur Museum at Winterthur, Delaware. It includes Valentines, marriage records, birth and baptismal records, and picture examples ranging from floral to abstract.

Hex Signs

The colorful hex signs on many Pennsylvania-German barns are not designed to scare witches away. They are purely decorative, their flower and geometric designs meant to be cheery and welcoming. Painting hex signs began in the southeastern corner of the state between 1830 and 1850. Ivan Hoyt, who paints hex signs today, speculates that the signs appeared when manufactured paint pigments were available and farmers mixed these with sour milk as a binder. The first signs were geometric designs in red, black, and yellow. Blue was seldom used since imported indigo was expensive. Farmers painted their own signs until the early 1900s when traveling barn painters picked up the art.

Some of the same hex designs seen on barns appear on Bibles, designs similar to early Christian symbols. Some popular symbols of hex signs are: tulips, representing faith; pomegranates, long life and fertility; hearts; and the *distelfink*. Either smooth sailing or a life of ups and downs is represented by the scalloped border, according to Hoyt.

This 12-inch original design hex sign is by Ivan E. Hoyt, a folk artist of Wapwallopen, Pennsylvania. The double rosette is for good luck in the grace of God for the 12 months of the year. It is also said to be the Trinity tulip as viewed by God. "As He looks down on the flower He is also looking down upon you."

Nutcrackers

Nutcrackers, a popular German woodcraft, were originally carved as functional devices in the early 1700s to crack nuts, but have since become popular collectibles. The stern nutcrackers usually are caricatures of authority figures, so there is a bit of irony that kings, policemen, officers, and noblemen are put to work for anybody with a nut to crack.

Bauernmalerei

Bauernmalerei, similar to Norwegian rosemaling, is a German folk art of painted decorating of furniture, clocks, woodwork and plates. Characterized by cheerfully colored designs on dark backgrounds, *Bauernmalerei* uses heraldic, geometric and floral motifs. The rose was a favorite subject, followed by the tulip, daisy, poppy, violet, and other garden flowers painted in simple or artistic arrangements.

German Americans painted all types of furniture. A popular piece was a dower's chest used to store a new bride's quilts and blankets. The German

Biedermeir style of furniture, popular among German professional classes, was also painted with warm landscape scenes and some amusing scenes.

Redware

Redware is a reddish brown, earthenware pottery often decorated with yellow, green, black, and blue. Colonists brought the first redware to New England, Virginia, and the Chesapeake Bay area, but it was the German-speaking immigrants who made the most elaborate pottery.

Three basic types of redware were: undecorated, slip-trailed, and sgraffito. Slip-trailed was created by drizzling a thin clay slip through a quill for lettering and design. By brushing the surface of damp clay with white or yellow liquid slip and using a stylus to design, sgraffito was made. Most elaborate sgraffito and slip-trailed redware are Pennsylvanian and were used as gifts. The undecorated redware was used as everyday dishes.

By the mid-19th century redware lost popularity as stoneware, glass, tin, and china were easily available to buyers. Today this folk art is enjoying a revival.

At Oley Valley Redware in Fleetwood, Pennsylvania, after more than 200 years, Gerald Yoder and William Logan have picked up the business that Yoder's great-great grandfather, George Adam Weidner, operated from 1745 until right before the American Revolution. Weidner made roof tiles and pottery used by settlers in Berks and surrounding counties. Yoder and Logan create traditional redware for an international market.

Quilting

Unlike *fraktur* and painted furniture, Germans did not bring quilting as a folk art with them to the United States. They borrowed it from their American neighbors and stitched their own identity into every quilt.

The Amish have created some of the most treasured quilts. Living in

Oley Valley Redware

Pennsylvania German Milk Pie Dish, Tree of Life motif: Milk pie was made from a left-over milk and flour batter with cinnamon sprinkled on top. Three tulips on one stem represent the tree of life of the Trinity.

Top: Pennsylvania-Dutch German Milk Pie Dish, Distelfink motif: Legendary bird representing good luck, perched on a sprig of the tree of life.

130

the world but not of it, they have separated themselves from outside influences, giving their quilts distinct characteristics.

The Amish use large fields of dark but vibrant fabrics stitched into bold patterns with as many as 20 stitches to an inch. The colors of their quilts reflect their own dress, for they wear deep, rich tones under their dark cloaks.

Quilting is a social art. Mothers and daughters often work on quilts together for the girls' wedding chests. Quilting bees, where several covers can be made, are still held today to make quilts for fund-raisers.

Beer Steins

Beer steins originated in Germany in the late 1400s when hordes of flies invaded central Europe in summer and the Black Death was a recent memory. Because most beer was consumed in outdoor gardens, beer drinkers decided to be cautious and put lids on their mugs equipped with a thumb lift.

Most early steins were made of wood or porous earthenware because pewter, silver, and glass were too expensive. Eventually stoneware was developed, an excellent material for steins. Renaissance artists lavishly decorated the steins with scenes from historical, allegorical and biblical tales. Shapes varied from conical to melon-shaped to the shape of a ram's horn.

Villeroy and Boch began creating steins in 1836 in Mettlach. They used Renaissance designs in brightly colored clays and glazes and enjoyed what was known as the golden age of Mettlach steins from 1880 until 1910. The company's trademark, the village's Old Abbey Tower, is on the bottom of most genuine Mettlach steins, which can sell for thousands of dollars today.

Hummels

A young nun from southern Bavaria was the creative genius behind the popular Hummel figurines. In 1927, at age 18, Bertha Hummel began studies at the Munich Academy of Fine Arts. She befriended two fellow students who were nuns, and through this friendship her interest in religious life blossomed. In 1931, she began her novitiate as a Franciscan nun at the Convent of Siessen, much to the disappointment of her professors. The nuns, however, recognized Hummel's talent of bringing wide-eyed children and religious subjects to life in her sketches. They encouraged Hummel, who by then was Sister Maria Innocentia, to return to the academy for more training.

Sister Maria Innocentia's charming sketches were made into cards which caught the eye of the enterprising German porcelain manufacturer, Franz Goebel. Goebel saw the cards in a Munich gift shop and knew he wanted to turn the sketches into figurines. He gave Sister Maria Innocentia and the Convent of Siessen final artistic control, and promised that the nun's signature would be on the base of each piece. Since Sister Maria's death in 1946 at age 37, the Convent supervises the modeling of Hummel art.

Hummel figurines first appeared in 1935. Known for their muted colors, soft glazing, and precious features, Hummels are popular collectibles. Authentic Hummels all have the M. I. Hummel signature incised on their base. Today the Hummel line has expanded to plates, prints, calendars, Nativity sets, plaques, bells, and lamps.

Dogs from Germany

Walter Schuerer of Amana, Iowa and Dixieland Luke, his German Short-haired Pointer, the No. 1 gun dog in 1990 American Kennel Club standings.

The Dachshund is older than recorded German history, but is so popular it is called the national dog of Germany. Dachshunds may be longhaired, shorthaired, or wirehaired, and red or black-and-tan.

The German Shepherd is also older than recorded history of the Germans, but is so named because Germans adopted it early and liked it. In addition to being a pet and a friend, it serves soldiers and police, often does best in obedience tests, and excels in guiding the blind.

The German Short-haired Pointer not only points game for the hunter but also will retrieve from land or water. Its color is usually a combination of liver and white, or solid liver, as is the coloring of the German Wire-haired Pointer, another popular dog.

The gray Weimaraner was developed in Weimar, Germany in the 19th century and is a good pointing and hunting dog. It is a large dog, up to 27 inches high and weighing as much as 80 pounds.

The Schnauzers, with their cropped ears, were bred in Württemberg. They come in three sizes—giant (up to 25 inches tall), standard, and miniature.

The Doberman Pinscher was developed in Germany as an attack dog and was named for Louis Dobermann, who did the original cross-breeding. It may be black, or brown with rust markings. The Miniature Pinscher was developed later and is about 11 inches tall at the shoulder.

The Rottweiler was brought to Germany by the Romans, and has been a favorite dog ever since at Rottweil on the Neckar River in south Germany. It was used in developing the Doberman Pinscher, and is of the same coloring but is a larger and slower dog.

Other dogs popular in Germany include the Great Dane and the Hanoverian Schweisshund.

German-style Food in America

By Joan Liffring-Zug

By the millions, Americans flock to German- or Bavarian-style restaurants in leading tourist sites and cities. One reason: they'll never leave hungry. If there is a sign featuring Bavaria or Germany at a restaurant, you have arrived at a table of abundance. You are likely to find sauerkraut and red cabbage, sausages, brats, pork, and beer, followed by an interesting choice of tortes and cakes. Any German-style celebration, virtually anywhere in America or Germany, means beer and sausages and plenty to eat. The pencil-thin, high fashion image does not usually depict German people.

German-style cooking is found in every Amish or Mennonite community in Pennsylvania, Ohio, Missouri, Indiana, Illinois, Iowa, and Kansas, with restaurants serving the foods of these plain people. In the Pennsylvania Dutch country of Lancaster County in southeastern Pennsylvania, the people's closeness to the soil is evident in the bounty of produce seen at the roadside stands. The production, preparation and preservation of food plays a main part in setting the pace of life. There seems to be such a celebration of food that in "Twenty Most Asked Questions About the Amish and Mennonites" (written by a young Mennonite couple), one of the questions asked is: "Is food a part of their religion?" Recipes reflecting German heritage are handed down from generation to generation. These family "hand-me-downs" are served typically family style at tables laden with soup, main dishes, side dishes of vegetables, sweets and sours, noodles, and salads. Sweets of pudding or cake are sometimes served before the main meal because there may not be room after the hearty feast. The Amish themselves usually do not own and operate the restaurants; the more liberal Mennonites run the restaurants and the tourist industry featuring the Amish foods. Amish women, however, may cook in the restaurants where the ingenuity of the Amish and Mennonite cultures flourish. Some communities offer tours that include the opportunity to eat in an Amish or Mennonite country home.

Today, many Americans are exploring their German heritage with pride. In Kalona, Iowa, Amish-Mennonite dinners usually include different kinds of tapioca puddings. In Pennsylvania Amish-Mennonite restaurants, Pickled-Red-Beet Eggs are a treat, and Shoo-fly Pie is a traditional dessert. People come to Frankenmuth, Michigan, for the famous chicken dinners. In New Braunfels, Texas, the local speciality is smoked turkey—a native American bird advertised with a Tex-German accent. German restaurants in Fredericksburg, Texas offer a variety of choices that may include: sausages such as Bratwurst and Bockwurst made with veal, pork and traditional spices; or a dinner of Schnitzel Holstein (breaded veal cutlet topped with poached eggs, gravy and anchovies).

Lovers of Tex-Mex food have a German to thank for the perfect combination of spices, with extracted and ground pulp from the chili pod, that gives their

133

favorite dishes the right taste. Born in Germany, William Gebhardt came to the United States, and in 1892 opened a café in the back of Miller's Saloon in New Braunfels, Texas. He soon discovered that the German community loved chili, but couldn't make it until the season of the home-grown chilies. In 1894 he developed the first commercial chili powder by running pepper bits through a small home meat grinder. Two years later Gebhardt and Albert Kronkosky opened a factory in San Antonio for the production of chili powder.

The Amana Colonies of Iowa, although not Amish, are famous for their German-style foods served family style featuring Amana hams and beef and full bowls of side dishes, which may include applesauce and cabbage. Each restaurant in the Amanas has its own version of Rhubarb Pie, and it is a treat to compare the double crust, single crust, meringue topped, and many other taste delights, particularly during the fresh rhubarb season. In season, the rhubarb is used, also, to make Piestengel, a favorite wine.

From Iowa, Missouri, Wisconsin, Texas and other states where many Germans settled, meat markets ship products stressing the traditions of old Germany. The Texans ship smoked turkeys as well as the traditional bacons, hams and sausages. Among the products available from Pennsylvania and Ohio are their specialties: pretzels, jellies, and jams.

Many German immigrants founded breweries, especially in Wisconsin and Missouri. *Oktoberfests* nationwide feature beer and bratwurst. The *Wurstfest* in New Braunfels, Texas, lasts for several weekends and draws thousands of tourists. Beer and brats and other German foods appeal to the ninety-thousand people attending Milwaukee's weekend, Summertime German Fest, an annual event with a year of preplanning and a cast of hundreds of volunteers. There are joyous celebrations of heritage, with all the traditional fare, throughout the country.

While the immigrants had to adapt to the foods of a new country, they kept many of the time-tested recipes of the Old World. In her essay on German cooking, Lynn Hattery-Beyer, a former Iowan, who lives with her editor husband and children in Hamburg, Germany, explores the culinary heritage of the over fifty-million Americans of German descent. Hannelore Bozeman of Iowa City, where her husband is a professor of religion at the University of Iowa, writes about German foods and includes many favorite recipes from her family in Germany. Other recipes in this collection of German-American cookery are from people and organizations that share a strong German heritage.

Amish Quilt Designs: *Baskets, Cross in the Square, Bear Paw*

 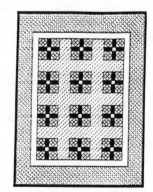 

The Heritage of German Cooking

By Lynn Hattery-Beyer

German meals traditionally revolve around meat. During the late 18th and early 19th centuries the main meal of the day for many Germans included several courses featuring fish, pork, and game. Those who could not afford such extravagance at least had nice chunks of meat in their stew. Most German meat dishes are pan-cooked; roasts frequently are cooked on the stove top.

The importance placed on pickling and marinating is another distinguishing feature of German cuisine. *Sauerbraten* soaks in a spicy brine for two to four days to develop its distinctive flavor; herring is pickled in a mixture of vinegar and juniper berries before being prepared in numerous ways; sauerkraut is shredded and salted weeks before it is ready to be made into a salad or cooked. From a historical point of view, pickling was a necessity. The German climate limited the growing season to four or five months a year. Food therefore had to be preserved by pickling, smoking and curing.

The preparation of marinated and pickled food usually involves making a sauce out of the marinade and sugar, honey or fruit. The result is a delicate blend of sweet and sour, a taste so characteristic of German food. Germans began adding fruit to their meat to break the monotony of their meals during the long winter months. They enhanced their usual stews and roasts with raisins, prunes, dried pears, and apples in dishes. If fruit is not added during the cooking process, it is often served as a side dish. Applesauce and freshly grated horseradish accompany boiled beef and mild sausage. Game is unthinkable without *Preiselbeeren*, wild, small, red berries similar to our cranberries, also called lingonberries. The German love of fruit becomes evident on travels through the German countryside. Many back roads are lined with an assortment of fruit trees, and pastures often look more like small orchards. Given the choice—and climate conditions—a German homeowner would rather plant a fruit tree than a shade tree. Many Americans of German descent carry on this tradition of having lovely fruit trees in their yards.

Another characteristic of German cooking is the importance of potatoes, rice, and noodles. Any meal including meat (which is almost every main meal) must include one of these—if not as a "filler" to make up for smaller portions of meat, then as a "*Soßenträger*," or means of soaking up meat juices or gravy.

In Swabia, noodles have a long tradition. There, *Spätzle* take the place of potatoes. They are made out of a flour-egg dough which is cut or pressed directly into boiling water. *Spätzle* are not only served plain along with a roast and gravy, but also are combined with the local cheese, *Allgäuer Emmentaler*, to make *Käsespätzle*, with sauerkraut to make *Krautspätzle*, or served with lentils and bacon as a one-dish meal.

One characteristic of the German cuisine which Americans notice immediately is the absence of big desserts after meals. Usually no dessert is served after the evening meal, which is traditionally a light supper often consisting of open-faced sandwiches and salads. The main meal of the day usually includes a light dessert of fruit, pudding or ice cream, if dessert is served.

It's not that Germans don't have a sweet tooth—they do—but most Germans find American food too sweet. They dislike pancake syrup, sprinkling their pancakes and waffles with powdered sugar instead. Germans eat a lot of whipped cream: on cakes, on ice cream, even in coffee. They add little sugar to it, however, and it tastes light and airy. It is a far cry from the calorie bomb that American whipped cream represents. The American cookie and cake recipes that I make for my German friends are most successful when I use only one-third to one-half the sugar given in the recipe.

Northern Germany stretches from the North Sea and the Baltic Sea south across rolling plains to the mountains of central Germany. This is countryside populated by fishermen and farmers, with several large, wealthy cities: Berlin, Hamburg, Bremen. Its cuisine is geared to the cold, damp climate and the hard-working life of the inhabitants, using the excellent products of the sea and local farms.

Herring, the most popular fish, is prepared in many ways: fried (*Brathering*), pickled and placed in a cream sauce (*Matjeshering*), rolled (*Rollmops*), or combined with other pickled vegetables to make a salad (*Fischsalat*). Eel is considered a delicacy and is usually smoked. A specialty of Hamburg is Eel Soup, which not only includes eel but also dried fruit, herbs, and several different kinds of vegetables.

The plains extending south from the coast are famous for their smoked meats and bacons (*Räucherspeck*) as well as excellent ducks and geese. The Pomeranian geese have a reputation for meatiness and tenderness.

The northern plains also have produced many well-known recipes for hearty soups and stews made with cabbage and bacon, all of which taste best when chased down by a "*Klarer*," a glass of clear *Schnaps* distilled from local grains.

Among central Germany's rolling hills and fertile valleys are huge fields of potatoes and sugar beets, pastures for sheep, orchards, and vineyards. The people who live here are used to "*Hausmannskost*," the simple, homemade food which many Americans consider typically German.

Most of the well-known central German specialties are simple meals meant to be enjoyed informally; pumpernickel and slices of Westfalian ham with a mug of beer and a glass of clear *Schnaps*; kale with sausage; and *Blindhuhn*, a stew made of beans, potatoes, carrots, onions, apples, and bacon, served with some good, dark bread.

When the main meal is simple, cakes and sweets gain importance. Central Germany has a lot to offer in this respect: *Obstkuchen*, thin-crusted yeast cakes covered with lots of fruit and sometimes topped with a custard meringue, and the well-known Christmas treat, *Dresdner Stollen*.

Abundance of potatoes in central Germany has produced a wealth of recipes for their preparation. The most elaborate are for *Klösse*, or dumplings.

136

One of Germany's favorite pork dishes is supposedly named for the central German town of Kassel: *Kasseler Rippchen*. These smoked pork chops are served individually or as a rack/roast with lots of sauerkraut and potatoes.

As for beverages, central Germany is renowned for its clear, very potent *Schnaps*, usually called *Korn*. It isn't made of corn, however. The German word *Korn* is a general term for grain, and this *Schnaps* is distilled from local grain. Of the many small distilleries in central Germany, one of the best-known is in Steinhagen, where the distinctive *Steinhäger*, a *Schnaps* flavored with juniper berries, is made and sold in an unusual brown ceramic bottle.

"*Apfelwein*," the Hessian apple wine, is potent cider made around Frankfurt. Since it cannot be stored and bottling is risky because fermentation is in progress, you have to go to Sachsenhausen in Frankfurt to enjoy it. The *Apfelwein* season in Frankfurt can be compared to the *Oktoberfest* in Munich, if not in size, at least in its revelry.

The cuisine of southern Germany is greatly influenced by the beer and wine made there in such abundance.

Bavaria is a country of wheat and barley fields, quick-flowing streams and thirsty people. What could be more natural than the many local breweries, each producing beer according to its own secret recipes? To drink as much beer as an average Bavarian does (60 gallons a year), you have to eat accordingly. Light, low-cholesterol meals just will not do. Huge platefuls of pork, sauerkraut, and dumplings are in order. Vegetables are not too popular in the average Bavarian cuisine, and salads usually are an assortment of cooked carrots, beans, celery, and cabbage. Meat is what Bavarians like best, and in Bavaria meat means pork, which can be found in every imaginable form. Munich is famous for its *Weißwurst*, sausage made of veal, brains, and herbs. *Weißwurst*, which do not contain preservatives, taste great with sweet Bavarian mustard or *Meerrettich* (horseradish), a pretzel and, of course, beer.

The vineyards of southern Germany are concentrated in the Rhineland, Baden, and the Palatinate. The cuisine in these areas is lighter and more graceful, fitting the character of the wine. One-dish meals, usually based on the ever-present potato, are common, but these are more refined than similar dishes in northern Germany. *Himmel und Erde*, a casserole of apples and potatoes served with sausage, and *Saumagen*, pig's stomach lining stuffed with ground meat, potatoes and herbs, are good examples.

Baden, which includes the Black Forest, is known for its smoked ham and bacon, and for Black Forest Cherry Cake. Blue fish, or the method of placing fish in vinegar for about five minutes before cooking which turns the fish blue, is said to have originated here.

Swabia, stretching north from Lake Constance across the Swabian Mountains and on past Stuttgart, has made its mark on German cuisine with *Spätzle*, noodles cut directly into boiling water.

German Beverage Traditions

In the Middle Ages, Germans used to drink mostly beer and wine because there were few safe alternatives. If you ask for water in a restaurant, the waiter will bring you a small bottle of cool mineral water, without ice, and charge you for it. A typical menu in Germany offers not only mineral water and carbonated soft drinks, but also ten to fifteen types of bottled fruit juices, from apple and grape juice to black currant and cherry juice. These drinks are served chilled but hardly ever on ice. At home, children drink a lot of fruit juices made from diluted fruit-flavored syrups. A favorite is *Himbeersaft,* made from one part raspberry syrup diluted with five parts water.

Coffee and tea are the beverages Germans consume the most, outranking both beer and wine. They drink coffee primarily at breakfast and at a special afternoon coffee break, but seldom by itself, or with, or after any other meal. Most Germans have an afternoon meal around 4 p.m., not unlike British tea time. Coffee is a must with pastries; it is nearly always brewed and filtered, and tends to be stronger than American coffee. Specialty coffees, often even stronger, are also served. Coffees are served with light or whipped cream. The first decaffeinated coffee, *Kaffee Hag,* was developed in Germany. Tea is popular as a beverage to go with the traditional cold, light supper. Occasionally people add a little rum to their tea, especially in the winter. Most common is black, English tea, served with a squeeze of lemon juice and sugar.

—*Hannelore Bozeman*

Beer

Although beer was first brewed in ancient Egypt, it has become known as a true German beverage. Beer was the favorite drink of the Germanic tribes. The first evidence of beer brewing on German territory dates from 800 B.C. At that time, beer was flavored with myrtle, oak bark, and honey. Just as women baked bread, it was women's work to brew beer, and when the beer turned out especially well, the women often invited other women over to taste it—the first "tea parties."

In the monasteries, the brewing of beer was developed into an art in the Middle Ages. Any pilgrims or wanderers who stopped at the monastery doors were given as much beer as they wanted.

The brewing process remained unchanged from Roman times until the 15th century. In the 15th and 16th centuries, a revolution in German beer brewing swiftly spread through Europe: hops were added to beer. This gave beer its now traditional bitter taste and allowed it to be stored longer. In the late 16th century, bottom-fermented beer was developed in Bavaria; it was stored for a longer period of time before drinking to permit further fermentation.

Because beer was an important dietary staple and its sale was lucrative, quality controls for its production were established early. The first edict regarding beer was issued in Munich in 1363. In 1420, both the brewers' guild and the reigning dukes called for regulations governing the production of beer produced in and around Munich. In 1487 a Pledge of Purity statute was enacted, applicable to Munich and expanded in 1519 to include all of Bavaria. This *Reinheitsgebot* (Pledge of Purity) not only determined standard prices for beer, but also decreed that beer could be brewed only from barley, hops, and water. Yeast was later added to the list. This Pledge of Purity is one of the oldest laws on the production of food and drink which is still in effect.

During 1986-87, the Common Market countries tried to convince West Germany to drop the *Reinheitsgebot* for beer to open the German beer market to all member countries. German brewers and beer drinkers were adamant about adhering to this age-honored tradition. Traditionally, beer is tax free.

Any American who tastes German beer immediately notes that it tastes different than American beer. The differences are in the type of hops and starch used. The finest hops (the hops with the most delicate flavor) grow in Czechoslovakia and southern Germany, and are used by most European brewers. American brewers generally use only a small percentage of the more expensive European hops (if any), relying heavily upon lower-grade domestic hops from Washington, Oregon, and California, or simply hops syrup.

The type of starch used in the brewing process also is responsible for major taste differences. The barley malt traditionally used for brewing gives beer flavor, body (in the form of sugars and protein), head, and color. If barley malt is used, no further coloring agents or syrups are necessary. It is expensive. German brewers, bound by the *Reinheitsgebot*, must use pure malt barley. American brewers (and ten to twenty-five percent of other European brewers) use malt adjuncts instead (high-starch materials such as corn, rice, unmalted barley, malt syrup or tapioca).

The brewing process also is responsible for the difference in taste. During fermentation carbon dioxide gas is naturally produced. American brewers remove this gas and store it. German brewers allow it to remain in the beer. After the aging process, American brewers reunite the natural carbon dioxide with the beer and add artificial carbonation during the bottling process. This high level of carbon dioxide content produces beer which is crystal clear, fizzes, and produces a creamy foam even when ice-cold. It also increases the storage life of the beer. The German method of natural carbonation produces beer which is smooth and non-gassy. Optimally, it should be served at a temperature of 45°, which is warmer than most Americans prefer.

If overchilled, German beer becomes cloudy and its proteins separate. Most Americans do not know that regular German beer is perishable and should be consumed within six weeks of bottling. Like draught beers—even American draught—German beer is not pasteurized. American beer (and German export beer) is pasteurized, though, to ensure safe storage for four months (cans) to six months (bottles).

139

The final difference between German and American beers is in the serving temperature. There is a ritual to pouring German beer. As mentioned, the temperature of the beer is crucial; it shouldn't be chilled lower than 45°. (To the chagrin of many American tourists who are dissatisfied with the temperature of their beer in Germany, one often sees "beer warmers" in German taverns. These are metal test-tubes with a screw-on lid and side handle, which are filled with hot water and lowered into a mug of beer until the beer reaches the desired warmer temperature.)

Beer warmers

The size and shape of the beer mug or glass is also important. Many types of German beer are served only in a certain type of glass. *Weizenbier*, a light summer beer with a high yeast content and level of carbonation, always is served in a tall version of our traditional Coca Cola glass. *Altbier*, a speciality of the *Düsseldorf*, is served in a short, straight-sided glass similar to our juice glasses. In any case, the glass must be dry and at room temperature.

Some of the largest German breweries are *Hofbräu, Spatenbräu, Becks Dortmunder* and *Aktienbräu*.

Well-known types of beer are: *Alt, Kölsch* (from Cologne), *Weizen, Berliner Weiße* (served with a shot of raspberry syrup), *Bock* (dark beer brewed in the spring) and *Pils* (the lager beer, based on the traditional Czech *Pilsner Urquell*).

More than 250,000 gallons of good German beer are consumed during Munich's two-week *Oktoberfest*, the world's biggest beer bash. The celebration of the wedding of Crown Prince Ludwig (later King Ludwig I of Bavaria) and Princess Therese von Saxony-Hilburgshausen on October 12, 1810, was the beginning of this annual custom. The site of the celebration is the same patch of ground used for the royal wedding festivities that started it all.

The American brewing industry owes a lot to its German roots. Beer has been brewed since the first colonists landed, and several important colonial Americans (Samuel Adams, William Penn, George Washington) brewed their own beer. It was not until the 1840s, which brought a great influx of German immigrants, that the brewing industry truly started to flourish. The German settlers brought with them a new type of yeast for producing lager beer. This beer could be kept longer and tasted better than the previous American brew. Many German settlers started their own breweries, and areas with large German populations became centers of the brewing industry. The names of many breweries reflect their German origins: Strohs, Heileman, Anheuser-Busch, Schlitz and Pabst.

—*Lynn Hattery-Beyer*

Isn't this a carving bench?
Yes it is a carving bench
Short and long   back and forth   this way and that   shooting gun
wagon wheel   crooked and straight   big glass   oxen bladder
pile of manure   Schnickel Fritz*   fat lady   fat sow

*a silly, rascally little boy, a folklore character

This German-American drinking song with drawings originally appeared as a poster at Mader's Restaurant in Milwaukee, Wisconsin, in the 1930s and 1940s. Now available as a card or a poster, the *Schnitzelbank* is loved by German-Americans, but is rarely heard in Germany. Karin Gottier explains, "It is reflective of the German carnival entertainers who set up a little bench at fairs; climbed up on it; unrolled a paper with pictures, and while pointing to illustrations, told a story in the style of ballad singers."

141

Iced Coffee
Eiskaffee

Hannelore Bozeman

4 cups brewed or instant coffee, extra-strong
4 scoops vanilla ice cream, divided
1 cup whipped cream, divided
coffee powder or chocolate shavings for garnish, optional

Prepare the coffee, using about twice the regular amount of coffee. Let cool; you may want to put the coffee into the freezer for a while or add a couple of ice cubes. Put 1 scoop of vanilla ice cream into each of 4 tall glasses. Pour the cold coffee over the ice cream and garnish with the whipped cream. Sprinkle with a little coffee powder or chocolate shavings, if desired. Serve immediately with straws, long iced tea spoons, and a cookie for each person. Serves 4.

Fruit Punch
Bowle

6 ripe, peeled peaches, or 8 unpeeled apricots, or 1 sliced pineapple, or 1 quart strawberries
1/2 cup powdered sugar
1 cup dry sherry
4 bottles dry white wine

Slice the selected fruit and place in a large bowl. Sprinkle with the powdered sugar. Pour the sherry over the fruit, cover, and let stand for at least 4 hours. Add the wine and stir. Serve cold. Serves 20.

Gemütlichkeit

There are said to be more than 500,000 words in the English language as spoken in America, compared with 125,000 words in the German language. So, naturally, the German word *"Gemütlichkeit"* should have a one-word counterpart in English, but such a word is yet to be heard.

Carl Oehl of the Colony Market Place in South Amana, Iowa, says:

English should be on probation
For failure of translation
Of this nice word that really
Should captivate the nation.

Pronounce it Ga-MEET-Lic-Kite,
You'll get by.
Hard to translate?
Let's give it a try:

Geniality, Contentment,
Similar words we hear.
Hospitality, Good Fellowship,
All are very near.

So let's hear it tonight:
Gemütlichkeit!

The Zither
From F. H. Ehmcke's Graphic Trade Symbols by German Designers, 1907.

German Wines

Many Americans who have bought German wines have probably been perplexed by the label. Information on the label tells a lot about the quality of the wine inside the bottle. It names the region where the wine originated (i.e., *Moselle, Rheingau, Rheinhessen, Rheinpfalz, Nahe, Franken*); vintage, the year the wine was made; the village or town where it was grown (i.e., *Rudesheim, Deidesheim*); the grape used for the wine (i.e., *Riesling, Sylvaner, Müller-Thurgau, Gewürztraminer*); the particular vineyard where the grapes grew (i.e., *Sonnenhügel, Schlossberg*); the taste of the wine, dry (*trocken*), medium-dry (*halbtrocken*). (No style indicated usually means a balance of sweetness and acidity.) The label also states if the wine was bottled by the grower (*Originalabfüllung*), and includes the official registration number for the particular wine. This official number (*A.P.Nr.*) is the wine's "birth certificate," which allows it to be sold commercially. —*Lynn Hattery-Beyer*

Rhubarb-Grape Wine Cocktail

Mixing equal parts of Piestengel (rhubarb wine) and grape wine creates a popular drink in the Amana Colonies in Iowa. Piestengel is a relatively dry wine; its sweetness is determined by the grape wine with which it is mixed.

Viticulture
From F. H. Ehmcke:
Graphic Trade Symbols
by German Designers, *1907*.

Rhine Wine Cup
Rheinweinbowle

1/2 cup water
1 cup sugar
1 1/2 cups lemon juice
1/2 cup brandy
1 1/2 cups dry sherry
3 bottles dry white Rhine wine
1 quart carbonated water

Combine the water and sugar in a saucepan. Boil for 5 minutes. Chill. Mix all the ingredients together in a chilled punch bowl. Add ice and serve. Serves 20.

Mulled Wine
Glühwein
From "It's Tasting Good"
New Ulm, Minnesota

A favorite at Christmas time or other holidays during the cold season.

3 cups red wine
2 tablespoons sugar
1 cinnamon stick
3 cloves
2 orange slices
1 tablespoon rum

Bring all to a boiling point, but do not allow to boil. Strain and pour into mugs. Serve hot. Serves 4.

Appetizers and Snacks

German dinners often start with a soup. They include appetizers only at the more formal occasions. Most of the following recipes would be served as part of the *Abendbrot*, the informal meal in the evening, rather than as an hors d'oeuvre in the classical sense.

Sweet-Sour Pumpkin
Süßsauer Kürbis

Rosemarie Petzold
Iowa City, Iowa

Rosemarie was born in Saxony and fled East Germany in 1956. After completing her education as a medical technologist in West Germany, she emigrated to the United States in 1965.

Pickled pumpkin is a regional specialty from East Germany; it is almost unknown in West Germany. "I associate this dish especially with my grandmother," Rosemarie says. "She'd always have an extra supply at hand when I visited her. Since garden space was always at a premium, she'd plant the pumpkin seeds in otherwise useless spots—to cover up the unsightly compost heap, for example. My grandfather, who worked for the railroad, also would plant some seeds near the railroad tracks."

1 yellow pumpkin, about 5 pounds
1 cup white vinegar, divided
3 cups sugar
1 or 2 sticks cinnamon, or to taste
10 whole cloves

Cut the pumpkin into wedges, remove the seeds, and peel, then cut into 1-inch squares. Place into a large bowl, pour half the vinegar over the pumpkin, and mix well. Let it stand overnight, or for at least 12 hours. Drain, reserving the liquid. In a large saucepan, combine the reserved liquid and the remaining vinegar; add the sugar, cinnamon, and cloves. Boil until the sugar is dissolved, then add the pumpkin, and boil until the pumpkin is glossy. Pack the pumpkin and the liquid into 5 sterilized pint jars. Seal immediately, let cool, and store in a cool place.

Note: You may also use butternut squash or the light green parts of watermelons.

Die Hausfrau
Mai 1994 Jahrgang 87.

Seit 1904 Das FENSTER nach drüben

Left: A cover of Die Hausfrau, *the oldest and largest German language monthly magazine published in America. Published since 1904, it contains articles on a wide range of subjects: a serial novel, short stories, poems, and regular columns covering environmental concerns, interesting facts from Germany, needlework, science and research, health, and other topics of interest. Published in Athens, Georgia, it is a great source for information and material in the German language. The cover picture is of "Schloss Charlottenburg" in Berlin.*

Mustard Pickles
Senfgurken

Rosemarie Petzold

4 pounds large, firm cucumbers
1 1/2 tablespoons pickling salt
4 small onions, sliced
6 tablespoons mustard seeds, divided
20 whole allspice, or to taste
32 black peppercorns, or to taste
1 cup white vinegar
1 cup water
1 1/2 cups sugar
1/4 teaspoon salt

Peel and quarter the cucumbers and remove the seeds. Place them in a large bowl, sprinkle with the pickling salt, cover with water, then put a tight lid on the bowl. Let stand for 24 hours in the refrigerator. Drain the liquid and discard. Cut the cucumbers into 1x2-inch pieces and place into 4 clean pint-sized pickling jars, along with the onions. To each jar, add 1 1/2 tablespoons mustard seeds, 5 whole allspice and 8 peppercorns.

In a medium-sized saucepan, combine the vinegar, water, sugar, and salt. Heat and boil until the sugar dissolves, stirring frequently. Pour the hot liquid over the cucumbers. Cover the jars securely and let cool. Store in the refrigerator for at least 3 to 4 weeks before serving; longer storage improves taste.

Note: You may substitute zucchini if you wish.

Horseradish Cream
Meerrettichsahne

1 cup heavy cream
4 to 5 tablespoons grated horseradish
1 1/2 teaspoons lemon juice
1/2 teaspoon salt
1/2 teaspoon white pepper

In a mixing bowl whip the cream. Fold in the horseradish, lemon juice, salt, and pepper. Good served with boiled beef, tongue or pork. Makes 4 servings.

Note: Fresh horseradish must be washed thoroughly and peeled before grating. If fresh is not available, horseradish ready-grated in jars can usually be found.

Half a Rooster
Halber Hahn

Hannelore Bozeman

The name of the recipe is a joke. This dish has nothing to do with chicken. It is a Rhineland specialty from my mother.

2 large pretzels or 1 rye roll
3 ounces Edam or caraway-seed cheese
butter to taste, optional
parsley sprig

Arrange the ingredients on an individual serving plate. Serve with *Kölsch* or *Alt* beer, or some other light or dark beer. Serves 1.

Pork Liver Pâté
Landleberwurst

Helen Kraus
Amana, Iowa
From The Story of An Amana Winemaker, *the book about the Kraus family's winery.*

1 1/2 pounds pork liver, minced
1 1/2 cups finely ground pork
2/3 cup chopped salt pork
strong dash of nutmeg, or to taste
strong dash of oregano, or to taste
1/2 teaspoon freshly ground pepper
1/4 teaspoon crushed bay leaf
3 cloves garlic, crushed
2 tablespoons brandy
1/2 cup dry rhubarb wine
uncooked bacon slices

Mix the liver, pork, and salt pork. Add the nutmeg, oregano, pepper, bay leaf, garlic, brandy, and wine, and mix thoroughly. Line a terrine or any 1-quart, oven-proof casserole with the bacon slices and fill with the liver mixture. Press down firmly and top with more bacon slices. Cover with aluminium foil and bake at 350° for 1 1/2 hours. Cool and refrigerate at least 8 hours before serving.

From Graphic Trade Symbols by German Designers, *by F. H. Ehmcke, 1907.*

Pickled Herring Rolls
Rollmops

4 to 6 fresh herring fillets
2 tablespoons prepared mustard
1 tablespoon capers
2 small pickles, sliced
2 onions, finely sliced
6 to 8 peppercorns
2 small bay leaves
1 1/2 cups white vinegar
1 cup water, boiled and cooled

Brush one side of each herring fillet with the mustard and cover it with the capers, pickles, and onions. Roll up carefully and secure with cocktail sticks or toothpicks. Place the *rollmops*, peppercorns, and bay leaves in a jar. Cover with the vinegar and water. Chill for 6 to 8 days. Remove the *rollmops* and serve with boiled potatoes, or on a piece of lightly buttered bread as a sandwich topping.

After School Snack

Submitted by Gloria Reuber
Monett, Missouri
From Authentic German Recipes, Old Time Remedies, Historical Sketches of Freistatt, Missouri, *by Senior Citizens.*

In years past, children coming home from school were hungry and there were no refrigerators to raid, so mother spread lard on a piece of bread and sprinkled sugar on it. This was called *Fettbrot.* If people were a little more well-to-do, they gave the children a piece of butterbread with a molasses cookie on it. When no butter was available, sour cream was used on the bread and sprinkled with salt and pepper, or sugar.

Ham and Cheese Toast
Überbackener Toast

Helga Wagner
Bonn, West Germany

8 square slices of white bread
tomato paste to taste
8 slices of pineapple, fresh or canned
8 ham slices
8 slices of cheese

Spread the bread slices with a thin layer of tomato paste. On each slice, place 1 pineapple slice, cover with a ham slice, and top with the cheese, cutting each piece to fit the shape of the bread, if necessary. Bake in an oven at 350° for 10 minutes or until the cheese is melted. Serves 8 as an appetizer, or 4 as a main dish if served with a salad.

Variations: Instead of the pineapple, you may use thinly sliced mushrooms. Or you may omit the pineapple and the cheese and top the unbaked sandwich with a fried egg instead. This is called *Strammer Max*, literally, "Strong Max."

Sweet Green Tomato Pickles

5 large onions, sliced
1 cup salt
2 gallons green tomatoes, quartered
2 quarts water
2 quarts vinegar, divided
1 3/4 pounds brown sugar
2 heaping tablespoons ground
   mustard
1 1/2 tablespoons cloves
2 tablespoons cinnamon
1/2 teaspoon cayenne pepper

Sprinkle the onions with the salt and let stand overnight. Drain. Combine the tomatoes, onions, water, and 1 quart vinegar. Bring to a boil and simmer 5 minutes. Drain. Combine the remaining vinegar, sugar, mustard, cloves, cinnamon, and cayenne pepper; pour over the tomatoes and boil together 3 or 4 minutes. Put into sterilized jars and seal.

Note: Good served with fried potatoes. These pickles are very sharp.

Smoked Salmon
Räucherlachs

Hannelore Bozeman

This is a great appetizer for a formal dinner.

4 servings of horseradish cream
   (recipe on page 145)
3/4 pound smoked salmon
1 whole lemon, divided
4 to 8 slices of French bread
butter to taste
4 parsley sprigs

Prepare 4 servings of the horseradish cream as directed; chill. Slice the salmon as thinly as possible and arrange on 4 individual serving plates. Cut the lemon in half. Sprinkle the juice of 1/2 lemon over the salmon. Cut the remaining lemon into 4 equal pieces and use as garnish with the parsley sprigs. Serve immediately with the horseradish cream and slices of the bread and butter. Serves 4.

> Idleness is the
> beginning of all evil.

Cooked Cheese
Kochkäse

Loretta Schmidt
Fredericksburg, Texas

Loretta and her husband Charles own Gästehaus Schmidt, a bed and breakfast lodging service.

2 cups buttermilk
5 gallons whole milk, preferably
   unpasteurized
2 tablespoons salt

To cook 2 cups of the cheese:
2 tablespoons butter
pinch soda
1/2 cup hot water or milk
1 teaspoon salt
caraway seeds, if desired

In a large crock, combine buttermilk and milk. Let stand until clabbered, 1 to 1 1/2 days. Heat clabber over low heat until very warm, do not boil. Pour into a colander lined with cheesecloth and press to drain all moisture. Let cool; then crumble into a large crock. Stir in 2 tablespoons of salt. Cover with foil and a plate and set in a warm place for 3 to 4 days or until hard. This mixture may be cooked or stored in the refrigerator or freezer until ready to cook.

To cook 2 cups of the cheese: Place 2 cups of cheese and butter in a saucepan over low heat to melt cheese, stirring occasionally. Stir in soda. Add water, remaining salt, and caraway seeds if used. Serve on hot homemade bread or refrigerate and cut into slices.

Corn Relish
Pennsylvania Dutch

2 cups sugar
2 cups cider vinegar
1 cup water
2 bay leaves
2 teaspoons mustard seeds
2 teaspoons celery seeds
1/2 teaspoons ground turmeric
6 cups corn kernels, fresh or
   canned and drained
2 cups chopped onion
1 cup chopped green pepper
1 cup chopped red pepper
2 cups chopped cabbage

Mix sugar, vinegar, water, and spices and bring to boil. Add remaining ingredients and simmer for 15 minutes if using canned corn, 30 minutes if fresh. Discard bay leaves. Ladle into clean jars, cover and refrigerate overnight, at least, before serving. To preserve: pack in sterilized canning jars; seal and process in boiling water bath for 15 minutes. Makes 3 quarts.

Red-Beet-Pickled Eggs
Pennsylvania Dutch

2 1-pound cans sliced beets
1 1/4 cups cider vinegar
3 tablespoons sugar
1 teaspoon salt
1/4 teaspoon pepper
1 tablespoon mixed pickling spice
6 (or more) hard-cooked eggs

Peel eggs. Drain beets; reserve juice, and set beets aside. To the juice, add remaining ingredients, except eggs; heat to boiling and simmer 5 minutes. Strain and pour clear juice over eggs. (Pour small amount over beets, if pickled beets are desired.) Refrigerate overnight; turn occasionally. Serve eggs whole or sliced.

Soups

Apple Soup with Meringue
Apfelsuppe

2 1/2 cups plus 2 tablespoons water,
 divided
1 1/2 cups white wine
1 small cinnamon stick
3 medium-sized apples
3 tablespoons lemon juice
1/4 cup cornstarch
8 tablespoons sugar, divided
1 egg white
1/4 teaspoon vanilla extract

In an enamel saucepan heat 2 1/2 cups water, the wine, and the cinnamon stick over low heat for 10 minutes. Remove the cinnamon stick. Peel and core the apples; slice finely. Add the apples to the warm liquid. Poach the apples briefly, being careful not to overcook. Combine the lemon juice and cornstarch; add 2 tablespoons water and stir the mixture into the apple soup. Add 5 tablespoons sugar, stirring until dissolved.

Meringue: Beat the egg white until nearly stiff. Gradually beat in the remaining 3 tablespoons of sugar, and the vanilla. Drop by spoonfuls onto the surface of the hot, but not boiling, soup. Cover; cook 3 to 5 minutes or until set. Using a slotted spoon, carefully remove the meringue drops; set aside on a plate. Transfer the apple soup to individual bowls or a terrine. Garnish with the meringue drops. Serve warm in the winter, or as a cold soup in the summer. Good with a sprinkling of toasted almonds. Serves 4 to 6.

Potato Soup
Kartoffelsuppe

Madeline Roemig
Amana, Iowa

Madeline Roemig relates, "This is an ideal way to use chicken broth one may have at hand from cooking chicken for a salad or casserole. My family usually treated potato soup as 'peasant food' and had been only slightly interested in having it served to them. I countered this by adding egg yolks and sour cream, which creates an elegant soup. To impress them further I remind them that this might also be served cold as a very classy vichyssoise."

4 slices lean bacon, diced
6 leeks, sliced thin (or use 2
 large onions instead)
1/4 cup chopped onion
2 tablespoons flour
4 cups chicken broth
3 large potatoes, sliced thin
2 egg yolks, beaten
1 cup sour cream
3 tablespoons chopped parsley

Sauté the bacon in a deep saucepan for 5 minutes. Add the leeks and onion and sauté another 5 minutes. Stir in the flour. Slowly add the chicken broth, stirring constantly. Add the potatoes and simmer for 1 hour. Mix in a blender or food processor until creamy. Combine the egg yolks and sour cream; add mixture to the soup. Simmer for 10 minutes, stirring constantly. Garnish with fresh, chopped parsley. Makes about 2 quarts.

149

Kirchweih Soup

Vic and Marie Mader
From Mader's Recipes of
Continental Europe.

*Mader's is a famous restaurant special-
izing in German foods and Germanic
decor in Milwaukee, Wisconsin. This
soup is served on the third Sunday in
October which is celebrated as* Kirchweih,
a church consecration day, in Germany.

1/2 pound shoulder of lamb, diced
1 1/2 quarts cold water
1 teaspoon salt
3 peeled tomatoes, seeded
   and chopped
3 green peppers, seeded and chopped
1 large onion, chopped
2 tablespoons rice
2 tablespoons butter
2 tablespoons flour
2 egg yolks
1/4 cup yogurt
juice and grated rind of 1/2 lemon
salt and pepper to taste
finely chopped parsley

In a large kettle, combine the lamb
and water. Bring to a boil and add salt.
Cook until the meat is tender, about
20 minutes. Add tomatoes, peppers,
onion, and rice. Cook for 15 minutes.
In a saucepan, melt butter and stir in
flour. Cook until bubbly, then gradually add 1 cup of the lamb broth,
strained. Cook, stirring constantly
until thickened. Stir into boiling soup
and cook for 5 minutes. Blend the egg
yolks, yogurt, and the juice and grated
rind of the 1/2 lemon. Reduce heat so
that the soup does not boil and add
the yogurt mixture. Season to taste.
Serve with finely chopped parsley.
Serves 8.

Broth with Liver Dumplings
Leberknödelsuppe

Hannelore Bozeman

This soup is popular in Bavaria.

6 cups beef stock
3 tablespoons butter
1 egg, separated
1/2 cup fresh, fine bread crumbs
1 small onion, minced
1/4 pound calf liver, ground
1 teaspoon salt
1/2 teaspoon marjoram
dash of nutmeg
grated rind of 1/2 lemon
3 tablespoons finely chopped
   parsley, divided
1 tablespoon flour, or as needed

Heat the stock in a large saucepan.
Meanwhile, cream the butter in a small
bowl and add the egg yolk, bread
crumbs, onion, liver, salt, marjoram,
nutmeg, lemon rind, 1 tablespoon
parsley, and the flour. Mix into a fine
paste. Beat the egg white and fold
into mixture. Form a 3/4-inch ball
and test by dropping it into the hot
broth; if it doesn't hold together, add
more flour to the mixture and try
again. Form the rest of the dumplings; their size and number will de-
pend on the number of servings you
are planning. Plan to have 1 or 2
dumplings per serving. Boil the
dumplings in the stock for 5 or 6 minutes, or until they rise to the top. Put
the soup in individual bowls and distribute the dumplings evenly. Sprinkle
with additional parsley, and serve
with a roll. Serves 4 to 6.

Vegetable Broth with Dumplings

Klare Gemüsesuppe mit Schwemmklößchen

1 quart vegetable broth
1 tablespoon dry sherry
1 teaspoon pepper
1 cup water
1 tablespoon butter
1/2 teaspoon salt
1/2 teaspoon ground nutmeg
1/2 cup flour
1 egg
2 tablespoons finely chopped
   parsley

In a medium saucepan, heat the broth, sherry, and pepper over medium heat. Meanwhile, combine the water, butter, salt, and nutmeg in a small saucepan and bring to a boil. Gradually sift the flour into the boiling water, stirring rapidly and thoroughly. Stir until the mixture forms a ball. Remove from the heat and cool slightly. Work in the egg, then shape the mixture into small, oval dumplings. Add the dumplings to the hot stock and simmer about 5 minutes; they will swell and become firm. Add more stock, if needed. Just before serving, add the parsley. Serves 4.

Oktoberfest, U.S.A.
La Crosse, Wisconsin

Steve Pavela, Caryl Molzahn, Phil Addis and Marian Pavela are participants in the Oktoberfest. The colored maple leaf is the symbol of the annual festival in this Mississippi River town.

Left: Dolls dressed in Transylvania-Saxon costumes are the artistry of Katharina Breckner of Darren, Michigan. The Detroit Saxons perform at German and other ethnic festivals.

151

Pea Soup
Erbsensuppe

Hannelore Bozeman

2 cups dried split yellow peas
1 ham hock or ham bone
4 cups water
1 small onion, minced
1/2 cup minced raw potato
1/2 teaspoon marjoram
1 bay leaf
1/2 teaspoon salt
1/4 cup milk
3 tablespoons flour

Wash the peas and soak overnight. Drain. In a large saucepan, place the ham hock in the water; add the peas, onion, potato, and spices. Cover and simmer for 1 1/2 to 2 hours. Remove the ham hock from the soup, loosen the meat from the bone with a sharp knife, chop the meat into small pieces, and set aside. Remove the bay leaf from the pea soup and discard. Put the mixture through a food mill or sieve, or purée in a blender. In a separate bowl, blend the milk and the flour. Return the pea purée to the saucepan, add the flour mixture, and stir until creamy and slightly thickened. Add the chopped ham and heat through. Taste for seasoning and add a little sugar and salt, if needed. Serves 4.

Cabbage Soup
Weißkohleintopf

1/2 pound frankfurters or
  knackwurst
1/2 cup finely chopped onion
1/2 cup diced celery
1 cup diced raw potato
2 cups chicken broth
3 cups milk
2 cups finely shredded cabbage
2 teaspoons salt
1/2 teaspoon pepper
2 teaspoons brown sugar
1 teaspoon caraway seed
1 cup light cream

Cut the frankfurters or the knackwurst into 1/4-inch slices. In a 4-quart kettle, combine the frankfurters, onion, celery, potato, and chicken broth. Bring to a boil, reduce the heat, and simmer covered for 15 minutes. Add the milk, cabbage, salt, pepper, brown sugar, and caraway seed. Return to a boil. Reduce the heat and simmer, covered, for 30 minutes longer. Stir in the cream. Serve hot. Serves 6 to 8.

Hot Beer Soup
Heiße Biersuppe

3 12-ounce bottles or cans of
  light-colored beer
1/2 cup sugar
4 egg yolks
1/2 cup sour cream
1 teaspoon cinnamon
1/2 teaspoon salt
freshly ground black pepper

Pour the beer and sugar into a heavy 4 to 5-quart saucepan; bring to a boil, stirring until sugar is dissolved. Remove from heat. In a small bowl, beat the egg yolks slightly with a wire whisk; beat in sour cream. Stir about 1/4 cup of the hot beer into the egg mixture, then whisk mixture into the saucepan with the beer. Add the cinnamon, salt, and a few grindings of pepper. Return to low heat and cook, stirring constantly, until the soup thickens slightly. Do not let the soup boil as it may curdle. Serve at once.

Lentil Stew
Linseneintopf

1 1/2 cups lentils
6 cups cold water
4 slices bacon, diced
1 cup sliced leek
1 small onion, diced
1 carrot, diced
1/2 cup chopped green pepper
1 cup chopped tomatoes
3 tablespoons butter
3 tablespoons flour
2 cups beef broth
1 tablespoon salt
2 tablespoons vinegar
2 tablespoons prepared mustard

Place the lentils in a large kettle. Add the water and bring to a boil. Reduce the heat and simmer, covered, for 1 hour. Sauté the bacon in a large skillet until crisp. Add the leek, onion, carrot, green pepper, and tomatoes. Sauté 5 minutes over low heat. Add the bacon and vegetable mixture to the lentils. Melt the butter in the same skillet. Remove from the heat and stir in the flour. Gradually stir in the beef broth. Add the salt, vinegar, and mustard. Bring to a boil, stirring constantly. Stir into the lentil stew. Simmer for 30 minutes. Serves 6.

Blind Chicken Soup
Blindhuhn

2 1/2 cups dried kidney beans
1/2 pound bacon, unsliced
1 ham bone
2 1/2 cups green beans, cut
    into pieces
1 cup sliced carrots
1 pound potatoes, peeled and diced
1 1/2 cups sliced apples

2 onions, sliced
3 tablespoons bacon grease
salt and pepper
1 tablespoon chopped parsley

Soak the kidney beans overnight. Add the bacon and ham bone to the beans and the water in which they have soaked, and cook for 45 minutes. Add the green beans, carrots, and potatoes; cook for another 30 minutes. Remove the ham bone and bacon; add the apple slices. Fry the onions in the bacon grease until golden brown, and add to the vegetables. Season with the salt and pepper and sprinkle with the parsley. Slice the bacon and serve on top of the soup.

Cold Fruit Soup
Obstkaltschale

1 pound apples, cherries, rhubarb or
    gooseberries
2 quarts water
1 tablespoon cornstarch
1/2 cup fruit juice or water
2 tablespoons sugar
2 tablespoons lemon juice
1/2 cup white wine

Clean the fruit, pit if necessary, and chop into small pieces; set aside some fruit for garnish. Cook the remaining fruit in the water until soft. Drain and reserve the liquid. Press the fruit through a fine strainer. Return the fruit pulp and reserved liquid to the saucepan and bring to a boil. Dissolve the cornstarch in the fruit juice and stir into the hot fruit soup. Add the sugar, lemon juice, and wine. Stir until the sugar is dissolved. Garnish with the reserved whole fruit. Chill and serve cold. Serves 4 to 6.

Salads

In Germany, salads, or *Salate*, are usually served on the same plate as the meat and hot vegetables. They often are a part of the evening meal, or *Abendbrot*, as well. Other salads can be a meal in themselves.

Celery Root Salad
Selleriesalat

3 celery roots (celeriac)
2 large potatoes, washed and peeled
1 large onion
4 large eggs, hard-cooked and cooled, divided
3 stalks celery, sliced
4 stems parsley, chopped
1/2 cup vinegar
1 teaspoon dry mustard
salt and pepper to taste
1 pint cream

Scrub the celery roots, peel, and slice. In water to cover, simmer for about 25 minutes, or until tender. Meanwhile, cook potatoes in a separate saucepan for about 15 to 20 minutes. Drain both and refrigerate overnight.

Finely chop the celery roots, potatoes, and onion, and place in a large bowl. Mix well. Remove the yolks from 3 of the boiled eggs and set aside. Chop the egg whites and add to the celery-root mixture with the sliced celery stalks and parsley. Mash the egg yolks in a mixing bowl, then add the vinegar, mustard, salt, and pepper and blend well. Add the cream, mixing thoroughly. Add to the salad and toss. Refrigerate for 24 hours, stirring occasionally. Before serving, garnish with slices of the remaining egg.

German Potato Salad
Württemberger Kartoffelsalat

Metzger's Black Forest Inn
Ann Arbor, Michigan

2 pounds potatoes
1 teaspoon salt
1/4 teaspoon fine black pepper
1/2 cup finely chopped onion
1/3 cup apple cider vinegar
1/4 cup corn or olive oil
3/4 cup hot beef or chicken broth

Wash the potatoes, then boil with the skins on until tender. Peel while hot and allow to cool until you can slice them to a thickness of about 1/8 inch. Add the salt, pepper, onion, vinegar, and oil. Pour the hot broth over the potatoes. Mix together gently in order not to break up the potatoes. Let stand at room temperature for at least 1 hour. Mix again just before serving. Garnish. Serves 4.

Note: Leftover German Potato Salad can be stored in the refrigerator for several days. Store in a covered stainless-steel, glass, or plastic dish. Remove from the refrigerator and let warm to room temperature before serving. Or, if you prefer, heat this potato salad and serve hot.

> No prize without effort.

Fruited Cabbage Salad

Madeline Schuerer Schulte
The Brick Haus Restaurant
Amana, Iowa

2 oranges, peeled and sectioned
2 apples, chopped
2 cups shredded green cabbage
1 cup seedless green grapes
1/2 cup whipping cream
1/2 cup mayonnaise or salad
    dressing
1 tablespoon sugar
1 tablespoon lemon juice
1/4 teaspoon salt

Mix fruits and cabbage in a bowl. In a chilled bowl, beat the whipping cream until stiff. Put the mayonnaise into a bowl; fold in the whipped cream, sugar, lemon juice and salt. Stir into the fruited cabbage mixture. Serves 6.

Beer Dressing for Potato Salad

G. Heileman Brewing Company, Inc.
La Crosse, Wisconsin

1/2 cup diced onion
3 tablespoons salad oil
2 tablespoons flour
1 1/2 teaspoons salt
1/8 teaspoon pepper
2 teaspoons sugar
1 1/2 cups Old Style Beer
1/4 cup cider vinegar

Sauté onion in the oil for 10 minutes. Blend in the flour, salt, pepper, and sugar; gradually add the beer and vinegar, stirring constantly. Bring to almost boiling; reduce heat and simmer for 5 minutes. Cool slightly. Makes 1 3/4 cups.

German-Style Potato Salad

Kathryn Domeier De Marce
Mankato, Minnesota

Marlene Domeier of New Ulm, Minnesota, says, "This type of potato salad is made in every home in New Ulm where family roots are Austrian or German. My mother, Agatha Domeier, is still making it at age 92. Nobody makes it better than she! Like many good cooks, she uses a pinch of this and that, but my sister came up with this recipe that met Mama Domeier's flavor and consistency."

3 pounds small red potatoes
1/2 cup sugar (to taste)
salt and pepper (to taste)
1/2 to 1 pound bacon, cut into
    bit-sized pieces
3 medium-sized onions,
    finely chopped
3 tablespoons bacon drippings
3 heaping tablespoons flour
2 cups water
3/4 cup white vinegar

Boil potatoes in skins; let cool. Remove skins and slice potatoes in layers in a bowl; sprinkle sugar, salt and pepper over each layer. Fry bacon and onions together until onions are transparent and bacon is not yet crisp. Remove bacon and onions with a slotted spoon and place on top of the sliced potatoes. Reserve 3 tablespoons of the bacon drippings in the pan; stir in the flour, gradually add the water and cook until thickened. Add the vinegar and cook to a gravy consistency. Pour hot mixture over the potatoes, bacon and onions, and mix gently. Let stand a few hours so flavors blend. Serve warm.

Remove outer leaves and core from cabbage. Shred cabbage finely and rinse. Fry bacon in a large pot; add shredded cabbage and cook for 5 minutes, stirring constantly. Add water and simmer until cabbage is just tender. Combine oil, vinegar, salt and parsley and pour over warm cabbage. Cool before serving.

Dandelion Salad
Löwenzahnsalat

Salad:
4 cups chopped dandelion greens
3 eggs, hard-cooked, chopped
3 slices bacon, cooked and
      broken into small pieces

Dressing:
1 1/2 tablespoons flour
1 teaspoon salt
2 tablespoons sugar
1 egg
1/4 cup vinegar
2 cups milk or water
bacon drippings from slices fried
      for salad

German Coleslaw
Kohlsalat

1 medium-sized head white cabbage
2 slices bacon, diced
1/2 cup water
3 tablespoons salad oil
1 1/2 tablespoons vinegar
1/2 teaspoon salt
1 teaspoon finely chopped parsley

Salad: Gently toss salad ingredients and pour dressing over all.

Dressing: Mix flour, salt, and sugar together. Add egg, vinegar and milk or water. Stir. Cook this mixture in the bacon drippings until thickened. Cool slightly. Pour over the salad and mix.

Sauerkraut Salad
Sauerkrautsalat

Hannelore Bozeman

1 cup sugar
1/3 cup vinegar
1/3 cup oil
1/2 onion, chopped finely
1 small apple, chopped finely
1 celery stalk, chopped finely
1/2 green pepper, chopped
1 small jar pimientos, diced
1 teaspoon caraway seeds, optional
4 cups sauerkraut, rinsed and
    drained

Combine the sugar, vinegar, and oil in a bowl and stir until sugar is dissolved. Add the onion, apple, celery, green pepper, pimientos, and caraway seeds; blend well. Put the sauerkraut into a bowl; pour the dressing over it and toss well. Chill before serving.

Pepper Cabbage
Naomi Yoder
Gordonville, Pennsylvania

A typical Pennsylvania Dutch salad from Naomi, who is a receptionist in the quilt museum of The Old Country Store of the People's Place in Intercourse, Pennsylvania.

1 head cabbage, finely chopped
1/2 cup dark vinegar
1 cup sugar
1/4 teaspoon salt
3/4 teaspoon celery seeds
1 red or green pepper, or some
    of each

Combine vinegar, sugar, salt, and celery seeds. Let stand five minutes. Chop pepper in a blender and combine with chopped cabbage. Add vinegar mixture; mix well and refrigerate overnight or for several hours. Serves 6 to 8.

Winter Scene.
The Old Order Amish, Mennonites, and friends, Sarasota, Florida.

The German Love of Bread

By Lynn Hattery-Beyer

Bread has been the mainstay of the German diet since pre-Roman times, when it played an important role in pagan rites. The small size of many loaves stems from the use of bread as a sacrificial offering (the smaller the loaf the less expensive the offering). Some of the traditional loaf shapes were pagan representations of the sun (round, flat loaves), the moon (crescent loaves and rolls) and offerings of shorn hair (braided loaves). A more practical reason for the smaller loaves: German breads tend to be dense. A one-pound loaf is about half the size of an American one-pound loaf of bread. The importance of bread is documented in words such as *Abendbrot* (literally, "evening bread" or supper) and *Brotzeit* ("bread time" or snack time).

About 250 kinds of bread and 30 kinds of rolls are sold in Germany. Some traditional types of bread are *Graubrot* (rye), *Mischbrot* (wheat and rye), *Bauernbrot* (wheat), *Kommisbrot* (rye), *Vollkornbrot* (whole-meal), *Schwarzbrot* and pumpernickel (dark rye). The heavier, dark whole-grain breads such as pumpernickel are more prevalent in Northern Germany, whereas the light, more finely ground wheat breads prevail in the South. The present trend is definitely toward coarsely ground, whole-wheat bread which contains whole seeds and grains: *Dreikornbrot* and *Sechskornbrot* (contain three and six different sorts of grain), *Leinsamenbrot* (linseed bread), *Sonnenblumenkernbrot* (sunflower seed bread) and many more.

The variety of hard rolls and buns is extensive. In High German, the general term for rolls and buns is *Brötchen*, but almost every dialect has its own word for rolls in general or for the most popular regional variety: in Bavaria it is *Semmel*; in the Palatinate and Swabia it is *Wecken*; in Berlin, *Schrippen*. Not only the names vary, but also the types. There are rolls with poppyseed on top (*Mohnbrötchen*), sesame seed (*Sesambrötchen*), buns with raisins (*Rosinenbrötchen*), with diced, fried bacon (*Speckbrötchen*), with cheese (*Käsebrötchen*), and soft buns with extra sugar in the dough (*Milchbrötchen*). Southern Germany favors pretzels, buns, and crescent rolls.

The wide variety of breads and buns has made baking an art. In Germany, the bakers' profession has long been highly organized and regulated by laws. A three-year apprenticeship must be completed before a baker is allowed to ply his trade independently. Laws regulate what types of flour must be used for certain breads, how much the buns and loaves must weigh, and when a baker may start baking his bread—not before 4 a.m.

Professional bakers produce a wide variety of high-quality wares. Bakeries can be found in every village and on almost every city corner. There is scarcely a need for home-baked bread, but some families prefer to bake their own bread so they can enjoy the sweet-smelling warmth during baking and control the origin, quality, and freshness of ingredients.

Breads, Dumplings, Noodles

Potato Bread
Kartoffelbrot

This is a Pennsylvania Dutch recipe.

1 medium-sized potato, peeled
   and diced
2 1/2 cups water
2 tablespoons shortening
1 1/2 tablespoons sugar
2 teaspoons salt
6 cups bread flour, divided
1 package dry yeast

Cook the potato in the 2 1/2 cups water until tender. Drain and reserve liquid. If necessary, add more water to the reserved cooking liquid to make 2 1/4 cups; mash the potato in this liquid. Let stand 5 to 10 minutes. Combine the mashed potato mixture with the shortening, sugar, and salt. Blend thoroughly. Beat in 3 cups of the flour. When well-mixed, stir in the yeast. Add the remaining flour gradually, beating well. Turn onto a floured surface and knead the dough until smooth and elastic, about 10 minutes. Place the dough in a greased bowl, grease the top of the dough, cover the bowl, and let rise until doubled, about 1 hour. Punch down the dough and shape into 2 loaves. Place each loaf into a greased 8 1/2 x 4 1/2-inch loaf pan. Cover and let rise until doubled, about 30 minutes. Bake at 375° for about 40 minutes.

Pretzels
From F. H. Ehmcke:
German Trade Symbols
by German Designers, *1907.*

Pretzels
Brezeln

1 package dry yeast
1 cup lukewarm water
3 cups flour, divided
1 1/2 tablespoons butter
1/2 teaspoon salt
1/2 teaspoon sugar
4 cups water
5 tablespoons baking soda
coarse salt

Dissolve the yeast in the lukewarm water. Add 1 1/2 cups flour and the butter, salt, and sugar. Beat 4 minutes. Knead in the remaining flour until the dough is no longer sticky. Cover and let rise. Punch down and divide into 10 pieces. Roll into 20-inch lengths and loop each into a twisted pretzel shape. Place on a greased baking sheet and let rise until doubled in size. Preheat the oven to 475°. Bring 4 cups water and the baking soda to a boil. Using a slotted spoon, carefully lower the pretzels into the water. When they rise to the top, return them to the greased baking sheet and sprinkle with the coarse salt. Bake about 10 minutes until browned. Serve immediately.

Caraway and Poppyseed Rolls
Kümmelstangen und Mohnbrötchen

1 package active dry yeast
1 teaspoon sugar
1/4 cup lukewarm water
1 cup milk
1 egg
1/3 cup vegetable oil
1 teaspoon salt
4 to 4 1/2 cups wheat flour, divided
3 tablespoons milk blended with
    1 egg yolk for glaze
2 to 3 tablespoons caraway seeds
2 to 3 tablespoons poppyseeds

Grease two baking sheets; set aside. In a large bowl, dissolve the yeast and the sugar in the lukewarm water. Let stand until foamy, 5 to 10 minutes. Beat in the milk, egg, oil, and salt. Beat in 2 cups of the flour. Let stand 10 minutes. Add enough of the remaining flour to make a soft dough. Turn out the dough onto a lightly floured surface. Knead the dough 8 to 10 minutes or until smooth and elastic, then divide in half. Roll half the dough into a 1/2-inch thick circle. Cut into 6 triangles. Starting with the long side, roll up into a crescent. Place on a greased baking sheet. Brush each crescent with the milk glaze; sprinkle with the caraway seeds. Cover and let rise in a warm place, free from drafts, until doubled in bulk, about 30 minutes. Roll out the remaining dough into a long, fat, sausage-shaped piece; cut into 6 pieces. Roll each piece into a ball. Place on the second greased baking sheet. Brush each roll with the milk glaze; sprinkle with the poppyseeds. Make a crisscross slash in the top of each roll. Preheat the oven to 425°. Bake both kinds of rolls 15 to 20 minutes or until golden brown. Remove from the baking sheets; cool on a rack. Makes 12 rolls.

German Rye Bread
Deutsches Roggenbrot

Brush and Palette Club
Hermann, Missouri
From The Hermann Cookbook

2 tablespoons butter
2 tablespoons sugar
1 teaspoon salt
2 cups scalded milk
1 cake yeast
1/2 cup lukewarm water
6 cups rye flour, divided
1 1/2 cups bread flour
2 tablespoons caraway seeds

Put butter, sugar, and salt in the top of a double boiler; add the scalded milk. Dissolve the yeast in 1/2 cup lukewarm water. When the milk mixture is lukewarm, add the dissolved yeast and 3 cups of the rye flour. Mix with a spoon. Add the rest of the rye flour and mix thoroughly. Turn onto a floured board and knead the dough until it is smooth and elastic to the touch, and bubbles may be seen under the surface. Return the dough to the bowl, cover, and let rise until doubled. Punch the dough down and knead in the bread flour and the caraway seeds. Knead again, then shape into 2 or more loaves and place in greased pans, filling the pans halfway. Cover and let rise until doubled. Bake at 425° for 15 minutes, then reduce the heat to 375° and bake for another 30 to 35 minutes.

Fruit Bread
Schnitzbrot

Historic Hermann, Inc.
Hermann, Missouri
From The Art of Hermann
German Cooking

Dried fruits are used to make this bread of unusual flavor. The fruit is cut up (Schnitz) and added to the bread (Brot), thus the name.

1 12-ounce package mixed dried fruit
1 8-ounce package dried apples
1 package or cake of yeast
1/4 cup lukewarm water
1 cup plus 1 tablespoon sugar,
  divided
1 1/2 cups scalded milk, cooled
  to lukewarm
1 1/2 cups flour
1/2 cup butter or shortening
2 eggs, well beaten
1 teaspoon salt
1/2 teaspoon cinnamon
3/4 cup raisins
3/4 cup currants
1 cup chopped nuts, optional
7 or more cups flour, unsifted

Cover the mixed dried fruit and the dried apples with water and soak overnight. Pour the fruit and the water in which it has been soaking into a saucepan. Cook until the fruit is quite soft, about 15 minutes, then drain well in a colander. Chop, or cut up, the dried fruit. Dissolve the yeast in the lukewarm water, add 1 tablespoon sugar, and let stand 10 minutes. Add the milk, then the 1 1/2 cups flour to make a sponge and set aside until bubbles break on top. Cream the butter, add 1 cup sugar, and cream well. Mix in the beaten eggs. Add the sponge, chopped fruits, salt, cinnamon, raisins, currants, and nuts. Beat in 3 cups of the flour. Take out 1/4 of the dough and knead, adding enough flour to keep the dough soft, but not sticky. Continue doing this with each 1/4 of the dough until all the dough has been worked up. Then knead it all together, place in a greased bowl, cover, and let rise in a warm place until doubled. Knead lightly, divide into four portions, put into greased bread pans, cover, and let rise until double in size. Bake at 400° for 10 minutes, reduce the heat to 350° and bake 45 minutes longer, or until done.

Below: An exhibit at the Sophienburg Memorial Museum and Archives, New Braunfels, Texas, displays bags of flour milled at the Dittlinger Roller Mills at the turn of the century. The museum tells the story of the first group of German immigrants to Texas who were escorted by German Prince Carl of Solms-Braunfels. Prince Carl named the new settlement after his home in Germany.

Semolina Dumplings
Grießknödel

3 cups water
1 teaspoon salt
1/2 cup butter
3 cups semolina
4 tablespoons bacon grease
2 small onions, finely chopped

In a saucepan combine the water, salt, and butter. Bring to a boil. Slowly stir in the semolina until the dough pulls away from the pan and forms a lump. Remove from the heat. Fill a large kettle 2/3 full of lightly salted water. Bring to a boil. Form 8 dumplings out of the dough. When the water boils, carefully lower the dumplings into the water. Cover and simmer for 25 minutes. Meanwhile heat the bacon grease in a skillet; add the onion and fry in the grease until golden brown. When the dumplings are done, remove them from the kettle with a slotted spoon. Drain slightly and place in the frying pan with the onion. Turn the dumplings in the onion and place them on a serving tray. Good with roasts and goulash.

Bavarian Bread Dumplings
Bayrische Semmelknödel

10 slices white bread
1 1/2 cups lukewarm milk
1 tablespoon butter
1/2 cup diced bacon
1 small onion, finely diced
2 tablespoons finely chopped parsley
3 eggs
salt and pepper to taste
1/4 teaspoon nutmeg

Tear the bread into pieces and soak in the milk. The bread should soak long enough to become moist but not soggy. Remove from the milk, press out any excess liquid, and place the bread in a mixing bowl. Melt the butter in a frying pan. Add the bacon and the onion and fry until the onion is golden brown. Stir in the parsley. Add the fried mixture to the bread, along with the eggs and spices. Combine thoroughly. Let stand for 20 to 30 minutes. Bring a kettle full of lightly salted water to a boil. With wet hands shape the dough into dumplings and drop them into the boiling water. Simmer for 18 to 20 minutes. Remove, drain well, and serve immediately. Good with pork and sauerkraut.

German Pancakes
Pfannkuchen

Lucille Mauermann
Brodhead, Wisconsin

Lucille and her husband Harvey once operated a dairy farm. They sold milk to a Swiss cheese factory near their farm.

1/2 cup milk
1/2 cup flour
3 eggs, beaten
1/3 cup butter
powdered sugar
syrup

Combine milk and flour. Add the beaten eggs; mix well. Put butter in an 8-inch round cake pan, and place cake pan into a 400° oven until butter melts. Pour the batter into the pan and bake for 20 minutes. Serve with powdered sugar and syrup. Serves 2.

Dumplings

The Paul A. Maier Family
Kalamazoo, Michigan

1 egg
2 teaspoons salt, divided
1/2 cup milk
1 1/2 cups flour
4 cups water

Beat the egg well, add 1 teaspoon salt and the milk. Stir the mixture into the flour until a smooth batter is formed. In a large saucepan, bring the water with the remaining salt to a boil, and add the batter by spoonfuls. Let the dumplings cook for 15 minutes. Drain. Serve with sauerkraut.

Yeast Dumplings
Hefeklöße

4 cups flour
1 package dry yeast
3/4 cup lukewarm milk, divided
5 tablespoons sugar, divided
1/3 cup butter
1/2 teaspoon salt
2 eggs

Sift the flour into a large mixing bowl. Make a well in the center and crumble the yeast into it. Stir 1/4 cup milk and 2 tablespoons sugar into the yeast. Place flecks of the butter on the flour around the well and sprinkle the remaining sugar and salt over all. Mix to make a soft dough. Cover the bowl and put it in a warm place for dough to rise. After the dough has doubled, add the eggs and the remaining 1/2 cup of milk. Knead until the dough is firm, at least 8 to 10 minutes. Shape the dough into dumplings and place them on a floured surface to rise for 10 minutes. Bring a kettle full of salted water to a boil. Drop the dumplings into the boiling water and simmer for 10 to 15 minutes, turning frequently. Remove from the water, drain, and serve. Good with stewed plums, or sprinkled with poppyseed and sugar.

Swabian Noodles
Spätzle

4 cups flour
4 eggs, beaten
2 teaspoons salt, divided
9 cups water, divided

In a mixing bowl combine the flour, eggs, and 1 teaspoon salt. Add just enough of the water to make a firm dough. When pulled up on a spoon, the dough should tear at a height of 6 to 8 inches. Fill a large kettle with the remaining water, add the remaining salt, and bring to a boil. To make the *spätzle*, press the dough through a *spätzle* cutter, ricer, or colander directly into the boiling water. Rinse all the utensils in cold water before they come into contact with the dough. The water should boil at all times. The *spätzle* need only simmer for 2 to 3 minutes. Remove from the kettle with a slotted spoon, rinse, drain, place on a serving dish, and cover. Repeat the procedure until the dough is all gone. The *spätzle* may be kept warm for a short time in the oven before serving. Good with roast and gravy, or served by itself, tossed with lots of grated Swiss cheese.

He who begins much ends little.

Filled Dough Sandwiches
Verenike

Mrs. Leslie H. Harder
Mountain Lake, Minnesota

Mountain Lake is a community where "Russian Germans" settled more than 100 years ago. Originally from Germany, they fled to Russia to escape religious persecution in their home country. In the middle of the 18th century, Catherine the Great of Russia, recognizing their farming skills, invited Germans to settle in the Ukraine and Black Sea area to develop the fertile land into productive farms. In return they were promised 100 years of exemption from military service. After that period of time, the later czars tried to conscript them. Not wanting to fight for Russia any more than they did for Germany, they emigrated to the New World and found a haven in southwest Minnesota where their descendants live today.

They are a mixture of Catholics, Lutherans, Mennonites, Amish, and other Anabaptists. Their religious freedom has enabled them to maintain their native heritage in their foods, crafts, and customs. Every September they present an arts and crafts fair held at the Heritage House Museum where the old ways of life are displayed.

The following recipe, which is one of the most popular foods served at the event, shows the influence of their Russian sojourn. Fyodor Chaliapin, the great Russian operatic bass, loved cheese Verenike so much that he always looked for them in restaurants whenever he came to New York to sing.

Verenike (a Russian term with many spelling variations) are egg- and cottage cheese-filled dough sandwiches. They are of Russian-Jewish origin, and recipes for them are found in most Jewish cookbooks. They often are filled with cherries as well as cream cheese for dessert or with meat, potatoes, or kasha (buckwheat groats) as an accompaniment to the main dish. The dough is often a basic noodle dough, although this one is somewhat different.

Filling:
3 or 4 egg yolks
3 pounds cottage cheese
1 teaspoon salt
Dough:
3 or 4 egg whites
1 cup cream
2/3 cup milk
2 teaspoons salt
2 tablespoons oil
4 to 4 1/2 cups flour

Filling: Mix all the filling ingredients together.
Dough: Beat the egg whites slightly. Add the remaining ingredients to make a medium-soft dough. Roll out as for a pie crust. Cut into circles with a 3-inch cutter or fruit can. Place a spoonful of filling on each circle, fold in half and seal well. Drop into boiling water in a large kettle, and cook for 10 to 15 minutes, or until they rise to the top. Remove with a slotted spoon. May be served with sour cream and ham.
Note: This is a large recipe and can be cut in half easily. The Chinese call these *wontons;* the Italians, *ravioli.*

Mädchen und Eier muß man nicht aufbewahren.
Young girls and eggs shouldn't be stored.

Turkey Red Wheat

In the 1870s Turkey Red wheat (so named because it first grew in a little valley in Turkey, and Red because it has a reddish golden color) was brought by Mennonites to Kansas. This wheat is the grandfather of all United States hard winter wheat. It grew far better than the wheat the original Kansas settlers had and it produced the best flour. Before the Mennonites brought Turkey Red wheat to Kansas very little was grown there, now Kansas is one of the leading wheat-growing states and first in flour-milling.

Grist Mill Stone, circa 1875
The Kauffman Museum
Bethel College, North Newton, Kansas

The Museum tells the story of the Mennonites coming from Europe to the Central Plains in the 1870s, their encounters with and cultivation of the prairie environment, and their continuing global relationships through service, mission, and travel. On a five-acre site, the Museum is surrounded by prairie reconstruction: native grasses, wild flowers, a historic German-Mennonite farmstead and traces of the Chisholm trail.

Homemade Bread
Weißbrot

Loretta Schmidt

2 packages dry yeast
4 cups warm water
8 teaspoons sugar or honey
4 teaspoons salt
3 tablespoons vinegar, optional
1/2 cup shortening
13 to 14 cups flour

In a large bowl, dissolve yeast in water. Mix in all ingredients except flour. Add 2 to 3 cups of flour and mix until smooth. Gradually add enough of the remaining flour to make a stiff dough. Turn onto a floured surface and knead for 10 minutes or until smooth and elastic. Clean and grease bowl; place dough in bowl and turn to coat. Cover and let rise for 1 1/2 hours. Punch dough down. Knead lightly for 4 minutes and divide in fourths. Place into four 9x5-inch greased loaf pans. Cover and let rise for about 1 hour. Bake at 400° for 10 minutes, then reduce heat to 350° and bake for 35 to 40 minutes or until loaves test done.

Main Dishes

By Lynn Hattery-Beyer

Hunting (the stag seen by St. Hubert)
From F. H. Ehmcke: Graphic Trade
Symbols by German Designers, *1907.*

Germans are meat-eaters, but they tend to eat smaller portions at their main meal and consume much larger quantities of sliced meat, cold-cuts and wurst during their other two meals. Beef traditionally did not play a large role in their diet, but the advent of large-scale trade after World War II has changed that.

Pork is king of meats in Germany. Every bit of the hog is used—not even the innards go to waste. It is just as popular fresh (as pork roast, cutlets, and hocks) as cured. German butchers cure meat traditionally, using only natural ingredients. The meat is first pickled or salted (sometimes both) and then cold- or warm-smoked. World renowned examples of this art are the German smoked hams and *Kasseler* (smoked pork loin roast).

Veal, though expensive, is used quite a bit. *Kalbsbraten* (roast veal) and *Kalbsfrikassee* (thinly sliced veal braised in a cream sauce) are eaten frequently, but the favorite German cut of veal is the *Schnitzel*, or cutlet. *Schnitzel* may be prepared in a number of ways. It may be breaded (*Wiener Schnitzel*); simmered in sour cream (*Rahmschnitzel*); served with a fried egg and anchovies (*Holsteiner Schnitzel*), or simply pan-fried and served with lemon wedges (*Schnitzel Natur*).

Germans eat more game than Americans do, and hunting is not merely a leisure pastime. Rabbit and venison often are used year-round, while goose and duck are usually reserved for holidays and special occasions. A German hunter needs not only a license (for which he must pass an extensive test), but must also buy the hunting rights for a specific piece of land. Most farmers have hunting licenses and hunt their own farms; they may possibly sell some of the hunting rights.

Meat in the form of *Wurst*, sausage and cold-cuts, is just one of the categories in which German and American cuisines clearly differ. The bologna, summer sausage, and sliced meats Americans sometimes use on sandwiches are but a humble fraction of the selection Germans find at their local butcher shop or supermarket.

In general, German *Wurst* can be divided into four basic types, with regional variations and name changes. *Rohwurst* is cured and smoked by a butcher and may be eaten as is without further cooking. *Brühwurst* is not only smoked but

166

also scalded by the butcher and is eaten warm. *Kochwurst*, as its name implies, has already been cooked and sometimes smoked at the butcher shop. It corresponds to what we call cold cuts. The fourth kind of *Wurst*, *Bratwurst*, not only denotes the favorite "brats" so many Americans love, but is also a general term for raw *Wurst* which must be pan-fried before eating.

In butcher shops, orderly trays full of different kinds of hams, sliced roasts, pâtés and *Wurst* are embellished with pistachios, black peppercorns, and peppers. An average German family buys one or two pounds of assorted *Wurst* every week, and usually has a *Hartwurst* (like hard salami) hanging in the pantry in case it is needed.

Farm families still raise their own animals and have the local butcher come to slaughter them. This is an important occasion which usually takes place in late fall. The butcher comes early in the morning and sets up his equipment in the farm courtyard. After dividing the hog into the desired cuts, the butcher begins the more intricate process of making *Wurst*. Using old family recipes, the butcher chops up the leftover pieces of pork, including many of the innards, and adds herbs, spices, and vinegar. Some types of *Wurst* are then cooked in a big kettle before being put in casings or tin cans; others, for example *Bratwurst*, are not precooked.

The best part of the day is the *Schlachtfest*. After most of the work has been done (the meat is stored in the freezer, the courtyard has been hosed down and the butcher is busy making *Wurst*), a big kettle of water is put to boil. Small pieces of pork are thrown into the boiling water. Meanwhile, tables and benches are set up, pitchers of wine and beer or apple wine (depending upon the region) are brought up from the basement, and the family and neighbors sit down to enjoy fresh *Kesselfleisch* or *Wellfleisch* (meat boiled in a kettle).

I will never forget the first *Schlachtfest* I attended in a small village surrounded by vineyards in the Palatinate. Ten of us, including the eighty-three-year-old family matriarch, enjoyed the fresh meat, grated horseradish, thick slices of bread and glasses of the family's own wine. We were sitting outside in the courtyard, which faced the village square across from the Catholic church. After a while, the village priest wandered past and stopped for a chat. The conversation became quite lively, but my limited knowledge of the dialect did not allow me to follow it. Suddenly the family father rushed into the house and came back carrying a rifle. Shouldering it without a word, he aimed at the church steeple and fired, hitting the weather vane and making it spin about. Every man there burst out laughing, except the priest, who stomped off in a rage. They later explained to me that the priest had started to reminisce about a *Schlachtfest* in the very same courtyard in which he and his friend, the family father, had taken part as boys. He remembered how they had been drinking and had taken pot shots at the steeple, adding that they would never think of repeating this boyhood prank now. His friend obviously thought differently.

Venison Cutlets with Mushrooms
Rehschnitzel mit Pfifferlingen

8 venison cutlets
1/4 cup vegetable oil
1/2 cup red wine
4 bacon slices, diced
3 tablespoons flour
1 large onion, finely chopped
1/2 pound sliced mushrooms,
    preferably *Pfifferlinge** or
    chanterelles
1/2 cup cream
1/2 teaspoon thyme, or to taste
4 to 6 juniper berries, crushed
salt and pepper to taste

**Available in food specialty stores.*

Pound the venison lightly with a meat mallet, then brush both sides with the oil and arrange the cutlets in a shallow baking dish. Pour the wine over the venison. Cover and refrigerate overnight. Sauté the bacon in a large skillet; remove and keep warm. Drain the venison, reserving the marinade. Coat the cutlets with the flour and fry quickly over high heat in the bacon fat. Add extra oil if needed and turn once. Do not overcook. Remove the meat from the skillet and set aside on a warm plate.

Sauté the onion in the remaining fat and cooking juices until a light golden brown. Add the mushrooms, cream, thyme, juniper berries, and a little reserved marinade. Simmer the sauce 4 to 5 minutes. Season with the salt and pepper. Return the cutlets to the sauce and heat through. Garnish with the bacon. Serves 6 to 8.

Note: Serve with lingonberry preserves, currant jelly, or cranberries on the side. Goes well with potatoes or dumplings, and with red cabbage or Brussels sprouts.

Herbed Game Sauce
Kräutersoße für Wild

Madeline Schuerer Schulte
Brick Haus Restaurant
Amana, Iowa

1/2 cup butter
1/3 cup red currant jelly
1 teaspoon Worcestershire sauce,
    or to taste
salt to taste
1/2 teaspoon dried ground rosemary
1/2 teaspoon dried ground savory
1/2 teaspoon dried ground thyme

In a small saucepan, heat the butter and stir in the jelly. Cook over low heat, stirring just until the jelly melts. Do not allow the mixture to boil. Add the Worcestershire sauce, salt, and herbs. Bring just to the boiling point, but do not boil. Remove the sauce from the heat and allow to stand for 30 minutes. Makes about 1 cup. Serve with venison, duck, or goose. Do not serve with pheasant, quail, or grouse.

Note: When charcoal grilling, baste the meat lightly with the sauce just before removing from the grill. Pour the remaining sauce into a dish and use at the table.

> A good word costs nothing.

Fried Rabbit
Hasenpfeffer

Historic Hermann, Inc.
Hermann, Missouri
From The Art of Hermann
German Cooking

2 cups water
1/2 cup vinegar
3 tablespoons sugar
1 teaspoon salt
1/2 teaspoon whole cloves
1/2 teaspoon black peppercorns
1 bay leaf
1 rabbit
3 tablespoons butter
1 medium-sized onion, diced
1 1/2 tablespoons flour
3 tablespoons water
1/2 cup sour cream

Mix the first seven ingredients together in a saucepan and heat to the boiling point. Set aside to cool. Cut the rabbit into pieces and place in a glass or enamel bowl. Pour in the cooled diluted vinegar and spice mixture. Cover the bowl and refrigerate overnight. Remove the rabbit and strain the marinade; reserve. Melt the butter in a frying pan and sauté the rabbit pieces until brown, turning frequently. Add 1/2 cup of the strained marinade. Cover, and simmer for 1 hour, or until tender. Add the onion and another 1/2 cup of the marinade. Continue to simmer until the rabbit is very tender. Make a paste of the flour and the water and stir into the pan juices, stirring constantly. Boil for 2 minutes, stir in the sour cream, blend thoroughly and heat to boiling. Serve at once.

Berlin-Style Liver
Leber Berliner Art

2 tart apples
2 large onions, thinly sliced
5 tablespoons butter, divided
1/2 teaspoon salt
4 slices of calf liver
3 tablespoons flour
pepper to taste

Core the apples and slice into 1/4- to 1/2-inch thick rings. Separate the onion slices into rings. In a large skillet, heat 2 tablespoons butter and fry the apple rings in the hot butter for 1 to 2 minutes. Remove and keep warm. Fry the onion rings in the skillet until golden brown, adding more butter if needed. Season with the salt, remove from the skillet and keep warm. Remove any skin or fibers from the liver; coat lightly with the flour. Melt the remaining butter in the skillet. Sauté the liver quickly, turning once. Do not overcook the liver, or it will become hard and tasteless. Season with the pepper. Arrange on a warm serving plate and top with the fried apple and onion rings. Serves 4. Good with applesauce and mashed potatoes.

Note: This is a popular Berlin specialty. If you use pork or beef liver, soak in milk for 30 minutes before cooking.

Idleness is the
beginning of all evil.

Sauerbraten

Mark F. Sohn
Pikeville, Kentucky

Mark Sohn says, "My Dad's mother was German and she made Sauerbraten. My Mom makes it three or four times a year. Now I, too, have made Sauerbraten—a beef pot roast. The many days of soaking make me feel like an Old World cook. The roast presented below is very tender. The gravy is thick, mild, and creamy. This is among the best beef dishes I know. It takes me back to my German-American heritage.

"Because the cooked Sauerbraten improves with age, the entire dish can be prepared a day ahead and re-heated. Leftover roast can be re-heated or made into sandwiches or hash. Sauerbraten's tenderness and sour flavor come from the fact that it is soaked in a water and wine mixture for one to seven days—longer soaking makes it more tender and more sour. Sauerbraten is traditionally served with red cabbage and potato pancakes or potato dumplings. I recommend potatoes and cabbage; my parents serve it with Dad's specialty, Spätzle."

Marinade:
1 1/2 cups water
1 1/2 cups dry red wine
3 cloves garlic, cut each in half
1 medium-sized onion, peeled
    and diced
2 bay leaves
1 teaspoon peppercorns
1/4 cup sugar
Roast:
1 3-pound pot roast
1 carrot, cut up
1 stalk celery, cut up
1 medium-sized onion
    with 3 cloves stuck in it

Gravy:
1 teaspoon bouillon granules
1/2 cup red wine
1/2 teaspoon ground ginger
1 teaspoon salt
3 tablespoons instant flour, also
    referred to as sauce and gravy flour
1/2 cup sour cream

Marinade: In a medium-sized saucepan, heat the water and wine. Add garlic, onion, bay leaves, peppercorns, and sugar. Heat until sugar is dissolved, but do not boil.

Roast: Place pot roast in a glass or crockery pot. Add enough of the marinade to go halfway up the side of the roast. Reserve remaining marinade for cooking. Cover the pot and refrigerate. Turn roast in the morning and at night for 5 days. Place roast and marinade in slow-cooker, cover with remaining marinade and add carrot, celery, and onion. Cook it at 290° for 6 to 8 hours or until very tender. It should simmer; do not boil.

Gravy: Remove roast and vegetables from pot. Skim off the fat. Place 2 cups of the sauce in a saucepan. Add bouillon, wine, ginger, and salt. Bring to a boil. Gradually sift in the instant flour, stirring constantly. Boil for 1 minute. Reduce heat and keep warm. Slice roast and place it on a warm plate. Quarter the onion and arrange it with the carrot and celery around the roast. Pour 1/2 cup of the gravy over the roast. Add the sour cream to the remaining gravy, stir well and serve with the roast.

Note: If desired, serve with any red wine, such as Zinfandel.

German Meatballs

Historic Hermann, Inc.
Hermann, Missouri
From The Art of Hermann
German Cooking

1 slice of bread, 1 inch thick
1/2 pound of each: beef, veal,
    and pork or liver, ground together
2 eggs
1 tablespoon butter
1/4 cup finely minced onion
3 tablespoons chopped parsley
1 1/4 teaspoons salt
1/4 teaspoon paprika
1/2 teaspoon grated lemon rind
1 teaspoon lemon juice
1 teaspoon Worcestershire sauce,
    optional
5 cups vegetable stock, or 10 beef
    bouillon cubes dissolved in
    5 cups of water

Gravy:
6 to 8 tablespoons butter
6 to 8 tablespoons flour
salt and paprika to taste
2 tablespoons chopped pickles, or
    2 tablespoons lemon juice
2 tablespoons chopped parsley

Soak the bread in water to cover. Put the ground meat into a bowl. In a separate bowl, beat the eggs well and add to the meat. Melt the butter and sauté the onion until the onion is light brown. Add to the meat. Press the water out of the bread and add the bread to the meat mixture. Add the parsley, salt, paprika, lemon rind and juice, and the Worcestershire sauce. Mix well and shape into 2-inch balls. In a large saucepan, heat the stock, then drop the meatballs into the boiling stock and simmer, covered, about 15 minutes, until the balls rise to the top. Remove and keep warm.

Gravy: Measure the amount of stock; melt 2 tablespoons butter and stir in 2 tablespoons flour for each cup of stock. Add the stock and cook until smooth and boiling, stirring constantly. Season to taste with the salt and paprika. Add the chopped pickles or lemon juice and the parsley. Serve with boiled noodles or *Spätzle* (recipe on page 163).

Kasseler Pork Loin
Kasseler Rippchen

3 pounds smoked loin of pork
1 chopped onion
1 chopped tomato
1 stalk celery, diced
2 tablespoons butter
1 cup water
1 tablespoon flour
1/2 cup red wine
1/2 cup sour cream
salt and pepper to taste

Place the meat in a heavy kettle with the onion, tomato, celery, butter, and water. Cover and simmer for 1 1/2 hours, then turn to brown the meat on all sides in the pan juices. Remove the meat and place on a covered serving dish to keep hot. Stir the flour into the pan juices. Gradually add the wine, stirring constantly. Stir in the sour cream and season to taste with the salt and pepper. Strain the gravy over the meat and serve. Good with either sauerkraut and mashed potatoes, or red cabbage and potato dumplings. Serves 4 to 6.

Leg of Pork
Eisbein

1 leg of pork, about 4 pounds
1 onion, cut in quarters
2 bay leaves
2 whole cloves
1 teaspoon black peppercorns
1 small leek, cut into 1-inch pieces
1 small celery stalk, cut in half
1 carrot, cut in half

Place the pork in a large kettle and add the remaining ingredients. Cover with cold water and bring to a boil. Reduce heat and cook for 2 to 2 1/2 hours, or until tender. Serve with sauerkraut and boiled potatoes. In Berlin, puréed peas are the traditional side dish. Makes 4 to 6 servings.

Vienna-Style Veal Cutlets
Wiener Schnitzel

The Wiener Schnitzel *originated in Vienna, Austria and is found in German restaurants worldwide. These cutlets are typically a restaurant food; few women in Germany make them at home, possibly because veal is quite expensive.*

4 veal cutlets
2 tablespoons lemon juice
1/2 teaspoon salt
1 egg
3 tablespoons water
fine dry bread crumbs, as needed
2 tablespoons butter
4 lemon slices

Pound the cutlets slightly; slash the edges to prevent curling. Sprinkle each cutlet lightly with lemon juice and salt. In a shallow bowl, beat together the egg and water. Dip the cutlets in the egg mixture; coat with the bread crumbs. In a skillet, melt the butter and fry the cutlets until golden brown. Garnish with lemon slices and serve immediately. Sprinkle with additional lemon juice if desired.

Variation: For a *Holsteiner Schnitzel*, fry the cutlets as above, then melt another 2 tablespoons butter in the skillet. Fry 4 eggs and top each cutlet with a fried egg. Garnish each with an anchovy fillet, tomato slices, and a sprig of parsley.

Note: *Marlene Domeier says, "Nowadays, many Germans no longer eat veal so pork cutlets are substituted."*

Paprika Cream Schnitzel
Paprika-Rahmschnitzel

*Madeline Schuerer Schulte
Brick Haus Restaurant
Amana, Iowa*

4 slices bacon
1 1/2 pounds veal cutlets (cut into individual portions 1/2-inch thick)
2 tablespoons chopped onion
2 tablespoons sweet Hungarian paprika
salt to taste
1 cup sour cream
1/2 cup tomato sauce

Cook the bacon until crisp; remove from the skillet, crumble, and reserve. In the bacon drippings, brown the veal, add the onion and cook until lightly browned. Season with the paprika and salt. Stir in the sour cream and the tomato sauce. Cover and simmer for 20 minutes until the veal is tender (do not boil). Sprinkle with the bacon bits. Great when accompanied by egg noodles or rice. Serves 4.

Basic Bread Dough
for Ham Baked in Bread

2 packages active dry yeast
2 1/4 cups lukewarm water, divided
3 tablespoons sugar
2 teaspoons salt
2 tablespoons butter or shortening
6 1/2 to 7 1/2 cups flour, divided

Dissolve the yeast in 1/2 cup warm water in a large bowl. Stir in the remaining 1 3/4 cups water, the sugar, salt, butter, and 3 1/2 cups of flour. Beat until smooth. Stir in enough of the remaining flour to make a dough that is easy to handle. Turn onto a floured surface and knead until the dough is smooth and elastic, about 8 to 10 minutes. Place in a large greased bowl and rotate the dough so the greased side is up. Cover and let rise in a warm place until double, about 2 hours. Punch it down and divide it in half.

Ham Baked in Bread

one recipe basic bread dough
1 14-pound pre-cooked ham
melted butter
1 egg, beaten

Roll out one-half of the dough to about 15 inches in diameter, or large enough to cover the bottom and 2/3 up the sides of the ham. Place on a large greased baking sheet. With a brush or your fingers, use water to moisten 2 to 3 inches of the outer edge of the dough circle. Place the ham in the center of the dough. Roll out the second half of the dough to the same size and place over the ham. Pull the bottom dough up over the edge of top dough and press hard all around to make the dough stick together. Brush the entire ball with the melted butter to keep the dough soft. Let rise in warm place about 45 to 60 minutes or until double. Seal any cracks in the dough using a little water and pressing the cracks together. Brush the entire ball with the beaten egg and bake at 375° to 400° for 1 hour and 45 minutes. Cover lightly with foil if it begins to brown too much before the baking time is up.

German-Style Pickled Ham

Amana Meat Shop and Smokehouse
Amana, Iowa
Ideal for leftovers.

ham ends and pieces
water
vinegar
onion slices, optional
pimiento, optional

Cut ham into 3/4-inch cubes. Prepare a mixture of 1/2 water and 1/2 vinegar; prepare enough to cover the ham cubes. Add onion and pimiento, if used. Let stand refrigerated overnight. Serve cold.

Jack Hahn wraps a pre-cooked ham in bread dough at the Open Hearth Bakery in Middle Amana, Iowa.

Beef Rolls
Rinderrouladen

4 large thin slices top round of beef,
about 1/4 inch thick
salt and fresh pepper to taste
2 tablespoons prepared mustard
(German style if available)
2 1/2 cups finely chopped onion,
divided
4 strips bacon
4 dill pickle spears
3 tablespoons butter or margarine
1 tablespoon paprika
2 cups beef bouillon, divided

Sprinkle the meat with the salt and pepper. Spread each piece with about 1 1/2 teaspoons mustard and 3 to 4 tablespoons chopped onion. Cut each slice of bacon in half and then each piece in half lengthwise. Arrange 4 pieces on each slice of meat. Split each pickle spear in half lengthwise and arrange 2 halves between 2 bacon slices. Roll the beef up, enclosing the filling. Tie securely with a string.

Melt the butter in a skillet and sauté the remaining onion until golden; then sprinkle with the paprika. Cook a few seconds to blend. Add the beef rolls and turn in the paprika mixture until coated. Add 1 cup beef bouillon and cover. Cook over medium-high heat about 30 minutes, turning occasionally so that the meat does not stick. Add 1/2 cup bouillon, cover, and cook another 30 minutes. Add the remaining bouillon, cover, and cook an additional 15 to 30 minutes, or until fork-tender. Serves 4.

Stuffed Cabbage Rolls
Kohlrouladen

Hannelore Bozeman

1 cup dry bread crumbs
1 large cabbage head
3/4 pound ground beef
3/4 pound ground pork
1 medium-sized onion, minced
1 tablespoon Italian seasoning
1/2 teaspoon marjoram
salt to taste
1 beaten egg, optional
2 tablespoons butter
1 cup beef stock

Soak the bread crumbs in water, then drain, squeeze dry, and set aside. With a sharp knife, cut the outermost leaf from the cabbage head near the core, and remove the leaf from the head, taking care not to tear the leaf. Repeat until you have 8 large cabbage leaves; use the rest of the cabbage for some other dish. In a medium-sized saucepan, filled halfway with salted water, boil the cabbage leaves for about 3 minutes, until they are limp enough to roll but not cooked through. Drain; let the leaves cool. In a medium bowl, mix the ground beef and pork together well, then add the bread crumbs, onion, seasonings, and egg, if used. Mix well. Divide into 8 portions and place each portion on one of the cabbage leaves, roll up and secure each roll with a string or a toothpick, if desired. In a large skillet, melt the butter and place the cabbage rolls into the butter, seam side down. Add the stock and simmer, covered, for about 1 hour. Good with boiled potatoes and green beans. Serves 4.

Oatmeal Sausage
Goetta

Jerry Dorsel
The Dorsel Company
Cincinnati, Ohio

Goetta is a Cincinnati regional specialty. Many of Cincinnati's early settlers came from Germany; some of them were sausage makers. Goetta evolved from a similar dish made in some parts of Germany. It is very similar to oatmeal sausage, except for the shape and final preparation. It is normally a breakfast dish, served with eggs, but is also served as the main dish at lunch or supper.

The Dorsel company of Cincinnati, Ohio, with its current president, Jerry Dorsel, packages "pin-head" oatmeal (the local name for steel-cut oatmeal). The product is seasonal—it is not produced in the warm months—and is marketed only in the tri-state area around Cincinnati. The Dorsel company was started in 1897 by Jerry Dorsel's great-grandfather. "There are probably a thousand variations of the recipe locally, but the Dorsel Company chose to use that of my Grandmother Amelia. It's a recipe with which we all grew up."

8 cups water
3 teaspoons salt
pinch of pepper
2 1/2 cups pin-head or steel cut
   oatmeal*
1 pound beef and 1 pound pork,
   ground together
1 large onion, sliced, and 1 to 4 bay
   leaves, or 2 teaspoons dried
   summer savory
bacon fat

Put the water into a pan; bring to a boil, add the salt, pepper, and oatmeal. Cover, reduce heat to low and cook for 2 hours, stirring often; keep the lid on while cooking over low heat. Add the meat with the onion and the bay leaves, or the savory, to the oatmeal mixture, mixing well. Let cook for 1 hour, stirring often. Pour into bread pans and let cool. May be sliced and frozen for several months in the freezer, or put into the refrigerator, unsliced, where it will keep for days. When ready to use, slice the loaf of *goetta* and put the slices into a pan with a little hot bacon fat. Fry until well browned and serve.

Note: May also be prepared in a slow cooker. Use only 6 cups of water. Heat the water, salt, and pepper on high for 20 minutes, then stir in the oatmeal and cook, covered, for 1 1/2 hours on high. Add the meat and spices, mixing well, cover, and cook for 3 hours on low. Uncover, and if not thick enough, cook a little longer, stirring often. Put into bread pans and proceed as above.

Do not use regular rolled oats, they are too mushy.

Jedes Ding hat sein Ende und die Mettwurst hat zwei.

Everything has an end and a sausage has two.

175

Fish and Poultry

Fish and poultry take a modest, but nevertheless important, place in German cooking. The preparation is often simple: the chicken is frequently coated and roasted or baked; fish is stewed or baked. Because the preparation of these entrées tends to be simple, German-language cookbooks do not contain a lot of recipes for these, thus understating their importance.

Cod in Herbed Sauce
Kabeljau mit Kräutersoße

Hannelore Bozeman

Drawing by Ulfert Wilke, artist from Germany, who emigrated to the U.S. just before World War II.

1 1/2 pounds fresh or frozen
   cod fillets
juice of 1 lemon, divided
salt to taste
4 tablespoons butter
2 or 3 tablespoons flour
1 cup wine
1/3 cup milk
1 tablespoon finely chopped parsley
1 tablespoon finely chopped chives
1 tablespoon finely chopped dill

Wash the fresh cod or thaw the frozen fillets. Pat dry with paper towels. Sprinkle with some of the lemon juice and let stand for 30 minutes. Pat dry again, then add salt to taste. In a large saucepan, melt the butter, add the fish, cover tightly and simmer over very low heat for 15 minutes, or until fork-tender. Remove the fillets to a warm plate and cover. Add the flour, wine and milk to the cooking liquid, stirring constantly. Let cool for 5 minutes. Add the rest of the lemon juice and the finely chopped herbs. Mix well and taste for seasoning. Pour the sauce over the fish and serve. Goes well with boiled potatoes and green beans. Serves 3.

Herring in Sour Cream
Matjes nach Hausfrauenart

4 to 6 herring fillets
1 cup sour cream
1/2 cup plain yogurt
1 small onion, finely chopped
1 small apple, diced
salt and pepper
vinegar to taste

Cut the herring into bite-sized pieces. Combine the sour cream, yogurt, onion, and apple. Add the herring. Season with the salt, pepper, and vinegar to taste. Refrigerate for several hours. Serve with boiled potatoes and green beans.

Blue Trout
Forelle Blau

Hannelore Bozeman

4 fresh trout
2 1/4 cups white-wine vinegar
1/4 cup white wine
2 tablespoons salt
4 cups water or fish broth
lemon slices
chopped parsley to taste

Carefully wash the trout, holding it by the head and handling it as little as possible so as not to lose the sheen that gives the fish its color. Combine the vinegar and the wine and heat to boiling. Put the trout in a shallow pan and pour the vinegar mixture over it. Let stand 5 minutes. (The trout should turn blue.) Drain, reserving the liquid. Bring the water or fish broth and salt to a boil, add the reserved liquid, then carefully add the trout. Add more water to cover the trout, if needed. Simmer for 10 or 15 minutes. The trout is done when the fins can be pulled out easily. Drain and place on a hot serving platter. Garnish with the lemon slices and sprinkle with the parsley. Serve with salted potatoes and fresh or melted butter. Serves 4. **Note:** If you use frozen trout, thaw for about an hour; increase the cooking time by another 5 to 10 minutes.

Fishing From F. H. Ehmcke: Trade Symbols by German Designers, *1907.*

Chicken Fricassee
Hühnerfrikassee

Hannelore Bozeman

1 stewing chicken, cut up
salt and pepper to taste, divided
3 teaspoons lemon juice, divided
6 tablespoons butter, divided
2 cups chicken stock
1 carrot, cut into small pieces
1 bay leaf
5 whole cloves
3/4 cup finely chopped mushrooms
1/4 cup white wine
1/4 cup cream
2 egg yolks

Wash the chicken pieces, rub with some of the salt, pepper, and 2 teaspoons lemon juice. Boil in salted water for 5 minutes, then remove; reserve stock, and pat dry with paper towels. In a large saucepan, melt 2 tablespoons butter and fry the chicken pieces lightly. Add the chicken stock, carrot, and spices; cover and simmer for 1 1/2 hours, or until the chicken is tender. Skim off the froth and remove the chicken pieces, reserving the stock. Discard the bay leaf and also the cloves, if desired. Remove the skin and the bones and cut the chicken into bite-sized pieces. In a large frying pan, melt the remaining butter; add 1 cup of the chicken stock and stir until thickened. Add the mushrooms, season with additional salt and pepper, the remaining lemon juice, and the wine. Heat but do not boil. Add the cream. Beat in yolks and cook until thickened. Add the chicken pieces and heat through. Serve with rice and boiled white asparagus.

177

Roast Goose with Apples, Raisins, and Nuts

Gänsebraten mit Äpfeln,
Rosinen und Nüssen

Traditionally, roast goose has been to a German Christmas what turkey is to the American holiday. German housewives often save the drippings from the roast and let them congeal. This is called Gänseschmalz. *It keeps in the refrigerator for weeks and is used as a substitute for butter in cooking, or as a sandwich spread.*

1 8- to 10-pound young goose
goose gizzard and heart
3/4 cup seedless raisins
2 cups boiling water
3 tablespoons butter
1 cup finely chopped onion
1 goose liver
4 cups soft white bread crumbs,
    shredded with a fork
3 apples, peeled, cored, and coarsely
    chopped
1/2 cup coarsely chopped blanched
    almonds
1/3 cup finely chopped parsley
1 teaspoon dried marjoram
1 teaspoon sage
salt and pepper to taste

Wash the goose; pat dry inside and out with paper towels.

To make the stuffing, combine the goose gizzard and the heart in a small saucepan with enough water to cover completely. Bring to a boil over high heat, then simmer uncovered for 40 minutes, or until fork-tender. Meanwhile place the raisins in a bowl, pour the boiling water over them and let them soak for 20 minutes or until plump. Drain the gizzard and heart, chop finely, and place in a large mixing bowl. Drain and add the raisins. In a heavy skillet, melt the butter, then add the onion and cook until it is soft, about 5 minutes, stirring frequently. Chop the goose liver finely, add to the onion, and cook for another 2 or 3 minutes, until the liver is light brown, stirring constantly. Transfer the mixture from the skillet to the mixing bowl and add the bread crumbs, apples, nuts, parsley, marjoram, sage, salt and pepper. Mix together well and taste for seasoning.

Preheat the oven to 325°. Lightly salt and pepper the cavity of the goose and fill it loosely with the stuffing. Close the opening with skewers; fasten the neck skin to the back of the goose with a skewer and truss the bird. For a crisper skin, prick the surface around the thighs, the back, and the lower part of the breast with the tip of a small, sharp knife. Place the goose, breast side up, on a rack set in a large, shallow roasting pan, and roast, uncovered, in the center of the oven for 3 to 3 1/2 hours, or about 20 minutes per pound. As the fat accumulates in the pan, draw it off with a bulb baster or large kitchen spoon and save for *Gänseschmalz,* if you like. It is not necessary to baste the goose. To test for doneness, prick the thigh of the bird with a fork; if the juice that runs out is still tinged with pink, roast the goose another 5 to 10 minutes. For easier carving, let the goose sit in the turned-off oven with the door ajar for about 15 minutes. Transfer to a large, heated platter, and remove the string and the skewers. Serve with red cabbage and dumplings. Serves 6 to 8.

The Bethel Commune, a national historic site in Bethel, Missouri.
Bethel celebrates its heritage with traditional and seasonal events.
—*From* The Communistic Societies of the United States, *Nordhoff, 1875.*

Duck Breast à la Ratzsch
Entenbrust

John Poulos
Karl Ratzsch's Restaurant
Franklin, Wisconsin

4 10-ounce pieces raw duck breast,
   boneless
pinch of salt
pinch of black pepper
1 small clove garlic, minced
1/2 to 2/3 cup flour, divided
2 ounces butter
2 tablespoons diced onion
1 12-ounce can red, tart cherries
2 cups chicken stock
1 teaspoon Worcestershire sauce
2 tablespoons honey
1/3 cup brown sugar, or to taste
1/2 cup Burgundy wine
seasoning salt to taste, optional
sliced, toasted almonds

Season the duck breasts with the salt, pepper, and the minced garlic, then dredge in a little flour. In a sauté pan melt the butter, then brown the duck breasts on both sides in the butter. Add the onion, cherries, chicken stock, Worcestershire sauce, honey, brown sugar, and Burgundy wine, in that order. Preheat the oven to 350° and cook for 1 hour or until done.

Remove the duck breasts to a clean pan and keep warm. Skim the fat from the pan into another saucepan and add the remaining flour to make a roux. Simmer on low heat until it bubbles, then add remaining liquid. Blend well with a wire whisk until it comes to a simmer; add the seasoning salt or more brown sugar to suit taste. To serve, slice and top with the sauce and the toasted almonds.
Note: This dish may be garnished with fresh fruit and served with wild rice.

Vegetables and Side Dishes

Cabbage

Kohl is a household word in West Germany, a name shared by one of the nation's chancellors (Helmut Kohl) and by one of its favorite foods. *Kohl*, or cabbage, is a basic part of the German diet available in great variety: *Weißkohl* (white cabbage), *Rotkohl* (red cabbage), *Grünkohl* (kale), *Blumenkohl* (cauliflower), *Rosenkohl* (Brussels sprouts), *Wirsing* (savoy cabbage), and *Kohlrabi*. Cabbage is planted in roughly one-third of the total German vegetable fields.

Kale is just about the only kind of cabbage not popular throughout the country; its appeal is limited to northern Germany. The unchallenged king of cabbage is the white variety, used to make many of the hearty German stews and that national specialty, sauerkraut. Most sauerkraut is made in huge factories. White cabbage is the primary crop grown on farms around Stuttgart in southern Germany. (Filderstadt, a suburb of Stuttgart, is known as the cabbage capital of the country.) Many families in this area still make sauerkraut out of *Spitzkraut* themselves, shredding the tall, pointed variety of white cabbage with a gigantic grater. The shredded cabbage is layered alternately with salt in big wooden barrels. After adding each layer, the cabbage is stomped down with a wooden stamper (or with bare feet, depending upon the size of the barrel). When the barrel is full, the cabbage is covered with a wooden lid. This lid is weighted to force the brine to the top of the barrel. It is then allowed to stand until the cabbage has fermented, creating sauerkraut.   —*Lynn Hattery-Beyer*

Cabbage and Onions
Knabrus
This is a Pennsylvania Dutch recipe.

6 tablespoons butter, divided
1 head cabbage, finely shredded
3 sliced onions
1/2 cup water
salt and pepper to taste

Generously grease a saucepan or Dutch oven with 3 tablespoons of butter. Alternate layers of the cabbage and the onions in the pan. Add the water. Cover and set over low heat to steam until the cabbage is tender. Dot with the remaining butter and season to taste with the salt and pepper. Serve hot. Serves 6.

Sauerkraut with Caraway Seeds
Sauerkraut mit Kümmel

The Barn Restaurant, Amana, Iowa

2 pounds sauerkraut, drained
4 tablespoons sugar
1/2 cup chopped apples
1 tablespoon caraway seeds
4 tablespoons unsalted butter
1/2 cup water
1 tablespoon flour, optional

Combine sauerkraut, sugar, apples, caraway seeds, and butter. Add water, cover and simmer for 2 hours. If mixture has too much liquid, stir in flour and cook 10 additional minutes. Serves 8.

Sauerkraut

From "It's Tasting Good" at Home
in New Ulm, Minnesota

1 onion, chopped
2 tablespoons oil
1 1/2 pounds sauerkraut, drained
1 apple
2 cups (or more) of hot beef broth
ham bone or any small piece of pork
1/2 teaspoon caraway seeds, optional
6 slices bacon, chopped
1 1/2 tablespoons flour

In a saucepan, sauté the onion in the oil until the onion is light yellow and glossy. Loosen the sauerkraut with a fork and add it to the pan. Peel the apple, if desired; core and cut into small pieces; add to the sauerkraut together with the hot broth. Submerge the ham or pork in the kraut and add the caraway seed, if used. Cover and simmer gently a few hours (half a day, or longer). Add more broth if necessary, and stir occasionally with a wooden spoon. Just before serving, brown the bacon in a frying pan; drain off most of the grease. Dust the bacon with the flour and stir into the kraut to thicken.

Note: Pennsylvania Germans believed pork and sauerkraut should be eaten on New Year's Day in order to ensure health and prosperity in the coming year.

> *"America cultivates best which Germany brought forth."*
>
> —Benjamin Franklin
> 1706–1790

Braised Sauerkraut
Geschmortes Sauerkraut

3 slices smoked bacon
1 chopped onion
3 cups sauerkraut
2 medium-sized apples, peeled
  and chopped
6 to 8 juniper berries, optional
1 teaspoon sugar, optional
2 bay leaves
1 or more smoked ham hocks,
  optional
1 to 1 1/2 cups white wine,
  preferably Riesling
1 cup chicken stock
1 large potato, peeled and grated
salt and freshly ground pepper
  to taste

In a large skillet cook the bacon until the fat is transparent, then add the onion and cook until it is soft and glossy. Wash the sauerkraut carefully and drain. Add it to the skillet, along with the apples, the juniper berries, and the sugar, if used. Add the bay leaves, ham hocks, 1 cup wine, and the stock. Cover and simmer for 1 hour. Add the potato and continue simmering for 30 to 40 minutes. Stir occasionally and add more wine if needed. Season with the salt and pepper as desired. Serve hot. Serves 4 to 6.

Note: Braised sauerkraut tastes particularly good with beef sandwiches. This sauerkraut will actually taste better with reheating, so you may want to make a double batch.

Sweet-Sour Red Cabbage
Süßsauer Rotkohl

Connie Zuber
Bill Zuber's Restaurant
Homestead, Amana Colonies, Iowa

Bill Zuber's Restaurant was originally built as the Homestead Hotel in 1862. In 1949 Bill and Connie Zuber purchased the hotel. The red cabbage and potato dumpling recipes were used regularly in the old Amana community kitchens.

4 cups shredded red cabbage
2 medium-sized apples, sliced
1 cup water
4 tablespoons vinegar
4 tablespoons sugar
1 tablespoon butter
1/2 teaspoon salt
1/4 teaspoon pepper

Cook the cabbage and the apples in the water until tender, about 15 to 20 minutes. Add the vinegar, sugar, butter, salt and pepper, and cook a few minutes more. Reheats well. Best with roast chicken or pork.

Savoy Cabbage
Wirsing

1 head savoy cabbage,
  1 to 1 1/2 pounds
2 tablespoons butter
8 slices bacon, diced
1/2 teaspoon salt
1/2 teaspoon paprika
1/4 teaspoon curry
3/4 cup sour cream

Cut the cabbage into quarters; cut out and discard the core. Wash thoroughly. Cook in salted water over low heat for 20 minutes. Drain. Chop coarsely or shred. In a large skillet melt the butter and sauté the bacon until golden brown. Add the chopped cabbage, stirring well. Add the spices and cook for 2 to 3 minutes, until well-heated. Just before removing from the heat, stir in the sour cream. Serves 4. Good with poultry and boiled potatoes.

"Bluebill Decoys and Mallard Carvings"
Milton Geyer, Green Bay, Wisconsin

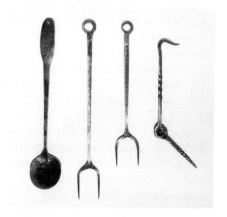

"Cooking Utensils,
Hook and Eye Fastener"
Robert C. Becker, Rice Lake, Wisconsin

The folk art above is from the book, From Hardanger to Harleys: A Survey of Wisconsin Folk Art, *a catalog of the 1987 exhibition at the John Michael Kohler Arts Center, Sheboygan, Wisconsin.*

Sign at Rosedale Hutterite Commune near Mitchell, South Dakota.

Green Beans with Bacon
Grüne Bohnen mit Speck

Hannelore Bozeman

4 slices bacon
1/4 cup onion, chopped finely
1 pound fresh green beans, cut
  into 1-inch pieces
1 cup hot water or beef bouillon
2 tablespoons chopped, dried savory
  leaf, or about 10 whole, dried
  savory leaves, tied
salt to taste
4 tablespoons butter, melted,
  (optional)

Over medium heat, cook the bacon until crisp. Remove, crumble, and set aside. Add the chopped onion to the bacon grease and cook until yellow and glossy, about 3 minutes. Add the beans, water or bouillon, savory, and salt; mix. Cover and simmer until done, about 15 to 25 minutes. Drain the water, remove the savory leaves if in a bundle, and put the beans in a serving dish. Pour the melted butter over the beans, if desired, and sprinkle with the crumbled bacon.

Baked Cauliflower
Blumenkohlauflauf

Hannelore Bozeman

1 medium-sized head cauliflower,
  about 2 pounds
8 ounces uncooked elbow macaroni
6 ounces cooked ham, cubed
4 tablespoons softened butter
  or margarine, divided
3 eggs
1/3 cup milk
salt and pepper to taste
grated cheese to taste

Trim off the leaves and the core of the cauliflower and remove any discolored parts. Place the cauliflower in a large pan filled with salted water and soak for 10 minutes, then drain. Divide the cauliflower head into flowerets and boil in 1/2 cup of water until tender, about 10 to 15 minutes. Meanwhile, boil the macaroni according to package directions, about 10 to 12 minutes, until just tender. Drain.

Preheat the oven to 350°. Grease the bottom and sides of a casserole dish with some of the butter or margarine. Layer the cauliflower, cooked macaroni, and cubed ham; repeat once or twice, finishing with a layer of the cauliflower. In a small mixing bowl, beat the eggs and the milk; season to taste. Pour the egg mixture over the top cauliflower layer and sprinkle with the grated cheese. Dot with the remaining butter and bake for 30 to 40 minutes. Serves 4.

A hearth of one's own is
worth its weight in gold.

183

Brussels Sprouts in Cheese Sauce
Rosenkohl mit Käsesoße

2 pounds Brussels sprouts
3 tablespoons butter
3 tablespoons flour
3/4 cup milk
1/2 teaspoon salt
1/2 teaspoon ground nutmeg
1/2 cup shredded semi-hard cheese,
  preferably *Emmenthaler*

Remove the outer leaves from the Brussels sprouts. Cut off the stems and slash the ends in a crisscross fashion to ensure even cooking. Fill a large saucepan with 1 inch of water and simmer the Brussels sprouts uncovered until tender but still crisp, about 10 minutes. Drain and reserve the cooking liquid. Place the Brussels sprouts in a casserole dish. Preheat the oven to 400°. In a saucepan, melt the butter and stir in the flour. Cook for 3 minutes, stirring constantly. Gradually stir in the milk and some of the reserved cooking liquid until a thick consistency is reached. Season with the salt and nutmeg. Add the cheese gradually, stirring over low heat until the cheese is melted and the sauce has thickened. Pour the sauce evenly over the Brussels sprouts and bake for 10 minutes, until the sauce is lightly browned. Serve immediately. Serves 4.

Love your neighbor,
but don't pull down
the fence.

Glazed Turnips
Teltower Rübchen

2 pounds small turnips
3 tablespoons butter
1 tablespoon sugar
2 tablespoons flour
salt and pepper
1/4 teaspoon paprika

Cut the tops off the turnips and scrape them clean. Boil for 10 to 15 minutes in salted water. Drain and reserve the cooking liquid. In the same pan, melt the butter and add the sugar, stirring until brown. Add the turnips, stirring until they are covered with the butter mixture. Sprinkle the flour over the turnips. Add the reserved cooking liquid and more water, if necessary. Cover and simmer for about 30 minutes, or until tender. Season with the salt, pepper, and paprika. Good with lamb or pork roasts. Serves 6.

Onion Cake
Zwiebelkuchen

*Carol Schuerer Zuber
East Amana, Iowa*

6 large onions, slivered
1 tablespoon butter
salt and pepper to taste
1 egg, beaten
1-pound package frozen bread dough
1/2 pound bacon, cooked
  and crumbled

Sauté the onion in the butter until just limp. Season with salt and pepper. Cool and mix in the egg. Press the bread dough into the bottom of a 9-inch square baking dish. Pour the onion mixture over the dough and sprinkle with bacon. Bake at 400° for 30 minutes. Serve warm. Serves 6.

The Importance of Potatoes

The potato became popular in Germany long after it had been established in other European cultures. The first attempt to grow potatoes in Germany was in 1744. Frederick II the Great (1712-1786) of Prussia was convinced the potato could solve many problems (famine, poverty, unrest), and he tried to get the peasants to plant them. True to the German proverb *"Was der Bauer nicht kennt, frißt er nicht"* (If a farmer doesn't know what it is, he won't eat it), the peasants resisted, believing the potato to be poisonous. Not one to be put off, Frederick distributed free seed potatoes to the reluctant peasants and decreed that they had to plant them. He enforced his edict by posting soldiers in the fields.

The pure, unadulterated potato is king in the North, but dumplings reign in Bavaria. Dumplings can be made of cooked potatoes (with or without eggs), raw potatoes, or of both cooked and raw potatoes. Tricks for making them include using cheesecloth to squeeze moisture out of raw potatoes, using only semolina flour or potato starch to bind them, and using special ricers to press cooked potatoes. When my daughter, Inga, got to choose her birthday meal, all she wanted was mashed potatoes. —*Lynn Hattery-Beyer*

In Germany, potatoes (*Kartoffeln*) are probably the most important side dish. When I was growing up, my mother would serve them with almost any meat and vegetable dish. Rice, noodles, and similar starchy side dishes seem to be a more recent introduction. The most common way to prepare potatoes is as *Salzkartoffeln,* or boiled potatoes. The helpings tend to be larger than in America, but even so my mother often peeled a couple of extra potatoes, "just to make sure we have enough," then fried the leftover potatoes as *Bratkartoffeln*. A third common way to prepare potatoes is to mash them. New potatoes, especially, are often boiled in their skins and peeled before serving; that's called *Pellkartoffeln*. Potato skins are never eaten. Mashed potatoes are called *Kartoffelpüree* and are prepared the same way as in the United States; they are especially popular with children. —*Hannelore Bozeman*

Potato Ring
Kartoffelring

1 1/2 pounds potatoes
1/4 cup butter
3 eggs, separated
1 teaspoon salt
1 teaspoon ground nutmeg

Scrub and peel potatoes; boil until tender. Drain. Rub through a sieve or pureé while hot. Set aside to cool. Cream butter in a bowl; gradually blend in egg yolks. Stir in the cooled potatoes, salt, and nutmeg. Beat egg whites until stiff and fold into potato mixture. Put in greased tube pan and bake at 325° for 30 to 40 minutes. Reverse pan onto serving tray to remove ring. Center of ring may be filled with stew or steamed vegetables.

Potato Pancakes with Rosy Applesauce
Kartoffelpuffer mit rosa Apfelmus

Carol Schuerer Zuber
Amana Barn Restaurant
Amana, Iowa

Rosy Applesauce:
3 pounds McIntosh apples or
    other tart red apples
1/2 cup cold water
3/4 cup sugar

Potato Pancakes:
3 large potatoes, preferably Idaho,
    about 2 pounds
1 medium-sized onion
2 eggs
2 tablespoons flour
3/4 teaspoon salt
dash nutmeg
dash pepper
salad oil for frying

Artist Gustavus Grunewald drew this lithograph of the Moravian church and the Inspector's House in Salem, in the mid-1800s. The buildings still stand on the square in Old Salem, Winston-Salem, North Carolina.

Rosy applesauce: Wash the apples; drain well. Cut into quarters and core, but do not peel. In a 3-quart saucepan, combine the apples with the water. Bring to a boil, reduce the heat and simmer, covered, until very soft, about 15 minutes. Using a medium bowl, put the apples and the cooking liquid through a food mill, or press the apples through a colander, in order to remove the skins. (Unpeeled apples will impart a faint pink tint to the applesauce, and the peel also adds flavor.) Add the sugar; return to the same saucepan. Stir over medium heat until the sugar is dissolved, about 5 minutes. Turn into a serving bowl. Serve slightly warm, or refrigerate covered.

Potato pancakes: Wash and pare the potatoes. Grate the potatoes on a coarse grater into a large bowl filled with ice water. (This keeps the grated potatoes from turning brown.) Let stand for 15 minutes. Grate the onion; measure 1/2 cup. In a medium bowl beat the eggs with a wire whisk. Add the grated onion, flour, salt, nutmeg, and pepper. Mix well. Drain the potatoes; pat dry with a clean dish towel. Measure about 4 cups. Add to the egg mixture and mix well. In a large, heavy skillet slowly heat the oil, 1/8 inch deep, until very hot but not smoking. For each pancake drop about 1/4 cup of the potato mixture into the hot fat. Do not crowd in the skillet (make two or three at a time). With a spatula, flatten the pancakes against the bottom of the skillet to make each of them about 4 inches in diameter. Fry 2 or 3 minutes on each side, or until crisp and golden brown in color. Drain well on paper towels. Serve hot with applesauce or sour cream. Makes about 12 pancakes.

186

Potato Dumplings
Kartoffelklöße

Reingard Jordan
Iowa City, Iowa

Reingard is involved with the Intercultural Student Exchange, helping American students to visit Germany, France, and Spain, and European students to visit America. Reingard came to America from East Germany in 1959. She teaches German to elementary school students in an extracurricular program.

1 pound cooked potatoes
1 pound raw potatoes
1 tablespoon butter
1 teaspoon salt, or to taste
1 tablespoon flour

Peel cooked potatoes and grate. Peel and grate raw potatoes. Press grated raw potatoes through cheesecloth, a strainer or colander to remove as much liquid as possible. Mix all ingredients together and let stand about 15 minutes. Form into balls, about the size of a small egg. Drop each ball carefully into a large pot of boiling salted water. Cover pot, reduce heat and simmer 20 minutes. Don't let water boil. Remove dumplings with a slotted spoon. Makes about 10. Best served with pork or poultry.

"Heaven and Earth"
Himmel und Erde

Hannelore Bozeman says, "My mother used to serve a simple version of this dish, saying that it came from Silesia, where my father's family originated. Essentially, it consisted of chilled applesauce— the heavenly part—and hot mashed potatoes—the earthly component. I loved it as a child, especially for the applesauce; it seemed like having dessert."

1 1/3 cups water
1/2 teaspoon salt
3 1/2 pounds potatoes, peeled
    and diced
3 apples, peeled and quartered
1 teaspoon salt
1 tablespoon sugar
1 tablespoon vinegar
1/4 pound bacon, diced
2 onions, sliced

Bring the water and salt to a boil in a stockpot. Add the potatoes and boil until tender. Add the apples, return to a boil and cook until tender. Season with the salt, sugar, and vinegar. Fry the bacon and onion slices until brown. Pour over the potatoes and apples and serve.

Pastries and Desserts

Several world-famous cake recipes have originated in Germany—the best known is probably the Black Forest Cherry Cake, a delightful layered composition of spongy chocolate cake, cherries, and whipped cream. Tortes layered with whipped cream are just one of many different kinds of cakes made in Germany. Another favorite is the *Obstkuchen*, thin, round cakes piled high with seasonal fresh fruit and covered with a thin layer of gelatin. These cakes can be made in no time and taste delicious when served with whipped cream and coffee. Heavier cakes, often made with more ground nuts and grated chocolate than flour, are another favorite. All these cakes are very rich but not necessarily as sweet as American cakes. Icings and frostings are not made with as much powdered sugar and tend to be more like glazes.

—*Lynn Hattery-Beyer*

German Fruit Torte
Obstkuchen
Hannelore Bozeman

Obstkuchen is possibly the most common pastry in Germany, considering the large number of variations. It is to Germany what pies are to America. Bakeries and grocery stores carry the baked pastry used to assemble the Obstkuchen. *On occasion this pastry is for sale in American supermarkets. Look for the word* Tortenboden *(literally, cake bottom) on the package. It is the equivalent of a pie shell.*

Pastry:
2 cups flour, sifted
1 teaspoon baking powder
1/4 cup sugar
1/2 cup butter, softened
1 egg, beaten
1 to 2 tablespoons milk
Topping:
4 to 5 cups fresh or canned tart red
    cherries, pitted and drained
1 package glazing mix, or 1 cup
    sweetened fruit juice (from
    the cans) plus 2 tablespoons
    cornstarch
1 cup whipping cream, whipped

Pastry: Preheat the oven to 400°. Sift the flour, baking powder, and sugar together. Cut in the butter until the mixture resembles cornmeal. Add the beaten egg and milk. Mix together until the mixture is firm like a pie dough. Grease and flour a 10-inch springform pan. Distribute the dough evenly in the pan, using your fingers and the palm of your hand, and create a slightly raised edge. Bake for 20 to 25 minutes, or until golden brown. Let cool slightly and remove from the springform pan. Cool completely before assembling.

Topping: Cover the top of the cake with the cherries. Prepare the glaze according to package directions, or heat the fruit juice and the cornstarch in a small saucepan, stirring constantly. Cook over medium heat until thickened and clear. Pour the warm glaze evenly over the cherries, making sure all the fruit is covered. Serve the cooled cake with whipped cream.

Black Forest Cherry Cake
Schwarzwälder Kirschtorte

Irma Parrott
Iowa City, Iowa

1 4-ounce package German's
   sweet chocolate
1/2 cup boiling water
1 cup butter or margarine
2 cups sugar
4 egg yolks
1 teaspoon vanilla
2 1/4 cups flour
1 teaspoon baking soda
1/2 teaspoon salt
1 cup buttermilk
4 egg whites, beaten stiff

Filling:
2 16-ounce cans pitted tart red
   cherries, drained
1/2 cup kirsch (cherry brandy),
   divided
2 cups whipping cream
1/2 cup powdered sugar

Assembly:
3 ounces semisweet chocolate,
   finely grated
16 maraschino cherries, drained

In a small saucepan, melt the chocolate in the boiling water. Cool. Cream the butter and the sugar until fluffy. Add the egg yolks, one at a time, beating well after each. Blend in the vanilla and the melted chocolate. Sift the flour with the baking soda and salt; add alternately with the buttermilk to the chocolate mixture, beating after each addition until smooth. Fold in the beaten egg whites. Pour the batter into 3 9-inch layer pans lined with waxed paper on the bottom. Bake at 350° for 30 to 35 minutes. Cool.

Filling: Drain the cherries and cut each in half. Combine the cherries and 1/3 cup kirsch. Let the cherries soak while baking the cake, then drain, reserving the kirsch. With a fork, prick the top of each cooled cake layer and spoon the reserved kirsch over the cake layers. Whip the cream until almost stiff, add the powdered sugar and the remaining kirsch, and continue whipping until stiff. Place one cake layer on a cake plate, spread with 1/4 of the whipped cream and top with half of the drained cherries. Repeat, then top with the third layer.

Assembly: Frost the side of the cake with half of the remaining whipped cream. Using your hand, gently press the grated chocolate into the cream. Garnish the top of the cake with the remaining whipped cream and place the maraschino cherries in a circle around the top of the cake. Keep refrigerated but do not cover. Serves 12 to 16.

Hannelore Bozeman says: "For a variation, you may use raspberries in lieu of the cherries. I use about 3 cups of frozen raspberries from my summer garden. Do not thaw the raspberries completely when assembling the cake; the juice will enhance the flavor of the cake. Do not use frozen or thawed raspberries for garnish. Sprinkle the cake with additional chocolate."

Bundt Cake
Napfkuchen

Karin Gottier

This Napfkuchen *is Karin Gottier's Aunt Helen Schapperer's recipe. When Karin first came to America after World War II, she lived with her Aunt Helen in Ellington, Connecticut.*

Cake:
2 1/2 cups flour
3 teaspoons baking powder
salt to taste
1 4-ounce stick plus 2 tablespoons
    softened margarine
2 eggs
1 1/2 cups sugar
1/2 cup lukewarm milk
1 1/2 cups chopped dried fruit to
    taste, i.e. nuts, candied peel,
    apples, figs, currants, raisins

Icing:
1 1/2 cups powdered sugar
1 1/2 tablespoons lemon juice

Cake:
Mix together the flour, baking powder, and salt. Set aside. Beat together the softened margarine, eggs, sugar and warm milk. Mix dry ingredients into liquid mixture; stir in chopped dried fruit. Pour into greased Bundt pan and bake at 400° for 1 hour. Allow to cool for about 5 minutes before removing from pan.

Icing: Mix powdered sugar and lemon juice until smooth. Drizzle over the warm cake, allowing icing to run down the sides. Decorate with pieces of candied fruit, if desired.

Note: Sprinkle small amount of flour over dried fruit to coat lightly before chopping.

The Schwibbogen *below is a famous design that shows the major industries of the Ore Mountain region in Germany, namely the miners with their insignia, the woodcarver making toys and nutcrackers, and the lady making bobbin lace, which was an important home industry. To either side of the* Schwibbogen *are miners and angels holding candles. At Christmas it was customary to place figures of miners and angels like these in the window to indicate the number of boys and girls in a home. Although the* Schwibbogen *functioned originally as a source of light, its use today is ornamental. Depending on the subject depicted, it is now used at Christmas time or all year round.*

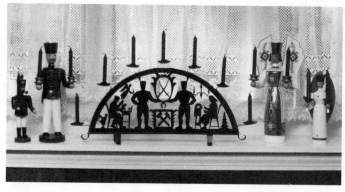

Wheat Berry Pudding
Weizenpudding

The Kansas Wheat Commission
Manhattan, Kansas

3/4 cup cooked wheat berries
3/4 cup milk
3/4 cup seedless raisins
1 egg, separated
2 tablespoons honey
1 teaspoon vanilla
1/4 teaspoon cinnamon
1/8 teaspoon salt

In a 2-quart saucepan, combine cooked wheat, milk, and raisins. In a small bowl, blend together egg yolk, honey, vanilla, cinnamon, and salt. Add to wheat mixture. Cook over medium heat, stirring constantly until mixture boils. Reduce heat and cook, stirring constantly until mixture is thick and creamy, about 5 minutes. Remove from heat and cool pan in ice water for 5 to 10 minutes. Beat egg white until stiff peaks form. Fold into wheat mixture. Spoon into dessert dishes and chill. Serves 4.

Below: The Warkentin House, a Victorian House Museum in Newton, Kansas. With the help of Bernhard Warkentin, 5,000 Mennonites brought Turkey Red, hard winter wheat, to Kansas during the years of 1878–1884. Warkentin's father, a miller, was instrumental in making the Ukraine the "Breadbasket" of Russia.

Frankfurt Tube Cake
Frankfurter Kranz

Cake:
2/3 cup butter
3/4 cup sugar
5 eggs
1 1/4 cups flour
3/4 cup corn meal
1 teaspoon baking powder
2 tablespoons rum
1 tablespoon lemon juice

Icing:
1 cup plus 2 tablespoons butter
2 cups powdered sugar
3 egg yolks
1 teaspoon vanilla extract

Topping:
2 tablespoons butter
1/2 cup chopped almonds
2 tablespoons sugar

Cake: Cream the butter in a large mixing bowl. Add the sugar and the eggs. Beat until light. Stir in the flour, corn meal, baking powder, rum, and lemon juice until well blended. Grease and flour a 10-inch tube pan. Pour the batter in and bake at 350° for 45 minutes. Cool slightly before removing from the pan.

Icing: Cream the butter and blend in the remaining ingredients until creamy.

Topping: Brown the almonds in the butter and sugar until golden. To assemble, slice the cake in half crosswise. Spread 1/3 of the icing on the bottom layer and cover with the top layer. Ice the top and sides of the cake with the remaining icing and sprinkle with the browned almonds.

Bavarian Apple Cake
Bayrischer Apfelkuchen

Irma Parrott

Crust:
1/2 cup softened butter or margarine
1/2 cup sugar
1/4 teaspoon vanilla
1 cup flour

Filling:
1 8-ounce package cream cheese,
    softened
1/4 cup sugar
1 egg
1/2 teaspoon vanilla

Topping:
4 cups apples, peeled and sliced
1/2 teaspoon vanilla
cinnamon to taste
1/2 cup sugar
1/2 cup chopped nuts

Crust: Cream the butter and sugar in a small bowl; stir in the vanilla. Add the flour and mix well. Spread on the bottom and 2 inches up the sides of a 9-inch springform pan.

Filling: Combine the cream cheese and sugar; add the egg and the vanilla, mixing well. Spread the cream cheese filling evenly over the pastry.

Topping: Place the sliced apples into a large bowl and add the vanilla. In a small bowl, combine the cinnamon with the sugar and mix well. Sprinkle the apples with the cinnamon-and-sugar mixture and stir to coat.

Spoon the apple topping over the filling and sprinkle with the chopped nuts. Bake at 450° for 10 minutes, or until the apples are tender. Reduce the temperature to 400°, and continue baking another 25 minutes. Cool before removing from the pan. Serves 8 to 10.

Heavenly Food
Himmelfutter

Lucille Mauermann

2 eggs
1 cup sugar
1 heaping tablespoon flour
1 teaspoon baking powder
1/2 pound dates, chopped
1/2 pound nuts, chopped
5 oranges
5 bananas
sugar to taste

Beat eggs and sugar together. Add flour and baking powder; mix well. Mix in dates and nuts. Pour into a 9x13-inch pan and bake at 350° for 35 to 40 minutes. Cool and store in the refrigerator. Slice oranges and bananas; add sugar to taste. Set aside for 1 hour. To serve, crumble the torte pastry and combine with the fruit mixture. Serves 14.

Fruit

From Graphic Trade Symbols by German Designers, *by F. H. Ehmcke: 1907.*

Funnel Cakes
Drechter Kucha

*Pennsylvania Dutch Folk Culture
Society, Lenhartsville, Pennsylvania*

*The Pennsylvania Dutch Folk Culture
Society fosters the preservation of the
culture, home life, dialect, and ancestry of
the Pennsylvania German people. The
society's museum complex, located in
Lenhartsville includes an authentic one-
room schoolhouse, the Dutch Corner
(lodge building and hotel with a restaurant and gift shop), a Colonial-era log
house, barn with antique farm equipment,
a turn-of-the-century house of fashions
and museum, and a genealogical and folklore library. They also sponsor an annual
"Harvest Jubilee," held over the Labor
Day weekend.*

3 eggs
1 quart milk
3 teaspoons baking powder
flour
vegetable oil
powdered sugar

Combine eggs, milk, and baking
powder in a bowl. Add enough flour
so batter will run through a funnel. If
it is too thick and will not flow well,
add more milk. If it runs too fast, add
more flour. Pour enough oil in a frying pan to cover the bottom. Heat oil
and test temperature: dip a fork into
the batter and then hold it in the hot
oil; if it sizzles, the oil is hot enough.
Pour a thin stream of batter into the
oil. Use a spiral motion, beginning in
the middle and moving out. Fry until
brown on one side, then flip the cake
over and brown the other side. Remove and sprinkle with powdered
sugar. Best when eaten immediately.

Note: Cover bottom opening of funnel with finger when filling; remove
finger to release batter into hot oil.
Try other shapes: initials, numbers,
seasonal, etc.

Apple Fritters
Apfel-Küchelchen

*Carol Schuerer Zuber
The Barn Restaurant,
Amana, Iowa*

1/2 cup flour
2 tablespoons sugar
1/4 teaspoon salt
2 eggs, separated
6 tablespoons milk
4 apples, peeled and cored
oil for deep frying

Pudding Sauce:
2 cups milk, divided
3 tablespoons flour
1 egg, beaten
1/2 cup sugar
pinch salt

Sift together dry ingredients. Beat
together egg yolks and milk; add to
flour mixture. Beat egg whites until
stiff and fold into the first mixture.
Cut each apple into 6 rings and dip
each ring into the batter, then deep fry
until golden brown. Serve with pudding sauce. Serves 6.

Pudding Sauce: In the top of a double
boiler, blend 1/4 cup milk, flour, egg,
sugar, and salt. Scald remaining milk,
then add to flour mixture. Cook in
double boiler over simmering water
for 15 minutes or until thickened.

Grape Tapioca Pudding with Vanilla Sauce

Florence Schuerer
Brick Haus Restaurant
Amana, Iowa

1 1/2 cups grape juice
1 cup water
3 tablespoons quick tapioca
1/4 cup sugar

Vanilla Sauce:
1 egg
1/2 cup sugar
2 cups milk
1 teaspoon vanilla
1 tablespoon cornstarch

For the pudding, combine the fruit juice and water, and heat. Add the tapioca and sugar. Boil for 3 minutes. Chill in a 9x5-inch loaf pan. Cut into squares to serve.

Vanilla Sauce: Beat the egg and sugar. Add the milk, vanilla, and cornstarch. Cook for 5 minutes. Chill until cold. Serve on top of the Grape Tapioca Pudding.

OLD GERMAN LOVE SONG
(THIRTEENTH CENTURY)
Since creation I was thine;
Now forever thou art mine.
I have shut thee fast
In my heart at last.
I have dropped the key
In an unknown sea.
Forever must thou my prisoner be!

Semolina Pudding
Grießbrei

Hannelore Bozeman

3 cups milk
pinch of salt
4 to 5 tablespoons sugar
1/2 cup semolina
grated lemon peel to taste
2 tablespoons raisins, optional

Heat the milk with the salt and the sugar. When the milk is about to boil, remove the saucepan from the heat and slowly stir in the semolina. Return to the heat and cook gently until done, about 10 minutes. Remove from the heat and stir in the lemon peel and the raisins, if used. Serve warm or chilled, topped with raspberry syrup or with stewed fruit.

Bread Pudding
Brotpudding

Florence Schuerer

1 loaf of bread (3 days old)
24 eggs
3 cups sugar
12 cups cold milk
butter to taste

Break the bread into bite-sized pieces. Put into a 12x18x2-inch pan. Beat the eggs and sugar lightly, add the cold milk and pour over the bread. Do not heat the milk before mixing. Dot with the butter and bake in a 375° oven for about 1 hour, until the custard is set. Cut into squares. Serves 48.

Apple Streusel Pie

1 unbaked 9-inch pie shell
3 cups sliced apples
1/2 teaspoon cinnamon

Cream Cheese Filling:
2/3 cup sugar
2 eggs
2 tablespoons soft butter
pinch of salt
1 1/2 teaspoons vanilla
3 ounces softened cream cheese

Streusel Topping:
1/3 cup brown sugar
1/2 cup flour
2 tablespoons softened butter
1/2 cup chopped pecans

Place the apples in the unbaked pie shell, and sprinkle with the cinnamon.

Filling: Cream the sugar, eggs, and butter for 2 minutes. Add the salt, vanilla, and cream cheese. Blend just until smooth and pour over the apples. **Streusel Topping:** Mix together the brown sugar, flour, butter, and pecans, and spread the mixture on top of the pie.
Bake at 375° for 45 minutes, then at 350° for 15 minutes.

The farm house, right, is one of the fourteen original buildings (circa 1894) at Amish Acres, restored farm site which tells the story of the Old Order Amish in Nappanee, Indiana. A step back in time, Amish Acres is open to the public May through October: there are guided tours, craft demonstrations, films, horse and buggy rides, and other attractions including the musical show "Plain and Fancy" during the summer season. The old barn restaurant features family-style dinners with thick bean soup in iron kettles, shoofly pie, and locally made apple butter.

Amish Lemon Pie

1 9-inch baked pie crust, cooled
4 eggs, separated
1 cup sugar
1 teaspoon grated lemon rind
3 tablespoons flour
1 tablespoon butter, softened
1/3 cup lemon juice
1 cup milk

Beat the egg whites until stiff. Set aside. Combine the sugar, lemon rind, flour, butter, and egg yolks and beat until well blended. Stir in the lemon juice and milk. Fold gently into the egg whites. Pour into the crust and bake at 325° for 35 to 40 minutes, or until a knife inserted into the center comes out clean. Cool completely before serving. If desired, garnish with fresh strawberries or other fruit in season. This custard-like pie will have a sponge-like topping.

Shoofly Pie

This is a favorite dessert, popular with natives of the Pennsylvania Dutch country for years. It is both delicious and inexpensive to make, thereby satisfying two basic needs of the Pennsylvania Germans—the love of good cooking and the desire for frugality.

Because it has a moist base, Shoofly Pie is sometimes called a "wet bottom" pie; it can be moister or dryer, depending upon the proportion of moist base to crumbly top. Its wonderful aroma attracts humans just as the molasses in this pie attracted flies in the early days when windows were not screened. The cooks were kept busy shooing them away, hence the name Shoofly.

1 9-inch unbaked pie shell
1 cup molasses
1/3 cup hot water

Crumb Topping:
1/2 teaspoon cinnamon
1/2 cup brown sugar
1/2 teaspoon baking soda
1 cup flour
1/2 cup margarine

Mix the molasses and the hot water. Combine the dry ingredients for the crumb mixture in a separate bowl. Cut in the margarine and mix until crumbly. Pour the diluted molasses into an unbaked pie shell, then top with the crumb mixture. Bake at 375° for 15 minutes, then at 350° for 45 minutes. Serve warm. Delicious with ice cream.

Note: Leftover Shoofly Pie is great served with eggs for breakfast.

Raisin Pie
(also called "Funeral Pie")

This is a Pennsylvania Dutch recipe.

1 cup raisins
1 1/4 cups sugar
3 1/4 cups flour, divided
1 1/2 teaspoons salt, divided
2 1/4 cups cold water, divided
1 egg, beaten
1 1/2 tablespoons grated lemon rind
3 tablespoons lemon juice
1 cup shortening

Rinse the raisins and drain. In the top of a double boiler combine the sugar, 1/4 cup flour and 1/2 teaspoon salt. Gradually stir in 2 cups of the water. Add the raisins. Bring the mixture to a boil over direct heat, stirring constantly. Cook for 1 minute and remove from the heat. Vigorously stir a small amount of the hot mixture into the egg, then stir this into the mixture in the top of the double boiler. Set over simmering water and cook about 5 minutes, stirring constantly. Take the top off the double boiler and stir in the lemon rind and juice. Cool.

Sift 3 cups of the flour with 1 teaspoon salt. Cut in the shortening until the mixture is coarse-grained in texture. Gradually sprinkle 1/4 cup water over the mixture, mixing lightly with a fork to form a ball. Roll pastry out on a floured surface and fit into a 9-inch pie pan. Pour the cooled raisin mixture into the pie shell. Cover with narrow pastry strips in a crisscross pattern. Bake at 450° for 10 minutes. Reduce the heat to 350° and continue baking for another 20 minutes.

Rhubarb Recipes

Florence Schuerer and her husband, Walter are two of the Amana Colonies' great cooks. For more than 40 years, they have served German foods family-style to the public. Florence uses only fresh green rhubarb from the garden for her double-crust pies. Her daughter, Madeline Schuerer Schulte, carries on the tradition in her Rhubarb and Strawberry Custard Pie (recipe on page 198) served at the Brick Haus restaurant.

Elaine Zuber, of Bill Zuber's restaurant, favors cutting rhubarb pieces into about 2-inch lengths and keeping the crust very full since it "settles down in cooking."

Rhubarb Custard Pie

*Ox Yoke Inn
Amana, Iowa*

3 1/2 cups chopped rhubarb
1 1/2 cups sugar
3 eggs, lightly beaten
1/4 cup half-and-half
2 tablespoons flour, divided
1/8 teaspoon salt
1 9-inch unbaked pie shell

Combine the first six ingredients (use 1 tablespoon flour). Sprinkle the second tablespoon of flour over bottom of crust. Pour the rhubarb mixture into the crust. Bake at 375° for 30 minutes; reduce the heat to 350° and bake another 25 minutes. Top with a meringue and bake for 10 to 15 minutes.

The Ox Yoke Inn's meringue recipe is a secret; below is a standard meringue topping recipe.

Meringue Topping:
2 egg whites
1/4 teaspoon cream of tartar
3 tablespoons sugar
1/2 teaspoon vanilla

Beat the egg whites until frothy. Add the cream of tartar and beat until stiff but not dry. Beat in the sugar 1 tablespoon at a time, just until incorporated. Beat in vanilla. Top the pie and bake at 350° for 10 to 15 minutes.

Zuber's Rhubarb Pie

*Bill Zuber's Restaurant
Homestead, Amana Colonies, Iowa*

"Our rhubarb pie is a double-crust pie," Elaine Zuber advises. *"If you make it at home, use a basic pie crust recipe."*

Pie crust for a double-crust pie:
**4 heaping cups fresh or frozen
rhubarb**
2 cups sugar
1/3 heaping cup flour
butter to taste

Prepare a basic pie crust recipe. Prepare the rhubarb and cut into 1-inch-long pieces. Mix the rhubarb, sugar, and flour together and pour into the crust. Dot with the butter and add the top crust, sealing the edges. Bake at 350° for 1 hour if you are using fresh fruit; for frozen rhubarb, bake 30 minutes longer.

Honesty lasts longest.

197

Rhubarb and Strawberry Custard Pie

Madeline Schuerer Schulte
The Brick Haus Restaurant
Amana, Iowa

Pastry for a 2-crust, 9-inch pie:
2 cups rhubarb, cut into 1-inch
  pieces
2 cups strawberries, quartered
1 1/4 cups sugar
3 tablespoons flour
1/2 teaspoon nutmeg
1 tablespoon butter
2 eggs, lightly beaten

Line a 9-inch pie plate with 2/3 of the pastry. Preheat oven to 400°. Combine rhubarb and strawberries and place in the pastry-lined plate. In a bowl, combine sugar, flour and nutmeg. Cut butter into small pieces and add to the sugar mixture. Add eggs and mix well. Pour sugar-egg mixture over the fruit. Roll out the remaining pastry and place over the pie. With a fork, pierce the center of the top crust. Place pie in oven; reduce heat to 350° and bake about 35 minutes or until pastry is done and rhubarb is tender.

Decorative Easter Eggs
A Springtime Collectible Craft in the Amana Colonies

For generations, groups of women in Iowa's Amana colonies have created beautiful, collectible Easter eggs using dried furniture glue mixed with water and dyes. The eggs pictured in the handcrafted willow basket on page 112 are of deep, rich colors with a shiny surface. Mottled patterns are created by rolling the dyed eggs between your hands.

Instructions provided by the Krauss Furniture Shop, South Amana, Iowa 52334. (Powdered furniture glue can be ordered from their shop.)

several dozen hot, hard-cooked
  eggs
disposable containers and stirrers
  (not plastic)
1/2 pound powdered furniture glue
1/2 cup water
food colorings or other dyes
waxed paper
non-stick vegetable spray
rubber gloves suggested

Cook eggs so they will be done about the same time the glue-dye mixture is ready. Place a disposable container in the top of a double boiler. Mix glue and water in the container and cook for about 45 minutes until glue is dissolved; stir often. Divide glue mixture into smaller disposable containers and add food coloring or other dyes to each. Mix well; let set about 30 minutes (mixture will be a gel-like substance). Roll hot, hard-cooked eggs in glue-dye mixture. To create a mottled design, pass eggs lightly between both hands. Egg and glue mixture will be hot and not easily removed so use rubber gloves. Spray waxed paper with the vegetable spray. Place eggs on paper and roll occasionally until completely dry. Rolling the eggs avoids plain spots underneath.

Teutonic Legend

An Easter Load

The Easter bunny dates from the pre-Christian era and the Teutonic legend of Ostara (also Eástre), the Saxon goddess of spring and returning life. At the spring festival celebrating the return of the goddess, it was customary to exchange gifts of painted eggs. As the German-speaking people became Christian, they adopted the festival as Easter and gave it a new meaning. The Easter egg was a symbol of reviving life, often colored in representation of flowers or, by Christians, of the blood of Christ.

The custom of the bunny and Easter eggs persists to this day. According to Karin Gottier, the bunny was bringing eggs to good children by the sixteenth century; earlier, a rooster, a stork, a fox, and the cuckoo brought the Easter eggs. The rabbit won out as the most fertile and, therefore, the best emblem of spring.

Easter Bunny Cookies
Osterhasenkekse

Mrs. Henry J. Meyer
Amana, Iowa

Mrs. Meyer acquired this recipe from her husband's side of the family where it has been passed down for several generations.

1 cup margarine
2 cups sugar
2 eggs
1 cup buttermilk
4 3/4 cups flour
2 teaspoons baking soda
1 teaspoon vanilla
1/2 teaspoon salt

An Easter Fancy

Cream margarine and sugar until light and fluffy. Add eggs one at a time, beating well after each addition. Add dry ingredients and buttermilk alternately. Add vanilla last. Divide dough into 4 parts. Wrap each part in plastic wrap and place in freezer for two hours. Take out one portion at a time and roll to 3/8-inch thickness on well-floured board. Cut into desired shape with cookie cutters. Bake at 350° until dough is set, about 8 or 9 minutes; do not over bake. This dough is very soft and hard to work with but the cookies will remain soft and not dry. Frost cookies, if desired, with pastel colored icing. Makes about 7 dozen.

An Easter Cradle

Illustrations from St. Nicholas Magazine, *April, 1878.*

Christmas Baking

Rummel Studios, Inc. photo

Nativity Scene, St. Francis De Sales Catholic Church, Muskegan, Michigan. Carved by Georg J. Keilhofer, Frankenmuth , Michigan.

Traditionally, Christmas baking begins in November. The enticing smell of *Stollen* begins to waft from the kitchens. Anise drops and cinnamon stars are busily made and stowed away in large tin boxes to "season" until they are whisked out on Christmas Eve to grace the well-loved Christmas trays that all children (and even some grown-up children) receive. It is not unusual to find up to 10 different kinds of cookies on these trays—not in huge amounts, though. It's the variety, not the quantity, that counts.

In traditional German cuisine, cookie baking is limited to the Christmas season. Although cookies can be purchased in stores throughout the year, hardly any German household has home-baked cookies except during late November and December. Then, however, the number and variety of cookies baked almost exceeds description. Each region has its own special Christmas cookie recipes, a custom preserved in the names of some of these cookies, such as *Aachener Printen* and *Basler Leckerli*. Cookie recipes from the rest of Germany have joined them. It is not at all unusual for a German housewife to bake 12 to 15 different sorts of cookies; she arranges a few of each kind on a Christmas plate, urging guests to try one of each. Many of these cookies are made with the traditional Christmas spices: cinnamon, nutmeg, cardamom, and cloves. When Germans eat baked goods containing one or more of these spices at any other time of the year they almost always say, "This tastes like Christmas!"

—*Lynn Hattery-Beyer*

Karin Gottier adds: "In November and early December when the sun sets and the sky turns red, children say that *Christkindl* is heating his bake oven to make Christmas cookies."

200

German Stollen

Dresdner Stollen

1/4 cup diced citron
1/2 cup golden raisins
1/4 cup brandy, rum or orange juice
1 package dry yeast
1/4 cup warm water
1/2 cup milk, scalded and cooled to
  lukewarm
1/2 cup sugar
1/2 teaspoon salt
3 whole eggs
1 egg, separated
3/4 cup butter, softened, divided
3 1/2 to 4 cups flour, divided
1/2 cup chopped blanched almonds
1/2 cup chopped red and green
  candied cherries
1 tablespoon lemon rind
1 tablespoon orange rind
1 tablespoon cold water
powdered sugar

Optional Topping:
1 1/2 cups powdered sugar
1 1/2 tablespoons milk
1/4 teaspoon almond extract
blanched almond halves
candied cherry halves

Combine citron, raisins, and brandy, rum, or juice. Let stand for 1 hour. Drain fruit and reserve the liquid. In a large bowl, dissolve the yeast in the warm water. Add reserved fruit liquid, milk, sugar, salt, whole eggs, egg yolk, 1/2 cup butter, and 2 cups of the flour. Beat until smooth. Stir in drained fruit, almonds, cherries, lemon and orange rinds, and enough of the remaining flour to make a soft dough that is easy to handle. Turn onto floured surface and knead until smooth and elastic, about 5 to 8 minutes. Place in greased bowl and turn to grease top. Cover and let rise in a warm place until doubled, about 1 1/2 hours. Punch dough down and divide in half. Pat each piece into an oval, about 10x7-inches. Spread each half with 2 tablespoons of butter. Fold lengthwise in half and press folded edge firmly. Curve into a crescent shape if desired. Place on a greased cookie sheet. Beat egg white and 1 tablespoon of water slightly. Brush over tops of stollen. Cover and let rise until double, about 45 to 60 minutes. Bake at 375° for 20 to 30 minutes, or until golden brown. Remove to rack to cool. Sprinkle with powdered sugar or frost and decorate with the optional topping.

Optional Topping: Mix sugar, milk, and extract until smooth. Spread or drizzle over tops of stollen. Decorate with almonds and cherries as desired.

Note: Stollen freezes very well.

Hannelore Bozeman says: *"This Christmas bread is in a class by itself. I grew up with it, since my mother came from Dresden, the town in Saxony for which this Christmas sweet bread is named. Each December she would bake several loaves for Christmas. Since our relatives from East Germany would often send us additional loaves for Christmas gifts (they ship well and are popular gifts), we had* Stollen *for our daily afternoon coffee break for weeks on end. By Easter I would get thoroughly tired of it—until the following year. In the United States, I can usually find imported loaves, although they can't beat the homemade varieties."*

Springerle Cookie History

The word *Springerle* is derived from a German dialect and means "small jumping horse." Originally the horse was the sacred animal of Wotan, King of Nordic Gods. The history of these picture cookies dates from the pre-Christian rites of Germanic tribles. During their celebration of Jufest or Winter Solstice, it was customary to sacrifice animals. It was said that those who could not afford to sacrifice animals offered instead tokens of dough baked in the shapes of animals. Wooden molds were made for embossing dough. Gradually the molds included the forms of people, birds, flowers, and fruit. These pale, hard cookies, often called "dunking cakes," have pleasant lemon-anise flavor.

In more modern times, the cookies were used for decorating the Christmas tree and as gifts to the children. Sometimes Grandmother would have a special mold for each grandchild at Christmas. It is not uncommon to find these delightful molds still used by Pennsylvania Dutch families as a tradition brought from the "old country." The molds can be found in the shape of cylinders, like a rolling pin with small designs carved on the curved surface; as a plate with several individual designs, or as single blocks. Modern machinery has provided the ability to mass-produce these molds. However, the hand-carved molds remain an object of value and are often displayed as an *objet d'art* when not being used to form a unique cookie.—*Carol Dillon*

Woodcarver *(Holtzschnitzer)* Don Dillon of Camp Hill, Pennsylvania, lived in Europe for several years, where he became interested in woodcarvings historically used by the European people, such as the molds used to make *Springerle*. His interest was enhanced by working with a woodcarver in Oberammergau, Germany. When he returned to the United States, he adapted the authentic European designs to Pennsylvania Dutch designs to to create a variety of molds. Some of these designs are pictured on page 203.

Each mold is hand carved with members of the Dillon family participating in the various processes. After the carving is completed, the plaques are stained, finished, and signed, ready for use or display. Some may be left unstained for individual preference.

Opposite page: Examples of the cookie molds produced by D.D. Dillon Carvings. Carol Dillon, wife of woodcarver Don Dillon, notes that original designs, some copied from a fabric trim found in Germany, or reproductions of antique molds, all have a similarity to Pennsylvania Dutch designs. The Dillons used Pennsylvania Dutch motifs in creating the multiple design mold.

Springerle

D.D. Dillon Carvings
Camp Hill, Pennsylvania

This recipe is for the well-known German Anise Cakes which are stamped with a wooden mold into quaint little designs and figures.

Carol Dillon says, "The symbolism of the Pennsylvania Dutch designs has been inspirational for us. The Springerle cookies have no shortening in them so they become hard faster than other cookies. Traditionally they were dunked in coffee or milk as they hardened."

4 large eggs
2 cups granulated sugar
1 teaspoon anise extract or
    4 tablespoons anise seeds
4 cups cake flour
1 teaspoon baking powder

Beat eggs till light, gradually add sugar and continue beating at a high speed until batter is thick and lemon colored. Add anise. Sift flour and baking powder, and blend with egg mixture at a low speed. Cover bowl with waxed paper or foil and let stand 15 minutes so dough is easier to work. Divide dough into 3 parts.

On a lightly floured surface roll dough to 8 inches square, 1/4 inch thick. Let rest 1 minute. Flour the mold and press design into the dough; cut around the design and place cookies on greased cookie sheet. Cover with a towel and let set at least 12 hours before baking.

Brush off excess flour and bake at 300° for 15 minutes. Cookies will brown slightly on the bottom, but not on the top; they should rise, but not spread during baking. Store in a tight container. Place a cut apple in the container if cookies become too hard.

Note: Lemon or almond flavoring can be substituted for the anise. After cookies have cooled, the design may be painted with food coloring and a fine brush. By punching a hole at the top of each cookie before baking, one can insert colorful ribbon and hang them on the Christmas tree as is traditionally done.

Anise Drops
Anisplätzchen

This is a Pennsylvania Dutch version of these popular Christmas cookies.

1 1/2 cups flour
1/4 teaspoon baking powder
1/8 teaspoon salt
2 eggs
1 cup sugar
1 teaspoon anise flavoring

Sift together the flour, baking powder, and salt. In a mixing bowl beat the eggs; gradually add the sugar and anise flavoring. Beat until very thick, about 20 minutes. Sift in and fold the dry ingredients into the egg mixture, about 1/4 at a time. Drop by teaspoonfuls onto generously greased cookie sheets, about 2 inches apart. Set the cookie sheets in a cool place (not the refrigerator) overnight. Do not cover and do not disturb. Bake at 350° for 5 to 6 minutes. Cookies should not brown. Remove to cooling racks to cool completely. Cookies form a cake-like layer on the bottom with a crisp "frosting" on top. Makes about 4 dozen.

Honey Cookies
Honigkekse

2 cups honey
1 tablespoon baking soda
2 tablespoons butter
1/2 cup granulated sugar
1/2 cup brown sugar
3 eggs, beaten
5 to 6 cups flour

Bring honey to a boil; remove from heat. Add soda and butter. Let butter melt in the honey and soda. Cool to lukewarm. Mix in sugars, eggs, and flour; chill overnight. Roll out on lightly floured board to 1/8-inch thickness and cut with floured cookie cutter. Bake on greased baking sheet at 325° for 8 to 10 minutes. Cool and decorate with powdered sugar frosting.

Chocolate Cookies
Schokoladenkekse

Terry Roemig, Amana, Iowa
The Colony Inn

Terry Roemig got this recipe from her late Oma Hermann. Oma means Grandmother in German.

1 1/2 cups butter
4 cups sugar
8 eggs
5 to 6 cups flour
3 teaspoons baking powder

Cream butter and sugar. Add eggs and mix until well blended. Blend in flour, baking powder and cocoa. Drop by teaspoons on lightly greased cookie sheet. Bake in 325° oven for 8 to 10 minutes.

Chocolate Shells

Mark F. Sohn

This German biscuit gets its special flavor from the combination of hazelnuts and chocolate. It can be made, also, with almonds. I would like to call it a chocolate hazelnut macaroon, but that is only partly correct because it is supposed to be shaped with a shell mold. I have simplified and modernized Mom's procedure and make it without the old, hand-carved wooden shell mold. I roll the cookie in sugar and drop it onto parchment.

At Christmas time, Grandma sent these with other German cookies. Grandma, Franziska Bender Sohn, was from Winweiler, which is in the Black Forest of southwestern Germany.

3 ounces semi-sweet baking
   chocolate
2 cups powdered sugar
1/2 pound hazelnuts
3 large egg whites
granulated sugar

Place chocolate in a large food processor and process until very fine. Add nuts and powdered sugar. Process until fine but not greasy. Add egg whites and process until mixed. Refrigerate for 30 minutes. Preheat oven to 275°. Line 2 cookie sheets with waxed paper. Roll teaspoonfuls of dough in granulated sugar and drop onto waxed paper. Bake for 40 minutes or until the center of the cookie is baked but still soft.

Note: With just four ingredients and one cooking step, this is an easy cookie. If you are in a hurry, don't refrigerate the dough.

Nikolaus Men

Lynn Hattery-Beyer

In Germany, December 6th is St. Nikolaus Day. *Any yeast dough is suitable to use for* Nikolaus *men.*

3 tablespoons butter or margarine
1/4 cup sugar
pinch of salt
1 cup lukewarm milk
1 package dry yeast
1 egg
grated rind of 1/2 lemon
4 cups flour, sifted
1 egg yolk, whipped

Add the butter, sugar and salt to the warm milk and stir until dissolved. Sprinkle in the yeast. Beat in the egg and grated lemon rind. Make a well in the flour and pour in the liquid mixture. Knead until air blisters appear on the surface. Let the dough rise for 15 minutes. Divide the dough into four equal parts. Out of each part form a thick ball for the head, a thick roll for the torso and legs (slit the bottom half of this roll and separate slightly for the legs), and thinner rolls for the arms. Connect the four parts of the body and use any remaining dough to form the facial features, buttons, etc. Brush the men with the whipped egg yolk and bake in a preheated oven at 400° for 20 to 25 minutes.

Apple Cookies
Apfelkekse

Edna Yoder
Kalona, Iowa

Edna is a member of the Old Order Amish church.

2 2/3 cups sugar
1 cup shortening
4 cups flour
2 teaspoons baking soda
2 teaspoons salt
1 teaspoon ground cloves
1 teaspoon cinnamon
2 eggs
2/3 cup milk
2 cups raisins or chopped dates
2 cups chopped apples
1 cup chopped nuts

In a large bowl, combine the sugar and shortening. In a separate bowl, sift together the flour, baking soda, salt, cloves, and cinnamon. Add the eggs and milk to the sugar mixture. Then add the flour mixture, raisins or dates, apples, and nuts. Mix well. Drop by spoonfuls onto a greased cookie sheet. Bake at 350° for 10 to 15 minutes. Frost while warm, or not at all. Makes about 10 dozen.

Ginger Biscuits
Pfeffernüsse

Lynn Hattery-Beyer

1 1/3 cups honey
1 1/4 cups sugar
3 eggs
1 teaspoon cinnamon
1/2 teaspoon ground cloves
pinch each of nutmeg, coriander,
    ground ginger, cardamom
1 teaspoon ground pepper
9 1/2 cups flour
4 teaspoons baking powder
2/3 cup powdered sugar

Warm the honey until liquified. Beat in the sugar, eggs, and all the spices. Sift the flour and the baking powder together and gradually work them into the honey mixture. Preheat the oven to 375°. Shape the dough into 1-inch balls and bake on greased cookie sheets for 15 to 20 minutes, or until golden brown. Remove from the cookie sheets immediately and let cool. Dissolve the powdered sugar in a small amount of water and heat to the boiling point, stirring constantly. Glaze the cookies with this mixture.

The various German regions had diverse structures at Christmas time. This Friesian arch, in Karin Gottier's collection, is trimmed with boxwood, candles, gingerbread figures, and apples.

Gingerbread Houses

Lebkuchenhäuser

Gingerbread houses are an all-time German favorite. The dough used to construct the houses is really quite simple to make. Walls and the roof are cut out after the dough is baked, and are "glued" together later with a simple powdered sugar frosting. The decorations on the houses vary greatly: some houses are elaborately adorned with various kinds of candy, some are decorated with raisins and other dried fruits; others are left plain letting the architecture and the smell of the delicious gingerbread speak for itself.

Gingerbread House Recipe

Carol Schuerer Zuber

Carol displays her houses made of honey dough during Christmas holidays at her family's Barn Restaurant in Amana, Iowa.

Note: Many instructions direct cutting the dough before baking. Carol cuts the pieces from the baked dough.

18 cups flour
1 cup plus 2 tablespoons baking powder
1 1/2 tablespoons cinnamon
3 teaspoons ground cloves
3/4 teaspoon nutmeg
3/4 teaspoon ground cardamom
1/2 teaspoon salt
2 1/4 cups honey
5 1/4 cups sugar
3/4 cup butter
1 cup fresh lemon juice
3 tablespoons grated lemon rind
3 eggs
3 egg yolks
3 to 4 batches of icing

Icing for Gingerbread House:
1 egg white, beaten
1 cup powdered sugar
Food coloring, optional

Grease and flour baking sheets. Sift together the flour, baking powder, spices, and salt. In the top of a double boiler, heat the honey, sugar, and butter until the butter is melted; add the lemon juice and the grated rind. Set aside to cool. Add the cooled butter mixture, eggs, and egg yolks to the flour mixture. Mix until a dough forms. Divide the dough and roll it into 1/4-inch thickness on greased baking sheets, covering the entire baking sheet. Trim the uneven edges. Bake at 350° for 35 minutes or until firm.

Remove the gingerbread from the oven and cut the baked dough by placing the pattern pieces over the warm sheets of dough. With a sharp knife cut dough around the pattern. Let the cut dough cool and trim away excess. If stained glass windows are desired, place crushed hard candy into window openings and return to oven for 1 minute or until the candy is melted; watch carefully so the gingerbread does not burn. *(continued)*

Icing: Beat the egg white until foamy; add the sugar. Beat until smooth. Pour into a pastry tube to use. Icing remaining after assembly may be divided and tinted with the food coloring for decorating.*

Assembling: Gingerbread pieces must be thoroughly cool. Join the pieces together with the icing. Dip the edges of smaller pieces into the icing. (Canned goods are useful for propping the pieces while drying.)

Decorating: After all the pieces have been assembled and are completely dry, the true artist is revealed through frosting, decorative flourishes, and candy. Windows, shingles, porches and other architectural accents can be created. This is definitely the most enjoyable part of creating a gingerbread house.

*Icing with uncooked egg white is for decorating only.

House Patterns

Lynn Hattery-Beyer says: "The easiest house for beginners to attempt consists of four pieces: two square slabs of gingerbread for the roof and two triangular pieces for the front and back. The roof is not held up by walls, but rather rests on the surface, making construction simple. Cut the patterns out of heavy cardboard. The size doesn't really matter—whatever you are prepared to decorate is fine! You will need to cut out two gingerbread pieces using each pattern. Feel free to cut windows and a door in the front and back pieces.

This simple pattern can be upgraded easily by adding side walls. In this case the side walls are as long as the roof is wide, and the front/back pieces must be lengthened to accommodate the height of the side walls.

For variety in decorating you can use: licorice, chocolate wafers, candied fruit, gum drops, and nuts.

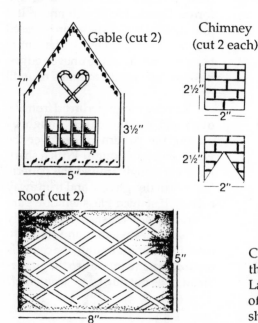

Gable (cut 2)

7"

3½"

5"

Roof (cut 2)

5"

8"

Chimney (cut 2 each)

2½"

2"

2½"

2"

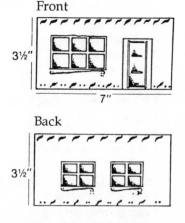

Front

3½"

7"

Back

3½"

Cut paper pattern according to size in the directions, or scale as you prefer. Lay the pattern over the warm sheets of dough, and cut around it with a sharp knife.